TERRORIST TRAIL

TERRORIST TRAIL

BACKTRACKING THE FOREIGN FIGHTER

ILLUSTRATED

H. JOHN POOLE
FOREWORD BY
MAJ.GEN. RAY L. SMITH USMC (RET.)

POSTERITY
PRESS

Published by Posterity Press
P.O. Box 5360, Emerald Isle, NC 28594
(www.posteritypress.org)

Cataloging-in-Publication Data
Poole, H. John, 1943-
Terrorist Trail.
    Includes bibliography and index.
    1. Infantry drill and tactics.
    2. Military art and science.
    3. Military history.
I. Title.   ISBN-10: 0-9638695-9-0   2006   355'.42
                  ISBN-13: 978-0-9638695-9-3
Library of Congress Control Number: 2006901815

Cover art © 2006 by Michael Leahy
Edited by Dr. Mary Beth Poole
Proofread by William E. Harris

First printing, United States of America, September 2006

To every American infantryman who has ever served.

GLORIFIED IMAGE OF A "HEAVY INFANTRYMAN"

(Source: Courtesy of U.S. Air Force, from its website, www.af.mil, "Aim High" graphic by Tech.Sgt. Cody Vance, afg_030409_002.jpg)

Contents

Illustrations

Maps

Figures

Foreword

Terrorist Trail is John Poole's latest attempt to interest the U.S. military in more light-infantry skills at the squad level. These are the skills with which a U.S. brigade could rely more heavily on surprise than firepower, and thus have less collateral damage. They can be loosely categorized as "sneaking," "hiding," and "escaping." He argues that such skills are prerequisite to winning a 4th-Generation war (one that is fought in martial, political, economic, and psychological arenas simultaneously). They would enable fourteen U.S. Marines or soldiers to outpost a volatile Iraqi neighborhood without much risk to themselves. When the militant mob showed up, they would simply melt into the woodwork—just like Asian and Islamic guerrillas have been doing for a century. All the while, they would be building rapport with the locals and protecting them from the *Hezbollah*-like terrorist element in their midst. Collectively, such outposts are a fledgling democracy's best chance at survival. Nothing is better at winning hearts and minds than some semblance of local security.

Through a detailed analysis of African history, Poole has revealed evidence of Sino-Islamic coalition. If it exists, U.S. leaders would be wise to adopt his fully tested squad training method. WWIII may well be fought in an unconventional manner by squad-sized units.

Within established guidelines, U.S. troops have performed superbly in Iraq and Afghanistan. Yet, Iraq is on the verge of civil war, and Afghanistan is heating up. Thus, one has to wonder about the applicability of those guidelines—or, more bluntly, whether U.S. units have been allowed to train and operate in the most effective way for this type of war.

My Marine Corps service began as an enlisted man. I often think back on how my fellow PFCs would have liked to have trained and operated like Poole suggests. Most would have loved the competition that drives his "combat experiments." They would have further jumped at the chance to operate alone. After commissioning, I saw combat in Vietnam, Grenada, and Beirut. I came to know the communist and Islamist way of operating from the "bottom up" instead of the "top down." Simply put, it takes self-sufficient U.S. infantry squads to beat such an enemy. Such self-sufficiency can only be acquired through more "light-infantry skills" than U.S. riflemen are currently being given. During my last few years as base commander of Camp Lejeune, I was often dismayed by the apparent lack of small-unit maneuver training. If it was going on, I couldn't find it on my many tours.

Through an overemphasis on technology and firepower, U.S. commanders may have failed to acquire what they will need most to win the Global War on Terror. In the name of "preserving life," they may have focused too hard on shooting and not hard enough on squad, fire team, buddy team, and individual maneuver. Their error is one of dimension—too much attention to the big picture and not enough to the little picture. Poole's chapter on Urban Tracking may help them to refocus. He claims 4th-Generation war is like high-intensity police work. He may not be right about everything, but without seriously contemplating this thought-provoking book, U.S. military men should not expect much of a change to the current situation.

M.GEN. RAY L. SMITH USMC (RET.)

Preface

Like most U.S. military personnel, the author tends to see the world's events as either friend or foe generated. In all probability, most are from local causes that have nothing to do with the United States. If too many are thought to be communist or terrorist inspired, then he or she who would try to help America, will end up doing her great harm. Violence begets violence, and polarity creates bias. Those who would consciously fuel either will be unable to win a modern war.

Terrorism is evil. By Christian doctrine, it can only be conquered by good. To win a "Global War on Terror," America must carefully measure its every response. If its military establishment projects too much force, it will only fan the flames. Such a mission creates a real problem for the U.S. Army and Marine Corps. They have traditionally directed overwhelming firepower against enemy strongpoints. In the vernacular of tactical evolution, they have been conducting 2nd-Generation Warfare (2GW). The 3rd Generation of war (3GW) involves bypassing the enemy's strongpoints to more easily get at his centers of gravity (headquarters, supply depots, and the like). With elaborately canned training, electronic surveillance, and "smart" ordnance, America has simply adopted a more technologically advanced version of 2GW. Its traditional adversaries have meanwhile devised a style of fighting that exploits the inflexibility of top-down bureaucracy and any overdependency on firepower. Called 4th-Generation Warfare (4GW), this new form of conflict is conducted simultaneously in the arenas of combat/tactics, politics/media, economics/infrastructure, and religion/psychology. Those who would try to counter 4GW with a 2GW response will only dig themselves a deeper hole—progressively eroding both local infrastructure and popular support.

To win 4GW conflict, America's military must shift to a less violent methodology—that which depends more on maneuver and surprise than on brute force. This can only be accomplished by tiny, semi-independent infantry detachments. They would always be outnumbered, so—to the uninitiated—their role appears more dangerous. In actuality, it would be less risky than what their fathers and grandfathers were routinely asked to do—move upright through a steady stream of machinegun bullets. The detachments that learned how quickly to hide and then exfiltrate enemy encirclements would be relatively safe.

To make a strategic contribution in such a conflict, U.S. military personnel must have only one preconceived notion—a thorough understanding of the cultural history of their theater. Then, when that history starts to repeat itself, they will know how strongly to oppose each apparent danger.

The American GI's mission must also be refined—from that of "kill or be killed" to one of "protect the weak." The U.S. service branches have yet to fully embrace their relatively recent shift to 3GW doctrine. Until they do, all U.S. soldiers and Marines must realize that the "basics" they are still shown are for 2GW, and only bare minimums for the higher variants. It is thus up to the individual to discover the vast body of knowledge that comprises the latter. There are any number of other ways to survive on one's own—like "shadow walking," hiding in plain sight, or eluding enemy mantrackers.

This book attempts to trace the world's terrorist problems to their source without catering to any particular political viewpoint. Because of America's traditional approach to war, its skirts are not completely clean in this matter. Nor is it totally responsible for the discord. But to prevail, it must remember how it countered communism after WWII—with the Marshall Plan. For in a global 4GW environment, any excesses in interrogation/incarceration or collateral damage will prove counterproductive. Central to the enemy's convoluted method is the provision of alternative basic services.

A wide range of details concerning U.N., Chinese, and Islamist activity in Africa and the Middle East has been provided. Many conflict with the U.S. "party line" and "conventional wisdom." They are only partially substantiated and should not be unconditionally accepted. They are only offered as an indication that history has begun to repeat itself. With enough knowledge of those details and that history, U.S.-sponsored detachments should be able to track down and *arrest* opposition recruiters and trainers. Only then will the fighting abate.

To make any sense of Eastern initiatives in the huge, multinational area that is "Africa and the Middle East," one must continually revisit the "whole" and other parts of that "whole." The average Western reader may find such an approach lacking in organization. However, it has a purpose. That's how Easterners think, so that's the best way to discover their plan.

H. JOHN POOLE

Acknowledgments

To the Lord, Jesus Christ, belongs most of the credit for this work. Without His knowledge, Africa's convoluted secrets would have remained hidden. Without His protection, the trip to Sudan would have turned out badly. Without His wisdom, "waging peace" would have seemed an inadequate response to Islamist/Chinese expansionism.

As with most worthwhile projects, the Lord has helped through many other people. To all who contributed, a heartfelt "thanks" is offered. Within their collective advice lies a way to disrupt the endless cycle of violence.

Introduction

What Has Drawn the World's Attention Back to Somalia?

Since the U.S. invasion of Iraq, *jihadists* have been entering that country from all over North Africa, with the largest contingent coming from Sudan.¹ In late 2005, Americans learned that those bound for Afghanistan were being trained in Somalia. They knew that *al-Qaeda* had been forced out of Sudan in 1996 and wondered if it had left a contingent nearby. (See Map 0.1.)

> Islamic extremists . . . are undergoing training at two terrorist training camps in Mogadishu, according to the *Somaliland Times*.
> The newspaper reported Dec. 12 that several dozen religious extremists were trained at the camps run by Hasan Aweys and Adan Hashi Ayro. At least 10 British nationals of Somali and South Asian [Pakistani] origin were at the training camps. . . .
> The camps are code-named Baytul-Amn (safe haven) and Salah Al-Diin. . . . Baytul-Amn is located near the Islamic courts headquarters in Mogadishu. The other training facility is at Shikaro, a neighborhood in Somalia's lawless capital.
> The training program . . . is based on Al Qaida manuals. Though most of the instructors are Somalis, Arab Afghans are teaching techniques for making powerful bombs and timers from easily available material.²

This was not the first time that Somalia had been in the news in 2005. An American cruise liner was attacked off the northeast coast in early November. Within 36 hours, Somali pirates went after two more passenger ships and three cargo vessels. By the end of the year, the number of reported piracy incidents in Somali waters had risen to 35, compared with two the previous year. By March 2006, the astounding total was up to 45 attempted hijackings.[3] A serious and growing problem had come to the forefront.

> For several months the International Maritime Bureau [IMB] . . . has warned ships to stay at least 240 km away from Somalia's coastline. . . .
>
> . . . [I]t said an increase in serious attacks off Somalia . . . after a quiet spell of nearly two years was particularly alarming.
>
> November 5 saw one of the boldest attacks. Two boats full of pirates approached the Seabourn Spirit, a cruise ship carrying Western tourists, about 160 km off Somalia and fired rocket-propelled grenades and assault rifles. . . .
>
> . . . In June, pirates hijacked a cargo ship carrying U.N. food aid for Somalis and held it for 100 days before releasing it. . . .
>
> "They were only hijacking the small fishing vessels. Now they are attacking the big merchant ships," he [an official] said. . . .
>
> Somalia has had no effective central government since opposition leaders ousted dictator Mohamed Siad Barre in 1991. They then turned on each other, transforming this nation of 7 million into a patchwork of battling fiefdoms ruled by heavily armed militias. . . .
>
> . . . [M]embers of the transitional government have been fighting among themselves and face serious opposition from warlords and religious extremists in Somalia.[4]
> — Associated Press, 16 November 2005

> A merchant vessel has been reported hijacked in the pirate-infested waters off Somalia. . . .
>
> . . . [T]he vessel was taken near the Somali town of Haradere [300 km north of Mogadishu near Hobyo]. . . .
>
> The town is considered a base for pirates. . . .
>
> The spate of attacks has . . . sparked calls for Somalia's unpatrolled waters to be declared a war zone.[5]
> — Agence France-Presse, 7 December 2005

Because the pirates had been holding crews hostage and demanding ransom,[6] one suspects *al-Qaeda* involvement. Kidnapping

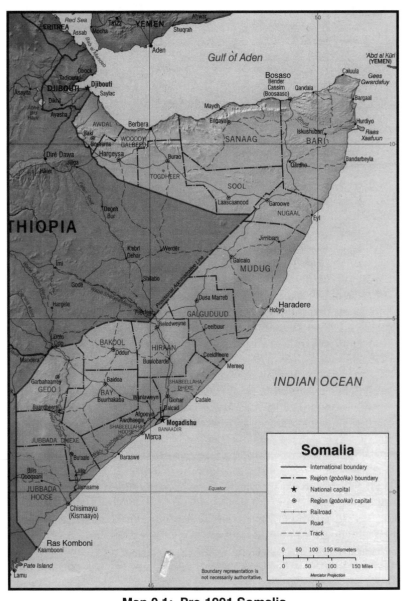

Map 0.1: Pre-1991 Somalia

(Source: Courtesy of General Libraries, University of Texas at Austin, from their website for map designator "somalia_rel_2002.pdf")

is, after all, part of the Islamic militants' formula. The attack on U.N. shipping was instead to discourage outside meddling. After American troops left Somalia in 1993, that country has inexorably slid toward Muslim militancy. For quite some time, *al-Qaeda* has had a base on the Somali island of Ras Komboni at the Kenyan border.[7] Of the three pirate gangs now operating along Somalia's 1,800-mile coastline, one is preying on the port of Kismayo, and another on the port of El-Maan (just north of Mogadishu). Only at issue is whether they are working for an *al-Qaeda*-affiliated militia or independent warlord.

> They [the pirates] may have been working for Somali warlords, who fund arms purchases by smuggling drugs, weapons, and people—and with piracy.[8]
> — *Christian Science Monitor,* 8 November 2005

As early as May 2005, the Marine general in charge of the U.S. Horn of Africa contingent warned that Somalia had become a safe haven for terrorists. He said it was "ungoverned space" being ruled by a regime in exile. Shortly thereafter, the African Union sent in 1,700 Sudanese and Ugandan troops to protect that regime's limited presence at Baidoa and Jowhar (towns west of Mogadishu). Somalia had been without a central government since 1991, and Mogadishu was far too dangerous to serve as its capital.[9]

> The new government is opposed by Islamic extremists and some of the dozens of warlords in the country.
> Ethiopian Prime Minister Meles Zenawi told the AP [Associated Press] on Thursday than an al-Qaida terror cell was "very active" in Mogadishu.[10]
> —Associated Press, 14 May 2005

When a U.S. Navy vessel captured some of the pirates on 18 March 2006, their parent organization was finally revealed. Their spokesman in "Harardhere" (Haradere) claimed that they were "militiamen . . . in an operation to protect the country's sea resources from illicit exploitation by foreign vessels." Geraad Mohamud (a subsequent spokesman) then warned, "They will kill any hostage they capture and would attack any ship unlawfully plying Somali waters unless their men were released."[11] An all-encompassing death threat for the entire Somali coast could only come from a radical fundamentalist with far-reaching power. In this part of the world that can only mean one thing—he works for *al-Qaeda.*

How All of This Relates to America's Tragic Experience in Somalia

Any discussion of *al-Qaeda* in Somalia would not be complete without an objective rehash of the events of 1993.

> Somalia, a "failed state," has no official government and is divided into three parts, each "ruled" by local warlords. Despite denials from Somali political leaders, Al Qaeda has been transporting men and material through its vast, unguarded coastline for many years. . . .
>
> As the Islamist vanguard, it was incumbent on Al Qaeda to manifest Muslim displeasure at the U.S. intervention in the Horn of Africa [in 1993]. Beginning in early 1992, Al Qaeda established a network in Somalia. Al Qaeda's then deputy Emir for military operations, Muhammed Atef, was entrusted with the mission, and frequently visited Somalia in 1992 and 1993. In early 1993, Al Qaeda's chief instructor, Ali Muhammad, came to train the attack team drawn from al-Itihaad al-Islamiya (Islamic Unity) *[AIAI]*, formerly known as the [Somali chapter of the] Muslim Brotherhood, an associate group of Al Qaeda. On October 3-4, Al-Qaeda-trained *[AIAI]* . . . fighters attacked U.S. forces in Mogadishu, killing eighteen U.S. personnel. The blame focused on General Muhammad Farah Aideed, but Osama was in fact behind this key operation. Although the world's attention was drawn to the deaths of American soldiers and the subsequent humiliating U.S. withdrawal, Al-Qaeda-trained Somalis killed Belgian and Pakistani peacekeepers too. On the Somalia operation, referring to Osama's role in the attacks, the CIA [Central Intelligence Agency] later stated: "Information from our sources confirms his involvement *(Background on Osama Bin Laden and Al-Qa'ida,* CIA, Washington, D.C., 1998, 10)."
>
> According to Indian intelligence interrogation of Maulana Masood Azhar, the then secretary of Harkat-ul-Ansar

[an al-Qaeda affiliate in Pakistan], . . . a number of Arab mujahidin . . . moved to Somalia. . . . [S]ome 400 went to Sudan and thereafter to Somalia, where they joined *[AIAI]* . . . in 1993. . . .

Al Qaeda's role in expelling U.S. troops from Somalia is acknowledged by local Islamists. . . . On June 8, 1998, the U.S. Attorney General indicted Osama for his role in training the tribesmen who killed eighteen U.S. soldiers in Somalia in 1993.[12]

— *Inside al-Qaeda,* by Rohan Gunaratna

Public-television's *Frontline* series confirms *al-Qaeda's* involvement with the U.S. withdrawal. It reveals that "Aideed's forces were getting help from Osama bin Laden's *al-Qaeda."* Osama, after all, was living in Sudan in 1993. It goes on to show that bin Laden had himself acknowledged *al-Qaeda's* intervention in Somalia in a 1998 interview. Aideed had also told Gen. Zinni from the U.S. Central Command (CENTCOM) that helicopters were the Americans' "center of gravity." That's why he positioned RPGs and machineguns on the rooftops around his headquarters.[13] The term "center of gravity" applies to 3rd-Generation (Maneuver) Warfare and is far too sophisticated for an "adviser-less" warlord. *Frontline* further confirmed that the "U.S. Justice Department had indicted bin Laden for providing support to Somali fighters in the way of training and assistance." It further linked Mohammed Atef to the U.S. embassy bombings in Kenya and Tanzania of 1998.[14]

When asked to leave Sudan in 1996, *al-Qaeda* must have moved part of its operation to Somalia. That might help to explain why "Somalia is [now] awash with some 60,000 militiamen."

As of early 2002, *[AIAI]* . . . had withdrawn from the ports of Merka and Kismayo and the inland center of Luuq, which its 3,000 armed fighters had dominated, using it as a staging-post till the mid-1990's for sortees *[sic]* into Ethiopia and Kenya (Hailes, "Somalia Provides Unsafe Haven," Janes Intell. Review, vol. 14, no. 1, 16). Ethiopian military intervention since August 1996 had in the mean time depleted its strength, but *[AIAI]* . . . has established a presence in northeastern Somalia, operating from the semi-autonomous region known as Puntland. Through its port, Bosaso, *[AIAI]*

. . . is also reported to have sent volunteers to fight with Al Qaeda in Afghanistan (Morrison, "Africa and the War on Terrorism," House Internat. Relations Committee Testimony, Washington, D.C., Nov. 2001).[15]
— *Inside al-Qaeda,* by Rohan Gunaratna

Like Lebanon's *Hezbollah* and Iraq's Mahdi Army, *AIAI* creates its own "state-within-a-state." It sponsors orphanages and schools, and provides pockets of security within Somalia.[16] Until the spring of 2006, Washington was content to let Ethiopia try to deal with the problem.

Washington . . . is likely to rely on neighboring Ethiopia—whose army has been fighting the al-Itihaad for at least four years. . . . There have already been allegations that Ethiopian troops have entered the breakaway Somali region of Puntland in the northeast to help the region's ousted leader, Abdullahi Yussuf. . . .

Analysts project that one early target may be the small island of Ras Komboni, near the Kenyan border. There is evidence that Ras Komboni serves as a base of operations for al-Qaeda, and that the organization ships people and supplies to and from Somalia through the island. . . .

. . . [T]he war-ravaged country remains a likely safe haven for bin Laden and al-Qaeda members if they flee Afghanistan. Somalia has been a sanctuary for al-Qaeda since 1993, when bin Laden sent several top associates to provide assistance to Mohamed Farah Aideed, whose supporters eventually killed 18 American troops in Somalia. The country was again a center of al-Qaeda activity in 1998 as its members plotted the bombings of U.S. embassies in Kenya and Tanzania. . . .

. . . In 1997, Ethiopia dispatched its troops to the western Somali town of Luuq to raid the offices of al-Itihaad. In addition to killing hundreds of the Islamic group's militiamen, Ethiopian forces reportedly seized three truckloads of documents detailing the group's link to al-Qaeda.[17]
— Center for Defense Info., 10 December 2001

A part of northwestern Somalia seceded from the rest of the country in 1991. Now calling itself Somaliland, it has a president, a freely elected parliament, and ambassadors. Hargeysa is its capital, and Berbera its port. Western aid workers have recently been killed in Somaliland, but it is still is a strong U.S. ally in the War on Terror.[18] Just across the Djbouti border is Camp Lemonier. It is home to 1,500 troops—the U.S. Horn of Africa task force. They have been "doing military-to-military training with five countries in the region," to include Ethiopia and Yemen. To their credit, they also work on community service projects in the undergoverned border area.[19]

So, *AIAI* controls the strategically important spit of land between the Gulf of Aden and Indian Ocean. Puntland is its name, and Bosaso is its port (and pseudo-capital). Thus, Puntland qualifies as a staging area for foreign *jihadists* headed for Afghanistan, Chechnya, and Europe. From the southern end of Somalia, *al-Qaeda* can also send fighters south and west—to places like Ethiopia, Kenya, Tanzania, and Nigeria.

> Al-Qaida-linked Islamist terrorists have set up a training camp in southern Somalia, near the Kenya border, according to eyewitness reports in the local press.
>
> The Nairobi East African Standard newspaper reported last week that Kenyan border guards are aware of the camp, which is a 20-minute boat ride from the underwater park at Kiunga, a border region.
>
> The Islamists at the camp are being trained with the help of a "white man sporting a thick moustache and believed to be of Eastern European extraction, presumably Yugoslavia," the newspaper reported.
>
> The camp at Ras Kiamboni [Komboni] is being used to recruit and train Islamist extremists linked to the Al-Ittiyad [al-Itihaad], a Somalia based group linked to Al Qaida.
>
> According to the report, Al-Ittiyad terrorists transit the Kenyan border with arms and equipment. The camp is said to employ turban-wearing sentries armed with AK-47 rifles.
>
> The terrorists are told that they would be sent to fight alongside Islamists in Chechnya. The fighters are part of the global "jihadist" or holy warrior movement that includes Al-Qaida.
>
> The accented trainer has been identified only as "David."

The report said fighters who were killed in friendly fire accidents are buried in the camp.

The facility is hidden in a thicket in the wilderness area of Somalia and is defended by a large caliber gun mounted on the coast targeted against approaching ships or boats.

An official in the Kenyan counterterrorist agency said the camp is supported by a Garissa, Kenya businessman and a series of lodges in the Majengo area of Mombassa.

Kenya agents visited the camp in May, June and July and obtained valuable details about its operations in an area almost 45 square miles in size.

The camp is inhabited by families of the jihadists and includes local police and courts.

The terrorists also have cells in Kenya and are supported by the Kenyan businessman. "He is the key financier of the group. Funds to bankroll the suspect activities of the outfit are channeled to the businessman from different banks in Kuwait," the official was quoted as saying.[20]

— *Geostrategy-Direct,* 14 December 2004

The Latest Developments in Somalia

To consolidate all of Somalia under *sharia* law, the "Union of Islamic Courts" (ICU) began an armed offensive against the warlords around Mogadishu in April 2006. As it had recently acquired a large arsenal and skilled militia,[21] the ICU is undoubtedly an *al-Qaeda* creation. Its leader is Hassan Dahir Aweys, a former cleric and head of *AIAI's* military wing.[22] In turn, the warlords formed the "Alliance for the Restoration of Peace and Counter-Terrorism." In April and May of 2006, it was reported to have U.S. backing, to include money and intelligence.[23] By some accounts, this backing undermined the authority of the transitional federal government.[24]

By 5 June, the Islamist militias had fully captured Mogadishu.[25] Against one warlord target within the city, they had launched a surprise attack with 300 militiamen and 30 technical vehicles. After morning prayers, some of the Islamists passed through the first line of defense in a truck bed covered by plastic.[26] To those who knew about *al-Qaeda's* longtime bastion at Bosaso, this came as no surprise. What did come as a surprise was that ICU forces had the help of *jihadists* from Saudi Arabia, Yemen, and Pakistan.[27] An *al-Qaeda* recruiting video was made of their exploits.[28] Thus, the flow of *jihadists* was going in both directions.

Then, the ICU troops started pushing north to seize more territory. They were also moving west toward Baidoa where the fledgling Somali government is based.[29] By 19 June, the U.S. had apparently returned the problem to the Ethiopians. On that date, Shekh Sharif Ahmed, ICU leader, reported that hundreds of Ethiopian soldiers had crossed the border and were heading for Baidoa.[30] It was soon established that 300 Ethiopians had made the incursion and that ICU forces had already imposed *sharia*-law on Jowhar—the other supposed government bastion.[31] On 20 July, fully loaded Ethiopian armored personnel carriers were sent to Somalia at the request of its president.[32] Within days, the ICU was calling for a holy war to expel them.[33] The ICU doesn't like to fight at night,[34] so that expulsion could be long and bloody.

U.S. officials have confirmed that Aweys is a high-level *al-Qaeda* operative who has replaced Ahmed as head of the ICU.[35] As Aweys also controls *AIAI's* military wing,[36] one could accurately now say that most of Somalia is now controlled by *al-Qaeda*.[37]

What Does This Have to Do with the War in Iraq

If *al-Qaeda* is sending *jihadists* to Afghanistan from Bosaso, and to Chechnya and Kenya from Ras Komboni, then someone else must be supplying fighters to the Iraqi theater from another country in the region. The background of that operation forms the fabric of this book. To short-circuit a Muslim revolution in the Middle East, the West must reduce the flow of *baseej* from North Africa.

Part One

Tail of the Viper

"The need to overcome oppression and violence
without resorting to violence and oppression."
— Dr. Martin Luther King

(Source: " 'Citizen King': The Life of the Rev. Martin Luther King, from 1963 to 1968," *American Experience*, NC Public TV. 16 January 2006)

1   *Baseej* from North Africa

- What has Africa to do with the war in Iraq?
- How deeply are terrorist elements embedded in Africa?

THE OTHER HOTBED OF SUNNI FUNDAMENTALISM

(Source: Corel Gallery, Corel Landmarks #26A017)

Al-Qaeda's Historical Link to Africa

Osama bin Laden is a Wahhabi Muslim from Saudi Arabia. Wahhabism is an early form of Sunni fundamentalism that dates back to the mid-18th Century. The Egyptian founder of the Muslim Brotherhood near Cairo in 1928 is said to have been influenced by the Wahhabis (who called themselves the *Ikhwan* or "Brotherhood"). His organization has been active throughout Egypt, Sudan, Syria, Palestine, Lebanon, and North Africa since before WWII.[1] An avowed enemy of Western "decadence," the Muslim Brotherhood has been trying for a long time to consolidate anti-

Western sentiment. As do Wahhabis, it claims to be purifying and restoring the original form of Islam. Like Wahhabi Salafis (those who follow the revered founders of Islam), the Muslim Brotherhood will be willing to cooperate with any fundamentalist Shiite movement that wants to evict Western occupiers and form an Islamic state.[2]

The Unwanted Answer to an Old Question

Many Americans have yet to make the connection between 1983 Beirut, 1993 Somalia, and present-day Iraq/Afghanistan. They see those battles as unrelated aberrations of an increasingly dangerous world. Sadly, there is a connection; and that connection has become impossible to ignore. There are four possibilities: (1) all regional Muslims are being discriminated against, (2) Islamists want to the Old Muslim Empire back, (3) a non-Islamic entity is unintentionally fanning Muslim discord, or (4) some foreign power is perpetuating that discord to pursue its strategic initiatives. (See Map 1.1.) Nowhere in the world are the last three possibilities more evident than in northeast Africa. For several years, the soldiers of virtually every nation along the Mediterranean and Red Sea approaches to the Suez Canal have had to combat an insurgency. (See Figure 1.1.) The catalysts for those insurgencies include the following: (1) Islamic Salvation Front, Armed Islamic Group, and Islamic Salvation Front in Algeria;[3] (2) *En-Nahda* in Tunisia;[4] (3) *Ga'mat al-Islamiya* and Egyptian Islamic Jihad in Egypt;[5] (4) Eritrean Islamic Jihad *(Jamal Jihad),* Eritrean Liberation Front, Eritrean Kunama Movement, and Red Sea Democratic Organization in Eritrea;[6] and (5) Islamic Union of Mujahideen of Ogaden in Ethiopia.[7] Most, if not all, of those insurgencies have had foreign support.

To maintain deniability, any movement or nation wanting to pursue empire building or strategic gain would have to do so through proxies and rebellion. They would need an unlimited supply of foot soldiers and a remote safe area in which to train those foot soldiers. Africa provides both. For lack of a better name, such foot soldiers will henceforth be referred to as *Baseej.* That's what Grand Ayatollah Khomeini called the 20-million-man "people's auxiliary" that he routinely expended as suicidal cannon fodder in his war with Saddam Hussein.

4

The Strategically Important Horn of Africa

Much of the world's trade flows through the Suez Canal. Without unlimited access to that canal, those who would reconstitute the old Muslim Empire or fully tap Africa's resources would have a hard time. Their holdings would be divided, and their trade restricted. Thus, every country along the Red Sea, Gulf of Aden, and northeastern coast of Africa has tremendous strategic value to a regional expansionist.

"About a third of Africa's 700 million inhabitants are Muslim, and Islamists see Black Africa as their newest theater."[8] That's

Figure 1.1: Egyptian Paratrooper
(Source: Courtesy of Orion Books, from *World Army Uniforms since 1939*, © 1975, 1980, 1981, 1983 by Blandford Press Ltd., Part II, Plate 110)

5

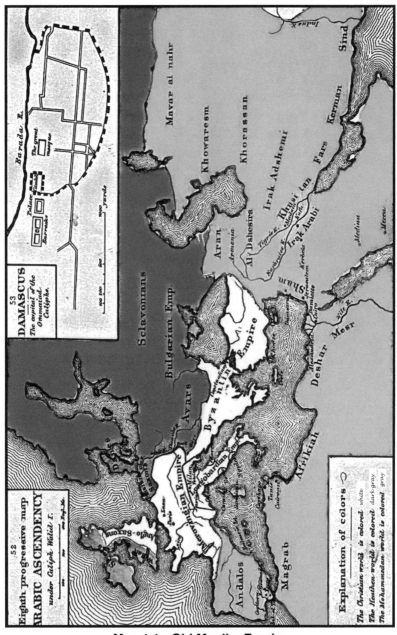

Map 1.1: Old Muslim Empire

(Source: Courtesy of General Libraries, University of Texas at Austin, from their website for map designator "arabic—ascendency 1884.jpg")

almost a quarter of the world's one billion Muslims. (See Map 1.2.)
In Egypt, Libya, Tunisia, Algeria, Morocco, Mauritania, and Sudan,
they are the population majority. In Somalia, Chad, Niger, Mali,
Senegal, and Guinea, they practice the majority religion. Muslims
constitute about half of the population in Nigeria, Eritrea, and Ethiopia; and there are sizable minorities in Ghana, Ivory Coast, Sierra

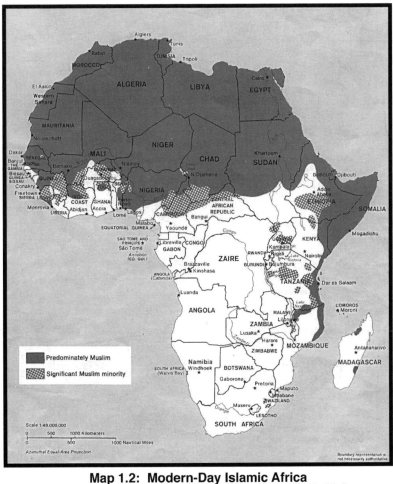

Map 1.2: Modern-Day Islamic Africa
(Source: Courtesy of General Libraries, University of Texas at Austin, from their website for map designator "africa_islam_1987.pdf")

Leone, Kenya, and Tanzania.[9] Thus, much of the "Dark Continent" qualifies as a lucrative recruiting ground for *jihadists*. (Africa is called the Dark Continent because it was little known until the late 19th Century.)

For years, the most dedicated of the Islamists considered Sudan to be their base of operations. Khartoum used Iranian and Saudi funding to promote Islamist uprisings throughout oil- and mineral-rich East Africa—most notably, Kenya, Uganda, Tanzania, Somalia, and Ethiopia.[10]

> U.S. authorities have evidence that Sudan harbors such militant Islamic extremist organizations as Hamas, Hezbollah, the Palestinian Islamic Jihad [PIJ] and Al Gamaat al-Islamiyya, and that it supports other terrorist groups in Algeria, Uganda, Tunisia, Ethiopia and Eritrea.[11]
> — Center for Defense Info., 10 December 2001

It was through an alliance of militant organizations in the 1990's that Khartoum tried to destabilize Eritrea,[12] Algeria,[13] Egypt, and Tunisia.[14] Though intentionally obscure, that alliance has been corroborated by several media sources. It was variously called the Armed Islamic Movement (AIM);[15] the International Legion of Islam;[16] Islamic People's Congress;[17] Islamic People's Conference;[18] and the Islamic National Front (INF).[19] The latter may be an intentional play on words. It might be easily confused with NIF (National Islamic Front), Sudan's ruling party. Of note, the Director of the Congressional Task Force on Terrorism and Unconventional Warfare has AIM "answering to NIF,"[20] instead of the other way around. Thus, NIF must be quite different from a Western-style political party. It may more closely resemble Lebanese *Hezbollah*—militarily minded, yet politically viable. Like *Hezbollah,* it may also be more of a "movement" than an "organization." Without much structure, it could safely serve as an umbrella for semi-autonomous subsects. It has been reported that NIF has a "cell-based structure" based on the Communist model.[21]

The NIF's Inception

The NIF initially arose from the Sudanese chapter of the Muslim

Brotherhood. Its head, Hassan Turabi, became the founder of NIF. While initially out of favor with the Nimeiri regime, he was named its attorney general in 1977 as a conciliatory gesture. From that office, Turabi helped other Brotherhood members to acquire positions of economic and political influence. Then, he again fell from official grace. "In 1989, a military coup brought to power a regime that was . . . a tool of the NIF."[22] This gave Turabi his chance to facilitate regional revolution. While he contended the NIF had been dissolved, it was more probably reconstituted as the Popular Defense Forces (PDF)—the regime's parallel army and trusted power base.[23]

As the PDF's role mirrored that of Iran's Revolutionary Guard *(Sepah),*[24] one could say that Sudan had become a revolutionary republic, and Turabi its pseudo-spiritual (ayatollah-like) leader. For Sunni fundamentalists, AIM would then serve the same purpose that the Party of God *(Hizbullah* or *Hezbollah)* had for Shiite activists. Under the financial backing (and indirect control) of hidden sponsors, they could also work together to emplace *sharia* law throughout the region. Like Lebanese *Hezbollah* in Lebanon,[25] Sudanese AIM acted as an umbrella for individual groups across North Africa. As such, it diverted unwanted attention from any particular group. So loose an arrangement might seem unproductive to a hierarchy-oriented Westerner.

Not surprisingly, three of those sponsors were the largest *sharia*-abiding states—Saudi Arabia, Pakistan, and Iran.[26] (See Map 1.3.) Saudi *Wahhabis* initially funded *al-Qaeda.* They and Pakistani *Jamiat-i-Ulema-i-Islam Fazlur Rehman Faction (JUI/F)* still support the Taliban's effort to recapture Afghanistan.[27] Pakistan's other legal religious party—*Jamaat i-Islami (JI)*—provided people and wherewithal to Hekmatyar's militia during the war with the Russians and probably still supports *Hezb-i Islami Gulbuddin (HIG).*[28] Not to be outdone, Iran has backed the Northern Alliance in Afghanistan;[29] *Hamas,*[30] *PIJ,*[31] and the Popular Front for the Liberation of Palestine General Command (PFLP-CG) in Israel;[32] and the Mahdi Army,[33] Ansar al-Islam,[34] and other Sunni factions in Iraq.[35]

Through the lead of Saudi Arabia, the Organization of Islamic Conference (OIC) had been formed in 1972 as a counter to the Egyptian dominated Arab League. Pakistan hosted an OIC in May 2005. In attendance were the representatives of several Islamic nations. While they openly agreed on a nonconfrontational stance with the

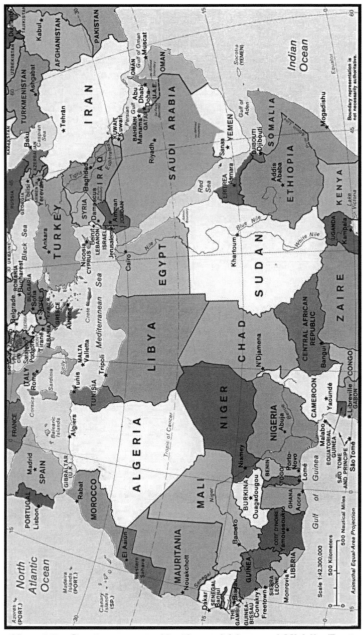

Map 1.3: Contemporary Northern Africa and Middle East
(Source: Courtesy of General Libraries, University of Texas at Austin, from their website for map designator "n_africa_mid_east_pol.95.jpg")

West,[36] several may have had hidden agendas. Those who were fundamentalist Shiite or Sunni would want more *sharia*-abiding states. While occupied by the West, such states will not be possible.

More About AIM's First Few Years

Turabi had assembled—on several occasions—some 40 Islamist parties, movements, and organizations under the guise of a Popular Arab and Islamic Conference (PAIC),[37] or Islamic People's Conference. The PAIC was formed as a counter to the Saudi-dominated OIC.[38]

These were AIM conferences at which the Muslim Brotherhood's Sudanese chapter did what it could to promote worldwide *jihad.* To augment (and possibly obscure) AIM's efforts, bin Laden (then living in Khartoum) created a parallel organization—the World Islamic Front for the Jihad against Jews and Crusaders (WIFJ). It would serve as an umbrella for about 20 other guerrilla and terrorist groups.[39]

These PAIC sessions were attended by some very interesting people. The guest list included top leaders from Pakistani Inter-Service Intelligence (ISI), *al-Qaeda,* Palestinian *Hamas,* Lebanese *Hezbollah,* and Iranian *Sepah.*[40] Because of Salafi beliefs, bin Laden and al-Zawahiri (though fundamentalist Sunni themselves) welcomed Shiite participation in their worldwide *jihad.*[41] In 1979, Ayatollah Khomeini called for a global revolution by both Shiites and Sunnis.[42] Thus, the stage was set for military cooperation between any number of Islamic factions with theological differences.

At some point, AIM operation centers were established in Tehran and Karachi.[43] Through Azzam and al-Zawahiri, the Muslim Brotherhood had spawned *al-Qaeda* in Pakistan and *Hamas* in Palestine.[44] That Brotherhood influenced the politics of Saudi Arabia through *Wahhabis,* and those of Pakistan through *JI.*[45] In the mid-1970's, Hekmatyar's *JI*-supported militiamen were locally known as the "Muslim Brotherhood."[46] Though Sunni, they too wanted to create an Islamic state like that of Iran.[47] Their Egyptian namesake is still very influential with Pakistan's *Markaz-ud-Dawa-wal-Irshad (MDI* or *"Jamaat ul-Dawa").*[48] *MDI's* military wing—*Lashkar e-Toiba (LET* or *"Khairun Nas")*—provides *al-Qaeda* with enough suicide bombers and special operators to support its cells.

Thus, the Muslim Brotherhood must be considered a major player in the Global War on Terror. It did finally create an Islamic state like that of Iran—in Sudan. With its new headquarters in Khartoum,[49] the Muslim Brotherhood is in a perfect position to provide trained *baseej* (foot soldiers) for Iran's Middle Eastern insurgencies and African initiatives. Through PAIC meetings, the leaders of Lebanese *Hezbollah, Hamas,* the Iranian Revolutionary Guard, and *al-Qaeda* have routinely conferred on strategy.

China became Iran's single largest supplier of arms in 1989. Since the year 2000, upwards of 4,000 Chinese military personnel have been stationed in Sudan (ostensibly to guard China National Petroleum Corporation facilities). The Sudanese Armed Forces have had Chinese aircraft and tank advisers since the mid-1980's.[50] If the revolutionary governments of China, Iran, and Sudan are now sharing notes on guerrilla warfare, world peace may be in considerable jeopardy.

Other Evidence of Sudan Instigating Trouble

Prior to 1991, the Sudanese Army and "Islamic fundamentalist militants from [other countries]" were being trained in Sudan by the Iranian Revolutionary Guard.[51] As of 1993, thousands of other *jihadists* were passing through camps built by Osama bin Laden.[52] "By early 1995, Iranian funding enabled the . . . [NIF] and *al-Qaeda* to establish twenty-three training camps throughout Sudan." At some of the *al-Qaeda* camps were *Hezbollah* and *Sepah* trainers.[53] Many stayed open after Osama's departure in 1996. Among them were the following: "[(1)] two camps for Arabs at Merkhiyat; [(2)] one camp for Eritrean, Ethiopian, Ugandan, Somali, and occasionally Palestinian Islamists at Al-Qutanynah; [(3)] one camp for training Palestinian, Libyan, Iranian, Iraqi, Yemeni . . . Islamists in Jabel al-Awliya; [(4)] one for training Egyptians, Algerians, and Tunisians in Shendi, near Port Sudan; [(5)] one for treating casualties in Soba; [and (6)] . . . one in Sejara near Omdurman [that] controlled training throughout Sudan."[54] In addition to the Somali island of Ras Komboni, *al-Qaeda* had a protected quay at Port Sudan's mechanized infantry barracks.[55]

All *al-Qaeda* facilities inherited by the Sudanese government may have been shut down after Turabi's arrest in 2001,[56] but those belonging to *Sepah / Hezbollah* probably stayed open. That would make Sudan the principal intake portal for Iraq's manpower pipeline.

Egyptian Islamic Jihad, Eritrean Islamic Jihad, Ethiopian Islamic Jihad, *Palestinian Islamic Jihad, Hamas,* and *Hezbollah* were just a few of the regional insurgencies supported by Sudan in the 1990's.[57] As *Sepah* is known to have also supported rebels in Algeria, Tunisia, and Egypt,[58] Sudan may have functioned as an Iranian satellite. The Iranian air force and navy were using Sudanese facilities. In 1979, Iran had called for a global Islamic revolution by both Shiites and Sunnis.[59] That would require the cooperation of fundamentalists from both sects, whether they liked each other or not. Azzam's *jihad* was global in scope, aimed at recouping the glories and lands of Islam.[60] Those lands include Palestine, Lebanon, Chad, Eritrea, Somalia, and Southern Yemen.[61] Thus, all of northeastern Africa must necessarily be included. Many of those lands are now under attack by insurgents. In December 2005, Chad declared war on Sudan, accusing Sudanese militias of making daily cross-border raids.[62]

Sudan's Internal Conflicts

Sudan is really two countries in one. Its northern population is largely Arab, while its southern population is black and non-Arab. The Khartoum-based Sudanese army (and its allied militias) had been fighting the south's Sudanese People's Liberation Movement/Army (SPLM/A) since 1983. Many of the SPLA fighters were trained and armed in Ethiopia.[63] To help derail the SPLA, Sudan's government has lent support to the brutal Lord's Resistance Army (LRA) of northern Uganda since the 1990's.[64] In 2004, a coalition government was formed and the former SPLM/A commander—John Garang de Mabior (a Christian Dinka)—made Sudan's First Vice President. Within months, he was killed in a helicopter crash.[65]

Then, the Sudanese Liberation Army (SLA) started clamoring for autonomy in the western, Darfur region. To defeat it, the Sudanese Army backed Arab militias, the *janjaweed,* with aerial bombardment of villages.[66] Sudan has accused Eritrea of aiding the Darfur rebels.[67] That support most probably goes to the Sudanese Justice and Equality Movement (JEM) that has been fighting for autonomy in both west and east. JEM, the Beja Congress faction, and other rebel groups now hold a strip of territory along the Sudanese-Eritrean border.[68]

> Created last year by the region's largest ethnic group, the Beja, and Rashidiya Arabs, the Eastern Front has similar aims to its counterparts in Darfur—greater autonomy and control over the area's resources.
>
> The rebel Justice and Equality Movement, active in Darfur, has also emerged as a key player in eastern Sudan. It demands a seat at the presidency as part of any peace settlement, but has not been invited to the Asmara talks.
>
> Sudan says the latest push to defuse the crisis in the east is part of an attempt to pacify the whole of Africa's largest country, by building on peace agreements reached recently with other rebels.[69]
>
> —*Sudan Tribune,* 10 June 2006

Other Regional Activity

Mostly Muslim Eritrea has been having a border dispute with largely Christian Ethiopia[70]—America's strongest ally in the area. From 1998 to 2000, that dispute claimed 70,000 lives—with the fighting often resembling that of WWI. At issue was which nation would control the town of Badme. The U.N.-backed boundary commission awarded Badme to Eritrea, but landlocked Ethiopia has failed to abide by the ruling. The Ethiopians claim that Eritrean troops are sneaking into their country disguised as militiamen. As of October 2005, U.N. forces were pulling back from the frontier.[71] Eritrea has since threatened to take Badme back by force, so the situation remains tense. Eritrea has been one of Africa's most repressive nations. It financed arms for Somali Islamic extremists in the mid-1990's and again in July 2006.[72] A month later, Eritrean, Afghan, and Pakistani trainers were spotted at an ICU boot camp.[73] That makes Eritrea a possible supporter of *al-Qaeda.*

The Certainty of an Islamist Coalition

The extent to which Shiite *Sepah* and Sunni Muslim Brotherhood have cooperated in the past in Sudan should be adequate proof of a coalition. For those who still doubt it, there was an interesting dialogue in late April 2006. First, while most of *al-Qaeda's* regional contingent was in Somalia, Osama bin Laden asked for *jihadists* to confront the U.N. in Sudan.[74] Then, Sudan indicated that no Western troops would be tolerated in Darfur.[75] Finally, Iran promised to share its nuclear technology with Sudan.[76] Sudan plays a larger role in world politics than just a rendezvous point for local subversives. While currently reeling from all the U.N. attention to its frontier squabbles, Sudan deserves a closer look.

Bilad as-Sudan

- Does Sudan still serve as an Iranian satellite?
- What are all the Chinese doing there?

BEYOND THE MIGHTY SAHARA

(Source: FM 90-3 (1982), p. 2-5)

The Strategic Key to Sub-Saharan Africa

Sudan is the largest country in Africa—comprising almost one tenth of its continental surface. The Sudanese describe their nation as the "whole of Africa in one country." Its terrain ranges from desert in the north to tropical forest in the south. Straddling the fault line between north and sub-Saharan Africa, the Arabs call it *bilad as-Sudan* or "land of the blacks."[1] As such, it is the most logical place from which to pump *sharia* law into the partially Muslim equatorial region. It is also the most logical place from which to exploit that region's vast petroleum reserves. Sudan borders upon eight other

17

nations. Its frontiers are so loosely controlled that foreign guerrillas cross them to seek shelter, and Sudanese proxies cross them to attack neighbors. (See Map 2.1.)

Sudan Has Changed since the Early 1990's

One cannot form an accurate picture of contemporary Sudan from history alone. As of June 2006, Khartoum's citizens enjoyed freedom of religion (a Catholic cathedral), press (independent newspapers), and dress (occasional uncovered female heads).[2] Yet, as in communist nations, a showplace capital doesn't mirror the welfare of a population.

Sudan's people are among the world's most hospitable.[3] Sadly, they have yet to benefit from any oil proceeds.[4] Since the mid-1990's, their Islamist government has made several concessions to the West. President Omar Bashir extradited Carlos the Jackal in 1994, expelled bin Laden's *al-Qaeda* faction in 1996, and jailed Hassan al-Turabi in 2001.[5] Yet, Sudan remains on America's list of countries supporting terrorism. Thus, its government may have learned how to more deceptively export "Islamic resistance."

The ruling faction in Sudan is the National Congress Party (NCP). "It was created in 1998 by . . . the former National Islamic Front (NIF)," and many Sudanese claim they are still one and the same.[6] According to the U.N. Mission in Sudan (UNMIS), "[the NCP] has its roots in . . . the Muslim Brotherhood movement in Egypt in the 40's." The followers of al-Turabi split from the NCP in 2000 to become the Popular National Party (PNP or PCP).[7] When their leader was released from prison in June 2005, the PNP became a legal opposition party.[8] Yet, everything was not going as well as it seemed.

As of May 2006, Turabi was calling for a "popular uprising" against the Sudan regime.[9] He is now associated with the JEM rebels at the Eritrean border and in Darfur.[10] It was JEM that, in May 2006, failed to join the SLA in signing the Darfur Peace Agreement (DPA). Thus, Turabi—though ostensibly pushing for the overthrow of the Bashir regime[11]—may be Sudan's new "infiltrator of rebel coalitions" and "delayer of U.N. accords." That might have been the condition of his parole. Such arrangements are commonplace in south Asia. That's how Eastern nations maintain deniability while bettering their odds in a regional power struggle. Is not the pro-Iranian Afghan regime opposed by both Pakistan-affiliated Taliban and Iran-affiliated Hekmatyar?[12] Just as Sunni Pakistan has been using proxy militias to influence Kashmir and Afghanistan, so too may Sunni Sudan be using proxy militias to control its remote border regions.

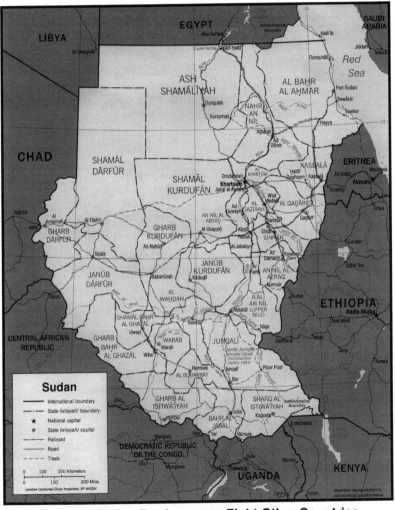

Map 2.1: Sudan Borders upon Eight Other Countries
(Source: Courtesy of General Libraries, University of Texas at Austin, from their website for map designator "sudan_pol00.pdf")

The Security Situation in Khartoum

Khartoum looks nothing like the center of a police state. It lacks the army checkpoints and bunkers that one might expect. The only visible downtown security is a sprinkling of police vehicles around the Presidential Palace and nearby street corners. On the nights of 30 and 31 May 2006, the SPLM bussed scores of supporters to rallies near the center of town. While those rallies were almost exclusively attended by hundreds of military-age males, there were no uniformed security personnel anywhere in sight.[13] Still, the absence of crime along Khartoum's poorly lit streets would indicate a no-nonsense criminal-justice system.

Now a Divided Nation

In January 2005, the Comprehensive Peace Agreement (CPA) was signed between the SPLM and Sudanese government. It made the former a legitimate political party, the Government of South Sudan (GoSS) autonomous,[14] and SPLM leader—Dr. John Garang—First Vice President of Sudan. Soon thereafter, Garang died in a suspicious helicopter crash at the Congolese border. Immediately, relations between the SPLM and Khartoum cooled among complaints that the latter had been stalling on the CPA's full implementation. Finally, after the DPA in May 2006, talks between the NCP and SPLM began anew.[15] Garang's successor—Lt.Gen. Salva Kiir Mayardit—became Sudan's First Vice President. The CPA had mandated that all oil revenues be divided equally between the Khartoum regime and GoSS during the six-year interim period, but the two sides had yet to decide on the demarcation line through oil-rich Abyei Province.[16] There were reports of Sudan's Popular Defense Forces moving into the disputed area.[17]

> The demarcation of Abyei, a contested area on the north-south border that contains one of Sudan's two main oil fields, was rejected by the NCP, although the boundary commission decision was supposed to be final and binding under the CPA. Abyei has been given autonomous status and will choose in a referendum in 2011 whether to remain part of the north or join a potentially independent southern Sudan.[18]
> — United Nations News Service, 1 June 2006

To make matters worse, the SPLM now wants its own refinery.[19] Simply agreeing on the distribution of revenue would have been hard enough, but the Khartoum government has an oil-hungry partner and record of agreement violations. Its willingness to fulfill the new promises has been questioned, and the status of three central and eastern provinces remains a point of contention.[20] Luckily, the CPA has guaranteed elections in 2007 and a secession referendum for GoSS in 2011, should the "Government of National Unity" fail to live up to expectations.[21] A lot can happen in five years, the Islamists may be just stalling for time.

As the leader of a nation in which one political party dominates, al-Bashir recently disclosed his perception of democracy.

> The President . . . asserted that the *game* of democracy must include both government and opposition because the presence of all forces with the same government will make it take the form of totalitarianism [italics added].[22]
> — President of Sudan, 31 May 2006

> Sudan is a one party dominant state with the National Congress in power. Opposition political parties are allowed, but are widely considered to have no chance of gaining influence.[23]
> — *Wikipedia Encyclopedia*

Meanwhile—through the hidden auspices of Khartoum—the LRA continues to undermine the viability of the GoSS. On 30 May 2006, the new First Vice President of Sudan accused the Sudanese Army of fueling instability in the south by helping the LRA.[24] Two days later, the LRA raided a village near Juba (the southern capital).[25] The fledgling GoSS has even tried to pay LRA leader Kony to stop raiding. Regional experts think the demented leader is in the process of moving his group farther west—to the border between Sudan and the Democratic Republic of the Congo (DRC).[26] Though the NCP and SPLM are now coalition partners, there have been few changes in NCP policies.[27]

Changes in Khartoum's Timeless Appearance

Much of the northern capital's Islamic influence resides in its sister city of Omdurman. At the southern end of Omdurman is the Islamic University (much less active than its Khartoum counterpart). Just north of there is Mahdi's Tomb and a one-acre, mud-walled prison that dates back to the days of Kitchener. Still farther north is the government-controlled radio and TV station.[28]

In June 2006, two new bridge/road networks were under construction (by the Chinese) across the Blue Nile. Their apparent purpose was to better link semi-industrialized Khartoum North and the Port Sudan highway with the city center.[29] The one over Tuti Island terminates (near what used to be the zoo) at the Sudanese/Libyan al-Fateh Project—a massive hotel grotesquely shaped like an on-end football. The other terminates near Khartoum university and the airport. The highway that runs north to the Red Sea from Omdurman may be under renovation to service the oil pipeline, because that which runs south from Khartoum airport was recently identified as the way to Port Sudan.[30] A tourist was not allowed by his Sudanese sponsor to travel (even for a short distance) along either route.[31] Thus, one wonders if the old *jihadist* training headquarters in Omdurman and trans-shipment points in Port Sudan may still be operational. Some 30 kilometers south of Port Sudan is the ancient seaport of Saikim.

Sudan's Traditional Turmoil

Because of its immense size, Sudan embraces both Arab and equatorial cultures. When facing a common foe (like British colonialists), those cultures cooperate. In 1898, Gen. Kitchener's expeditionary army was confronted by a combined force of "whirling dervishes" and "fuzzy-wuzzies."[32] Now that separatist movements have sprung up in the south and west of Sudan, those Arab and equatorial cultures are clashing. Because the south is largely Christian, its war could be sparked by religious differences. But in Darfur, dark-complected Arab Sunnis have been attacking black Sunnis.[33] Thus, Darfur's genocide has racial overtones.[34]

Darfur's Dance of Death

On 5 May 2006, the Sudanese government and main Darfur rebel group (the predominantly Zaghawa SLA/M of Minni Minawi) signed a peace accord in Nigeria. While there were indications that Sudanese leaders were now willing to accept a U.N. peacekeeping force, their previous opposition to such a force made its full deployment improbable. Those leaders have a history of not living up to agreements.[35] Two smaller rebel groups rejected the deal, and John Pendergast, head of the International Crisis Group's Africa Program, remained skeptical about the sincerity of Sudan's government. He pointed out that it had "previously shown a willingness to sign treaties (during the rebellion in the south of the country) and then delayed implementing them."[36] The two holdouts were a breakaway Fur tribe faction of the SLA led by Abdel Wahid Mohamed Nur and JEM led by Khalil Ibrahim.

Though the SLA/M is the largest anti-government faction in the region, it is tiny JEM that has tried to unify the opposition. On 20 January 2006, JEM declared a merger with SLM and other rebel groups to form the Alliance of Revolutionary Forces of West Sudan. That alliance must not have totally gelled, because JEM and SLM negotiated as separate entities during the recent peace talks.[37] JEM has had little military presence on the ground, but it is politically and propaganda savvy. This gives it the capability to spoil the agreement.[38] JEM is the group with an Islamist ideology that is linked to al-Turabi.[39] That's where the picture begins to blur. It was almost as if Turabi's radical Islamists were trying to create their own breakaway state.

In April 2006, Osama bin Laden had called for a holy war in Darfur. Two months later, his *al-Qaeda* deputy al-Zawahiri did likewise. Both wanted the Sudanese Muslims on both sides of the conflict to attack any U.N. peacekeeping forces that came into the region. They were also unhappy with the Sudanese government for agreeing to a U.N. military mission in Darfur.[40]

In March and April, JEM helped Chad's President Idriss Deby to repel attacks from Chadian rebels in Sudan. As both victims and perpetrators were black and Sunni,[41] this development is confusing. Deby is from the Zaghawa tribe like most of Minni Minawi's SLA.[42] Thus, Turabi may simply want Chad in his camp. Khartoum has been supporting and recently consolidating those Chadian rebels.[43]

Partially because of the U.N. arms embargo, Sudan has turned to China for military assistance. Unlike most Western nations, China is little fazed by human-rights abuses.

The manufacture in Sudan of Chinese weapons and ammunition complicates the enforcement of a UN embargo on supplies to militias in Darfur. Chinese-designed arms and radios are reported to have been used across the border in Chad–where France keeps a garrison–by rebels alleged to be operating with Sudanese support.[44]

— *The Financial Times* (UK), 28 February 2006

A Partial Solution for Darfur

Some of Darfur's problems can be traced to tribal hatred and Muslim expansionism, but others have a far more simple explana-

Figure 2.1: China National Petroleum Corporation "Guard"
(Source: Courtesy of Orion Books, from *World Army Uniforms since 1939*, © 1975, 1980, 1981, 1983 by Blandford Press Ltd., Part II, Plate 81)

tion. The northern part of Darfur has been hit hard by drought and desertification since the mid-80's. Much of its population has had to move south into central Darfur. The new arrivals were mostly camel herders (whose camels had died). Without any way to support their families or aid from Khartoum, many turned to banditry.[45] Such things are an unfortunate part of tribal dynamics in Africa (just as they were in early America).

Thus, the Western military has another paradoxical reminder of how to defeat an insurgency. By simply providing destitute peoples with a way to legitimately help themselves, it could turn the tide in the War on Terror. For, by so doing, it would eliminate the terrorists' recruiting base. In parts of Darfur, a single water well per village might be enough to get the job done.

The U.N.'s Existing Role in Sudan

UNMIS was established by the United Nations under Resolution 1590 of the U.N. Security Council on 24 March 2005. It was to support the CPA signed by the government of Sudan and SPLM on 9 January of that year. It was also to perform certain functions relating to humanitarian assistance, protection, and promotion of human rights. Some 10,000 military personnel were to have been involved. How many actually deployed is unclear. An undisclosed number of Chinese troops were sent to the "Wau" (Waw) Sector between the oil fields and DRC border. That sector includes the states of West Bahr el Ghazal, North Bahr el Ghazal, Warab, and Al Buhairat.[46]

China's Overall Involvement with Sudan

In the late 1970's, China replaced the Soviet Union as the principal supplier of heavy armaments to Sudan.[47] In August 2000, London's *Sunday Telegraph* reported a huge influx of Chinese troops into Sudan to help with its civil war in the south.[48] In March 2004, the *Washington Times* lowered that estimate to 4,000 and said their purpose was protecting an oil pipeline.[49] (See Figure 2.1.) (It further claimed that the original information was from a South African news service and in error.) That oil pipeline must be one co-built by the Chinese that stretches some 1,500 kilometers from the oil fields southwest of Khartoum, to the capital's refinery, and then on to Port Sudan.[50] On 1 May 2006, NPR reported that there was a widely held view within China that Chinese peacekeeping troops had already been sent to Sudan in support of U.N. resolutions.[51]

In 2004, there were 24,000 Chinese officially registered in Sudan.[52] As of June 2006, a longtime Khartoum hotel owner estimated almost ten times that number living there, with more coming in every day, and a projected total of a million.[53] In the capital, none are in uniform.[54] Many work at the refinery or on construction projects, while others represent a wide assortment of trades.[55] The relationship between China and Sudan has become more than one of a fledgling superpower helping an emerging nation.

> "The recent years have witnessed friendly exchanges between the Sudanese National Congress and the Communist Party of China [CPC] on all levels," it [the CPC message] said, adding that the CPC would exert more efforts to enhance the friendly ties with the NC[P].[56]
> — Official Chinese News Agency, 24 November 2005

A Troubling Similarity to China's Other African Projects

Though a pipeline carries the petroleum, China is building 25 locomotives for Sudan.[57] It has also been refurbishing the old British railway between the Angolan ports of Benguela and Lobito and the DRC towns of Luau, Lubumbashi, and Ndola (at the Zambian border).[58] If the Chinese-built "Tanz-Zam" railroad of 30 years ago is any indication, China's new Angolan enterprise may soon be carrying Chinese-trained replacements to an expanding Congolese War.

The Beijing government once had the authority to relocate any citizen to whatever part of China it wanted to develop.[59] For a long time, that was China's underpopulated west. That mandate may now extend to Tibet and its overseas colonies. Or, the hundreds of thousands of Chinese currently living in Africa may simply be employees of their government. A few thousand military trainers could easily hide among that many civilian workers. On 10 August 2006, Angolan President Dos Santos claimed that Chinese were coming to his country to work on temporary projects. This was in answer to a rumor that he had authorized the immigration of four million.[60]

What Interest Does South Africa Have in Sudan?

Prior to a surprise victory in South Africa's (SA's) 1994 elections, the African National Congress (ANC) was supported first by the Red Chinese and then by the Soviets. It has maintained many of those relationships and perceptions. For example, today's SA government reportedly prefers the Chinese-backed and dictatorial Mugabe to democratic reform in Zimbabwe. As of June 2006, it had rounded up, and sent back to an uncertain future, thousands of Zimbabwean refugees. While as many as two million may have crossed the border, South Africa has no formal asylum procedures and has only allowed "a handful" to legally stay.[61]

> The . . . (ANC) is a centre-left political party, and has been South Africa's governing party supported by a tripartite alliance between itself, the Congress of South African Trade Unions (COSATU) and the South African Communist Party (SACP) since the establishment of majority rule in May 1994.[62]
> —*Wikipedia Encyclopedia*

Possibly through a mutual dislike for European colonialists, the ANC has now formed a bond with African Islamists.[63] In Sudan, that bond has been combined with action. "South Africa is expected to assist Sudan in the process of demobilization and the integration of former [SPLM] combatants."[64] By 31 May 2006, SA and Sudan were about to sign some sort of treaty. The SA government has also been active in establishing a dialogue between the DRC rebels and government. It claims to be trying to assist the people of the area to prepare for elections.[65]

> "The [South African] ANC has never confined its efforts to making life better for its citizens only. It has always extended its efforts to uplifting the rest of the continent," says Dlamini-Zuma.[66]
> — SA Foreign Affairs Minister, May 2006

Within South Africa itself, the "democratic process" has produced one-party rule.[67] Amid accusations of corruption, "a small but growing number of blacks are arguing what once seemed unimaginable—that life was better under white rule."[68] As of May 2006, South African police are targeting any blacks they perceive to be foreigners.[69] One wonders how tightly it is protecting its interests or those of foreign partners. Many South Africans are not aware of the Chinese excesses in Tibet and elsewhere. They do not see the Chinese as neo-colonialists or any kind of a threat, for that matter.[70]

Let the Games Begin

On 25 June 2006, what longtime Sudan watchers had feared was starting to happen again. Sudan suspended (for a day) all U.N. mission work in Darfur after accusing the world body of transporting a rebel leader who had opposed the DPA.[71]

Is Sudan Still Exporting *Jihadists?*

Sudan is a huge country over which the Khartoum government can exercise only limited control. As in Pakistan, there may be vast areas that are virtually autonomous and thus perfect safe areas for Islamic radicals. Within the last chapter was evidence that Lebanese *Hezbollah* may still be running any number of guerrilla training camps in Sudan. To date, there is no direct evidence of Chinese light-infantry instructors at those camps. Still, that possibility exists.

For America, it is the *jihadists* headed for Iraq that pose the biggest problem. After leaving Khartoum, those trained by *Hezbollah* most probably travel through Lebanon.

Levant Passage

- How do the African *jihadists* get from Sudan to Iraq?
- What is the first stop on their journey?

WHAT'S LEFT OF A CRUSADER CASTLE

(Source: DA Pam 550-24 [1989], p. 179)

African *Baseej* Enter the Middle East through Lebanon

Several non-Lebanese, U.S. captives have admitted to visiting the Bekaa Valley en route to Iraq.[1] If African *jihadists* are being trained in Sudan by *Hezbollah,* then they are probably being escorted to the war zone by that same organization. Beirut is the terminus of the Shiite smuggling route out of Iraq,[2] so it would be the most logical place for *Hezbollah*-escorted and Iraq-bound Africans to enter the Middle East. Those destined for special-skill assignments or suicide missions could then be easily siphoned off in the Bekaa Valley for further training. (See Map 3.1.)

The radical Lebanese Shiite terrorist organization Hezbollah has been moving fighters to Iraq in recent months to battle American troops, according to a report in the Israeli newspaper Haaretz.

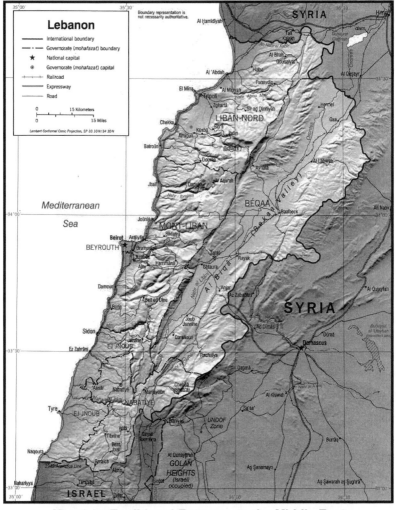

Map 3.1: Traditional Entrance to the Middle East
(Source: Courtesy of General Libraries, University of Texas at Austin, from their website for map designator "lebanon_rel_2002.pdf")

The report attributes the information to U.S. intelligence sources who say the transfer of fighters has been carried out through Syria, following an Iranian initiative. The transit through Syrian territory is permitted by Damascus along its porous border with Iraq.

The Hezbollah fighters in Iraq are part of a broader force of pro-Iranian militants operating in Iraq to destabilize the country and undermine U.S.-led coalition forces and the new Iraqi government.

Iran is eager to see the Hezbollah fighters establish operations in Iraq before a new regime is officially installed in Baghdad June 30 [2004].[3]

Many of the *Hamas* fighters for Gaza and the West Bank of Israel are also being trained in Sudan.[4] They would be expected to enter the Middle East through Lebanon. Lebanon's tiny army has yet to provide as much security as the now-departed Syrians did. It makes no attempt to guard the Israeli border. (See Figures 3.1 and 3.2.) A few too many military-age males arriving by private charter in the middle of the night at Beirut airport would draw little attention. After all, that airport lies at the center of a *Hezbollah* stronghold.

[T]he airport . . . [is] located by the seaside in the Lebanese capital's Hezbollah-controlled southern suburbs. . . .

. . . [T]he airport . . . is "a central hub for the transfer of weapons and supplies to the Hezbollah terrorist organization."[5]

— Associated Press, 13 July 2006

In the summer of 2004, British Airways was flying between London and Khartoum via Beirut. By June 2006, it had shifted its interim stop to Ankara.[6] One does not need too active an imagination to figure out why. Some of the passengers on the first part of the return leg had made the airlines a little nervous.

Whether the African *jihadists* were entering Lebanon through its principal airport or many seaports, Syria would be more than amenable to their trans-shipment to Iraq. In June 2006, Damascus and Tehran signed a military agreement . . . promising unrestricted passage through Syria for Iranian arms shipments to Hizbullah."[7]

Where arms travel freely, so too probably do armed personnel. Shortly, there would be an indication of how many heavy armaments had been flowing the other direction. (See Figure 3.2.) But the world would be caught by surprise, because Lebanese *Hezbollah* had been enjoying a long-term diversion near the Egyptian border.

The Unexpected Development in Palestinian Gaza

On 26 January 2006, fundamentalist *Hamas* had won a surprise victory over secular *Fatah* in the Palestinian parliamentary elections. Out of the 132 seats available, *Hamas* captured 74. After many years of *Fatah* rule, a faction dedicated to the violent overthrow

Figure 3.1: Lebanese Soldier
(Source: Courtesy of Orion Books, from *World Army Uniforms since 1939*, © 1975, 1980, 1981, 1983 by Blandford Press Ltd., Part II, Plate 117)

of Israel had "democratically" won the right to control the fledgling state and its Palestinian Authority. Among its representatives would be a woman who had happily sent three of her six sons on

Figure 3.2: Contemporary Beirut Street Scene
(Source: DA Pam 550-24 [1989], p. 39)

suicide missions.[8]   While U.S. leaders instantly downplayed the impact of this vote on regional peace, it created a long-term media diversion south of the Lebanese border.

The Palestinian election was overtly democratic, but its preliminaries were decidedly illicit. As do other fundamentalist factions in the region, *Hamas* relies for its power on a carefully choreographed mixture of financial destitution and charity, spiritual repression and emphasis, and nationalistic subversion and promotion. Of course, Israel—through its Westernized style of warfare (blockade, bombardment, and assassination)—has also contributed to the problem. Still, it was primarily through psychological manipulation that *Hamas* convinced the Palestinian people that it could deliver more Israeli concessions and a better way of life.

Israel had resisted *Hamas* participation in the election but finally bowed to U.S. pressure.[9] With only a few days to go, America contributed millions to *Fatah* advertising.[10] Unfortunately, it was too little and too late.

At first, armed representatives of the new *Hamas* government were happy to forcibly evict those from the outgoing *al-Fatah* faction. Then, in early June 2006, *Hamas* fighters tunneled into one of Israel's Gaza outposts to seize a hostage. Israel responded by bombing and entering parts of the Palestinian enclave.[11] On 12 July, *Hezbollah* upped the ante by crossing the Lebanese-Israeli border to capturing two more Israeli soldiers.[12] As the raid had been preceded by a short rocket barrage, Israel hit back hard.

Conduit Theory Buoyed by U.S. Reaction to Israeli Bombs

Something of strategic importance to America was happening in Lebanon, because Israel was permitted to bomb that country for almost a month without any serious attempts at a cease fire. Instead of condemning the destruction, the U.S. sent more and heavier "smart bombs" to Israel and offered to train the Lebanese army.[13] Among other things, it was taking full advantage of this opportunity to disarm *Hezbollah* in compliance with the 2004 U.N. resolution. Instead of attacking rocket sites in southern Lebanon, Israel was attempting to stem the flow of everything in and out of the entire country. Among its bombing targets were the following: (1) all seaports, (2) Beirut airport, (3) all bridges along the highway from Beirut to Damascus, and (4) all other roads into Syria.[14] While

Israel was supposedly curtailing the western flow of munitions from Damascus, America may have been curtailing the eastern flow of *jihadists* from Beirut.

By 7 August, *Hezbollah* had fired only a fifth of its 15,000 Iranian-supplied rockets and missiles at Israeli towns up to 45 miles from the border, to include Haifa. With other missiles that can reach over 100 kilometers, *Hezbollah* was also threatening to hit Tel Aviv.[15]

> Israeli officials think Hezbollah has dozens of long-range missiles capable of reaching Israel's largest city, Tel Aviv, but say it needs permission from its chief sponsor, Iran, before firing them.
>
> The missiles are . . . reportedly under the direct control of some 200 members of Iran's Revolutionary Guards who are deployed alongside Hezbollah in Lebanon. . . .
>
> Israeli officials quoted by the Associated Press said yesterday that at least one Iranian-made missile capable of reaching Tel Aviv was destroyed yesterday when an Israeli aircraft bombed a truck carrying several missiles. . . .
>
> The London-based Arabic newspaper al-Sharq al-Awsat yesterday quoted an Iranian military source close to the Revolutionary Guard leadership saying Iran has provided Hezbollah with C802 shore-to-ship missiles, which were copied from a Chinese [Silkworm] design and used over the weekend to hit an Israeli ship, killing four seamen.
>
> The newspaper said Hezbollah also has Fajr, Iran 130 and Shahin missiles with ranges of about 60 to 90 miles. The missile destroyed on the truck, shown in flames on Lebanese television yesterday, was identified as a Zelzal-2, an unguided missile with a range of up to 120 miles.[16]
>
> —*Washington Times,* 18 July 2006

The rockets kept coming despite Israel's edge in technology and firepower, so that country sent ground thrusts against selected *Hezbollah* bastions. Thus began a seemingly unrelated series of events. First, near Bint Jbail, elite Israeli troops were ambushed in a street that had already been "cleared."[17] Then, Israel's goal of raiding all the way to the Litani River (18 miles) was modified to creating a buffer zone 1.2 miles deep,[18] and remodified to bulldozing a half-mile-wide "no-man's land."[19] Finally, on 26 July, Israel

35

"mistakenly" bombed a U.N. border outpost containing a Chinese peacekeeper.[20] As both China and North Korea maintain embassies in Beirut,[21] the pieces began to fit.

Israel had sent mechanized infantry against a defense line that was very probably of Chinese or North Korean design. Just as U.S. troops had experienced trouble with the one just north of the 38th parallel in 1953, the Israelis were having a hard time with this one. *Hezbollah's* first bastion had been full of bunkers, caves, and tunnels.[22] On 30 July, Sheikh Naim Qassem—*Hezbollah's* second in command—boasted that *Hezbollah's* stockpiling of arms and preparation of numerous bunkers and tunnels over the past six years had been the key to its resistance. He further said, "If it was not for these preparations, Lebanon would have been defeated within hours."[23]

That sounds very much like a underground strongpoint defense—the current state of the art. Only highly skilled light infantry can deal with something like that without having to take heavy casualties. Unfortunately, neither Israel nor the U.S. has any true light infantry.

Now aware that *Hezbollah* could claim victory from a limited offensive, Israel sent 10,000 troops and scores of tanks across the border about 1 August. Its goal this time was to create a 5-mile-deep zone that U.N. peacekeepers and the Lebanese army could successfully occupy.[24] On 8 August, Israel's deepest penetration was reported to be only 4 kilometers in the direction of Taibeh.[25] The very next day, Israel announced an all-out assault on the border region involving many more troops and tanks. It also said it needed another 30 days to achieve its objective. Whether or not that objective had expanded in depth was unclear. Wisely, Israel had decided to attack the formation from east to west, instead of head on. *Hezbollah* defenders were negating Israeli air power by moving through tunnels that Iran had built.[26] While the terrain in southern Lebanon is not as daunting as that faced by U.S. forces just inside North Korea in 1953, this defense line has the advantage of modern technology. In addition to Fuel-Air-Explosive (FAE) anti-personnel missiles and infrared-detonated anti-tank mines above ground, it had an advanced command-and-control network below ground.[27] While the extent of the tunneling may never be known, *Hezbollah* fighters kept reappearing in places already under Israeli "surface control."[28]

[There were] bunkers housing . . . advanced eavesdropping and surveillance equipment and monitoring cameras. . . . [F]ighters [kept] constantly popping up . . . , firing, and then vanishing again.[29]
— *The Times* (UK), 10 August 2006

Israeli armor was particularly hard pressed by *Hezbollah's* "high-tech" anti-tank-missile methodology.

In one hidden bunker, Israeli soldiers discovered night-vision camera equipment connected to computers that fed coordinates of targets to the Sagger 2 missile.[30]
— *The Washington Post,* 14 August 2006

Further, *Hezbollah's* strongpoints were heavily disguised. To identify an enemy bunker, an Israeli soldier had to be "right there."[31] This sounds all too familiar to veterans of Iwo Jima, Korea, and Vietnam. Many still dream of bunker apertures they just spotted a few feet away. Yet, for whatever reason, contemporary leaders will continue to deny any correlation with the Asian model. Might the Chinese and North Koreans have been using Lebanon as a test of ways to incorporate modern technology into an already formidable defense scheme?

On 14 August, a U.N.-sponsored cease fire went into effect. Resolution 1701 forbade *Hezbollah's* from bearing of arms south of the Litani River. By the last day of the war, Israeli troops had reached the Litani in places. Yet, *Hezbollah* still managed to launch it biggest daily total of rockets and missiles—some 250.[32]

The End Result of the Israeli Incursion

Hezbollah's degree of control over Lebanon is hard for anyone to imagine who has not travelled there lately. Only part of that control emanates from Beirut's southern suburb of Haret Hreik. *Hezbollah* also has two cabinet ministers and 14 votes in the Lebanese parliament.[33] The duly elected Lebanese government does not recognize Israel and has depended on *Hezbollah* to guard is southern border for six years.[34] In early 2006, to escape the provisions of U.N. resolution 1559, that government designated *Hezbollah* as a "resistance group" instead of a militia.[35] On 17 August, it deployed its troops south of the Litani River, but their mission was not to confront *Hezbollah*. Lebanon's government had mandated that *Hezbollah's* arms be confiscated "only if carried in public." Thus, the fully sanctioned "resistance group" had only to keep their personal weapons out of sight.[36]

Israel's removal of the immediate threat to its northern border will be temporary at best. In the interim, *Hezbollah* may have more time to pursue its Iraqi initiatives. Amidst the ruins of southern Lebanese towns were signs that read "made in the U.S."[37]

How Will Events in Lebanon Affect the Iraqi Insurgency?

Only time will tell whether Israel's month-long isolation of Lebanon will help the Coalition to win in Iraq. There is irrefutable evidence that *Hezbollah* has been supplying Shiite and Sunni militias alike with advisers, equipment, foreign fighters. Its flow of people and materiel into Syria has only been briefly interrupted. One does not need roadways and bridges to move what little it takes to run an insurgency. (A hidden infiltration route will be the subject of the next chapter.) Additionally, Iraq's insurgency has become more self-sufficient.

Political wrangling does not easily supplant open warfare in the Middle East. Though a noble attempt to break the cycle of violence, the various elections won't produce viable democracies unless Israel and the United States adopt a less provocative style of war. That will take small-unit tactical reform—something that American arms manufacturers and rank enthusiasts have successfully dodged for 90 years. To lessen the *jihadist* impulse, missile sites must be inconspicuously sabotaged by *ninja*-like commandos. Terrorist leaders must be captured and tried, not summarily executed with bombs and rockets. This is a type of war in which high-level leaders play little, if any, role. More important to its outcome is the ability of security personnel to apply minimal force at short range.

Euphrates Pipeline

● Where along the Euphrates does the infiltration path run?

● What evidence is there of its exact location?

Mesopotamia's Only Concealment Was along Its Rivers

(Source: FM 90-5 [1982], p. 1-6)

Getting into Iraq Is the Easy Part

Once the African *baseej* transit Syria, they must still run the gauntlet into Sadr City or southern Iraq. Their most logical route would be along the Euphrates River. That route has been used by Shiite smugglers for centuries. It was undoubtedly improved during the pre-war boycott and possibly even taken over for a while by the Baathists.

In apparent preparation for nuclear war, Saddam Hussein had a whole series of heavily reinforced subterranean bunkers in Baghdad. To get around the U.S. embargo on nuclear proliferation materials and equipment, his intelligence agency—*Makhabarat*—utilized (or took over) the cigarette smuggling operation between Jordan and Iraq about 1995.[1] There is no telling how much of its traditional route may have been refined, but the world remembers well the cat-and-mouse game that U.N. inspectors played with Saddam's nuclear henchmen at its probable terminus—Abu Gharaib.[2] Saddam's intelligence agency may have taken advantage of the smuggling route from Syria as well (the one along the Euphrates). If so, that route may now have more of a subterranean dimension than before. "[By 1996] smuggling in Iraq, particularly with the burden of U.N. sanctions, had been refined to an art."[3]

Before the U.S. invasion, Saddam Hussein built "an extensive underground tunnel system . . . to ambush forces or for a quick get-away."[4] While many of his excavations were beneath the streets of Baghdad, there were others elsewhere. A large, well-maintained tunnel network was found under Fallujah.[5] Its passageways were steel reinforced, some big enough for bunk beds and trucks.[6] Others connected the mosques.[7] Fallujah is west of Baghdad on the Euphrates River. For an unobstructed exit to Syria, Saddam would have needed below-ground waystations all the way to the border. Thus, one might expect subterranean facilities farther west along the river. With enough evidence of such, one could plot the exact trace of the exit path. Routes of egress can also be used for reinforcement.

How an East-Asian Infiltration Route Operates

At the southern end of Okinawa during the latter stages of WWII, the Japanese expanded and stocked a series of caverns in which their units could rest and re-outfit during above-ground, reinforcing moves. On Vietnam's coastal plain 25 years later, the Viet Cong dug underground waystations along their infiltration paths into Danang. To protect those paths, the Viet Cong (VC) also established a 1500-meter-wide belt of fortified villages. Close enough to cover each other by fire, those villages constituted a "state-of-the-art" strong-point defense. Each had its own "below-ground hide facility." To keep one step ahead of U.S. intelligence, local guerrilla bands would shift their headquarters among ten or so of these hide facilities.[8] All of them had well-hidden front entrances and rear exits. The former was often below a village well's waterline, while the latter was below the surface of an irrigation canal.

The VC's early warning apparatus pales in comparison to that of the Muslim militant. The latter may not need fortified villages along his infiltration routes. To dampen Coalition interest in the entrances to underground facilities, he may only require boobytraps and snipers.

The Most Active of the Ancient Smuggling Routes into Iraq

For centuries, there has been a "rat line" up the Euphrates River into Syria and the Levant. It has traditionally handled the illegal smuggling of goods. Of late, those goods have included antiquities,[9] medicine, and medical supplies.[10] Its terminus is the port of Beirut.[11]

Within Iraq, that early rat line probably ran between above-ground transfer points or "safe houses." During the U.S. boycott, much of its trade started flowing in the opposite direction, and many of its waystations may have moved below ground (to elude satellite surveillance). The precise location of those waystations and of the route itself would have great strategic value to the Coalition. Where it crosses the border is anyone's guess. On 28 February 2005, an "Iraq Resistance Report" mentioned the "Makr adh-Dhib Road, a rocky trail that winds through a mountainous area where it is hard for helicopters to follow and observe people on the ground."[12]

Since the U.S. invasion, the rat line's Tigris River counterpart has been modified to handle not only supplies, but also people coming into Iraq.[13] (See Map 4.1.)

By the summer of 2003 . . . , the insurgency began to organize itself, and the call went out for volunteers.

Safe houses were established. Weapons were positioned. In the vast desert that forms the border with Iraq, passages through the dunes long used to smuggle goods now were employed to funnel fighters.

"We had specific meeting places for Iraqi smugglers," Abu Ibrahim said. "They wouldn't do the trip if we had fewer than 15 fighters. We would drive across the border and then into villages on the Iraqi side. And from there the Iraqi contacts would take the mujaheddin to training camps." . . .

In the summer of 2004, Abu Ibrahim got to go to Iraq. He crossed the dunes with 50 other volunteers, dodging U.S. patrols on the Iraqi side.[14]
— *Washington Post,* 8 June 2005

Such a transformation must have occurred at the entrance to the southern route as well. But, while the Tigris conduit supported Baathists and Sunnis, its Euphrates counterpart (because of its Lebanese origin and Iraqi destination) would better serve the Shiites. Why else would a ten-ton arms cache exist below the riverbank a full 25 miles south of the turnoff to Baghdad.[15] That supposition, in turn, raises the possibility that Lebanese *Hezbollah* may be supervising its operation. (See Figure 4.1.)

Figure 4.1: The Probable *Hezbollah* "Adviser"
(Source: Courtesy of Orion Books, from *World Army Uniforms since 1939,* © 1975, 1980, 1981, 1983 by Blandford Press Ltd., Part II, Plate 113)

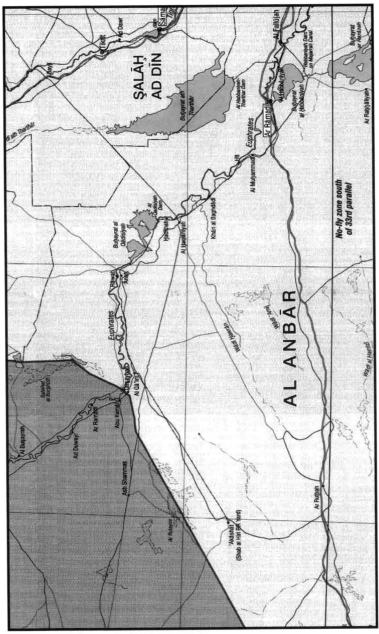

Map 4.1: Euphrates Reinforcement Route

(Source: Courtesy of General Libraries, University of Texas at Austin, from their website for map designator "middle_east_and_asia/iraq_cia_2003.jpg")

The border town most often associated with Euphrates smuggling is Al Qaim (on the south bank). During an operation in its vicinity in April-May 2005, the U.S. military captured smugglers who "confessed to bringing weapons, foreign fighters and money for terrorists across the Syrian border into Iraq." Included in that search was the tiny village of Ish, just north of Al Qaim.[16] As most maps show Al Qaim on the river's edge, Ish must be on the opposite bank. It was on the north side of the Euphrates that the Marines found "cave complexes."[17] At the end of the subsequent operation, they expanded that assessment to "numerous cave complexes."[18] In this part of the world, the term "cave" connotes human habitation. Might the rat line have followed the less-populated north bank of the river? That would have eliminated the requirement to cross over it to reach Baghdad and the majority of antiquity-producing ruins.

On Which Bank Have Most Smugglers Been Reported?

Several sources confirm that the purpose of Operation Matador (7-15 May 2005) was to investigate a "known smuggling route" in the al-Jazirah Desert just north of the Euphrates.[19] When the Marines took mortar fire from the south bank, they built a pontoon bridge and crossed over the waterway to the west of Obeidi.[20] That fire may have been an intentional diversion. One both sides of the river, the Leathernecks unexpectedly encountered strongpoints and regulars.

> [Lt.Gen. James] Conway said that the insurgents are well trained and equipped and have put up fierce resistance. "There are reports that these people [the insurgents] are in uniforms, in some cases are wearing protective vests, and there is some suspicion that their training exceeds that of what we have seen with other engagements farther east," he said.[21]
>
> —*Radio Free Europe/Radio Liberty,* 11 May 2005

> During that fighting, insurgents attacked in groups as large as 50 people, [Col. Bob] Chase said. . . .
> The offensive carried echoes of the Fallujah operation,

where Marines and soldiers also encountered formations of militants in well-defended positions.[22]
—*USA Today,* 10 May 2005

In early 2006, there were firsthand accounts of military materiel being smuggled by boat along the Euphrates.[23]

Which Frontier Residents Facilitate the Infiltration

On Operation Steel Curtain (5-22 November 2005), the Marines captured people using sheep for cover as they crawled away.[24] During the previous February, an "Iraq Resistance Report" had let slip that sheep and livestock smugglers were facilitating the infiltration."[25] With the advent of satellite-borne thermal imaging, such a ruse would make perfect sense.

In this region, the smuggling has been tribally based.[26] Which tribe is primarily responsible for the Euphrates sector is anyone's guess. Bedouins frequent both sides of the Syrian border. They are nomads and sheep herders. There is an old Bedouin route from Yemen to Damascus that runs just north of Karbala.[27] That would put it between Lakes Habbaniyah and Milh and along the south bank of the Euphrates or across the desert through a series of water holes. As sheep herds are often seen along the main road to Jordan,[28] it may be the latter. Still Bedouins are always short on funds, and those who live near Al Qaim may still be involved in the infiltration. Those along the Jordanian frontier are known to be protective of strangers.

What Happens at Tal Afar—the Tigris River Entry Point

Procedures at the Euphrates River portal may closely resemble those at its northern twin. At Tal Afar on 10 September 2005, several hundred insurgents put up a spirited fight in the city's ancient Sarai district and then mysteriously disappeared.[29] There is only one place they could have gone—into the city's subterranean ruins. A day later, the deputy chief of staff for Coalition forces in Iraq admitted to a network of "escape tunnels" beneath Sarai.[30] What he didn't realize was that the insurgents were probably still below his soldiers' feet—just waiting for them to depart. To find the exact locations at

45

which they disappeared below ground, his units would have needed "mantrackers." As most U.S. units lack mantrackers, they would also be unable to locate subterranean waystations. Within hours of their fruitless sweeps, enemy conduits can be up and running.

The commander of the U.S. assault force has confirmed that Tal Afar was an *al-Qaeda* stronghold.[31] In 2005, al-Zarqawi had reportedly shifted much of his operation from Mosul to Tal Afar.[32] That would suggest that Tal Afar is the entry point for those who would participate in the Sunni part of the insurrection. During the first half of 2005, 270,000 Saudis visited Syria. According to PBS's *Frontline*, the *jihadists* among them crossed into Iraq at Tal Afar.[33] The Sunni Arab tribes that live on both sides of the border make this passage possible. The Shamar is one such tribe. As it creates a diversion at one village in the area, it walks *jihadists* across the border into another. Those *jihadists* are told to shave their beards, carry cigarettes (most Salafis don't), and avoid shortening their robes (like Salafis do).[34] The same crossing method is, in all likelihood, used at the place where Shiite affiliates enter the country as well.

The First of Two Euphrates Pipeline Hypotheses

When people believed to be infiltrators were seen crossing the river at Obeidi,[35] Coalition commanders decided to curtail cross-river traffic through bridge removal. Thus, the infiltration route most probably now follows one bank or the other all the way to Ramadi.

> [Maj.Gen.] Lynch explains the tactic, "There were 12 bridges from the Syrian border to Ramadi. . . . There are now four. Those four that remain are under the control of the Iraqi security forces and coalition forces." . . .
> . . . Insurgents and terrorists wishing to transverse the river must now run the river gates established at Rawah [one bridge] and Ramadi [three bridges].[36]

After the infiltration route enters Iraq, it either follows the south riverbank to a point just southwest of Fallujah or the north riverbank to Fallujah. The first possibility (south of the river) will initially be examined. To avoid population centers, it would most likely parallel the rail line to just west of Ramadi and then skirt Lake Habbaniyah to Fallujah. (See Maps 4.2 to 4.20.)

46

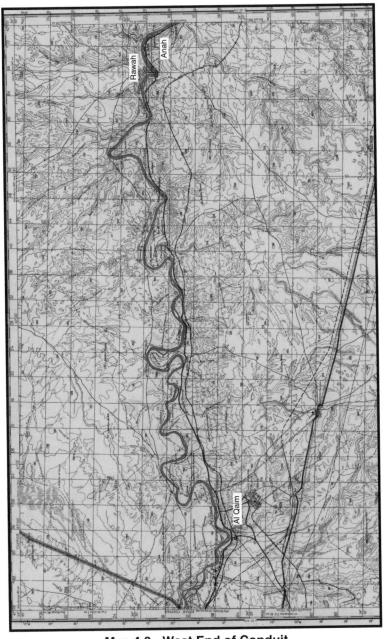

Map 4.2: West End of Conduit

(Source: Courtesy of Univ. of Cal. at Berkeley Lib., "8085/iraq/200k/i38_20.jpg," 1:200,000 Topographic Map, Soviet Union, Sovetskaia Armiia, Generalnyi shtab, 1972-1991)

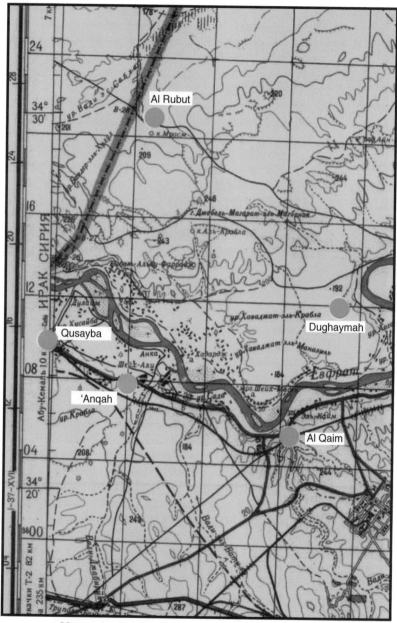

Map 4.3: Border Towns in Vicinity of Al Qaim
(Source: Courtesy of Univ. of Cal. at Berkeley Lib., "8085/iraq/200k/i38_20.jpg," 1:200,000 Topographic Map, Soviet Union, Sovetskaia Armiia, Generalnyi shtab, 1972-1991)

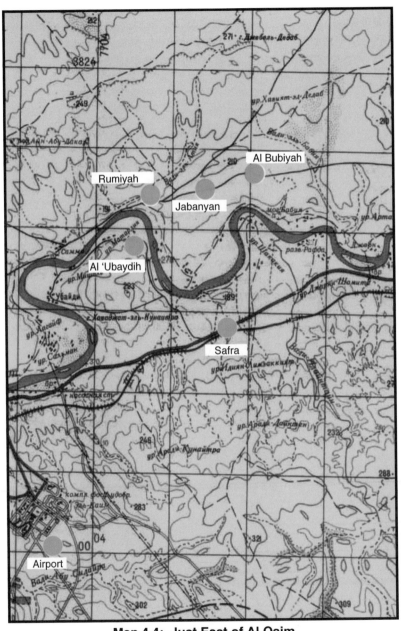

Map 4.4: Just East of Al Qaim

(Source: Courtesy of Univ. of Cal. at Berkeley Lib., "8085/iraq/200k/i38_20.jpg," 1:200,000 Topographic Map, Soviet Union, Sovetskaia Armiia, Generalnyi shtab, 1972-1991)

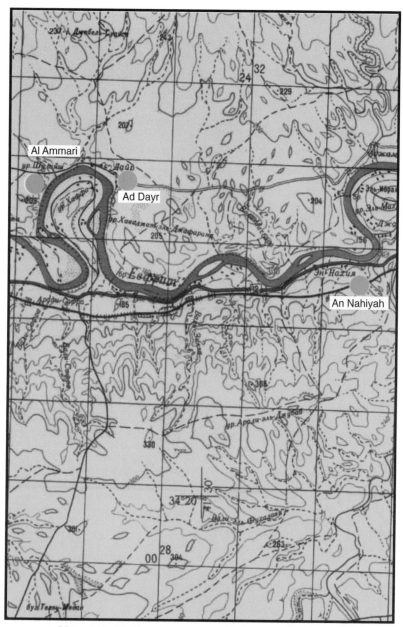

Map 4.5: Halfway between Al Qaim and Rawah
(Source: Courtesy of Univ. of Cal. at Berkeley Lib., "8085/iraq/200k/i38_20.jpg," 1:200,000 Topograhic Map, Soviet Union, Sovetskaia Armiia, Generalnyi shtab, 1972-1991)

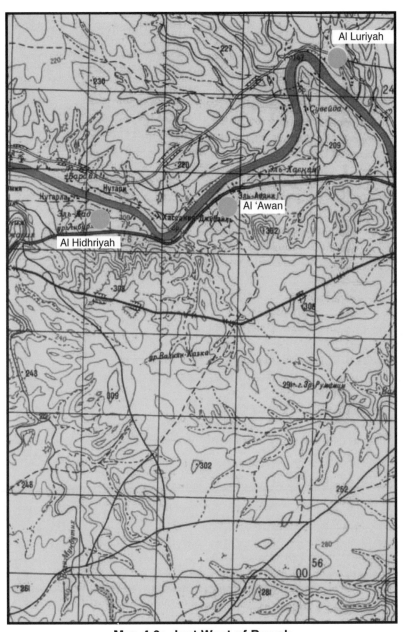

Map 4.6: Just West of Rawah
(Source: Courtesy of Univ. of Cal. at Berkeley Lib., "8085/iraq/200k/i38_20.jpg," 1:200,000 Topographic Map, Soviet Union, Sovetskaia Armiia, Generalnyi shtab, 1972-1991)

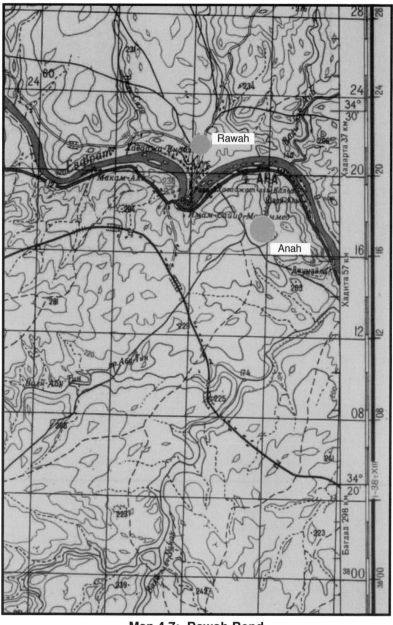

Map 4.7: Rawah Bend
(Source: Courtesy of Univ. of Cal. at Berkeley Lib., "8085/iraq/200k/i38_20.jpg," 1:200,000 Topographic Map, Soviet Union, Sovetskaia Armiia, Generalnyi shtab, 1972-1991)

Qusayba (Haseiba)

Qusayba straddles both highway and railway just east of the Syrian border. On 17 April 2004, just over a hundred Muslim fighters attacked a Marine battalion at Qusayba, fought for 24 hours, and inflicted a score of casualties.[37] Their degree of audacity and deception suggests an organized unit. First, a roadside bomb was detonated at Baath Party headquarters as a decoy. Then, the responding unit was met with machinegun and RPG fire. Finally, U.S. reinforcements were mortared and taken under small-arms and RPG fire from both sides of the road. When several Marines tried to clear a house, they were ambushed in its courtyard. Their killers were wearing black uniforms and laughing.[38] The Marines returned to Qusayba during Operation Steel Curtain in November 2005 and vowed to create a long-term presence in Qusayba, Karabilah, and Obeidi (as they already had in Fallujah and Ramadi). This was a change in policy. Before, they had only occasionally swept through those places.[39] During Operation Steel Curtain, they found 36 weapons caches and 107 IEDs.[40] As their search spanned both sides of the river, there is no way to tell which side contained more evidence of an infiltration route. From Qusayba, the rail line closely parallels the road to Al Qaim.

'Anqah and Karabilah

An Iraqi road map shows 'Anqah as the first town on the road east of Qusaybah, but there are actually others.

Karabilah is seven miles from the Syrian border and on the main road to Al Qaim. On 18 June 2005 during Operation Spear, U.S. Marines found what they interpreted to be a training facility at Karabilah.[41] The town was further investigated during Operation Steel Curtain in November.[42]

Al Jaramil, Khutaylah, Sa'dah (Saadah), and Ba'lujah

These towns lie along the riverbank and off the main road. Eight miles from the Syrian border, Saadah has gotten the most attention. During Operation Iron Fist (1-15 October 2005), U.S. Marines searched Saadah after giving its 2,000 residents time to

53

leave. According to the *San Francisco Chronicle,* this is one of the places where the insurgents had instituted *sharia* law.[43] Many had hidden in the houses and planted IEDs throughout the town.[44]

Saadah was also searched during Operation Steel Curtain in November,[45] but nothing of major consequence was discovered at that time.

Al 'Ushsh and Al Qaim

Al 'Ushsh is not very big. It lies just south of the main road and west of Al Qaim.

Al Qaim itself is located between the river's most southerly bend and the road. On Operation Matador in May 2005, U.S. forces swept the area. As soon as they left, heavily armed insurgents returned to its streets. Among them were many foreign fighters who were trying to impose *sharia* law on the population.[46]

U.S. forces laid siege to Al Qaim again in August. Since the autumn of 2005, Al Qaim and its outlying villages along the south bank of the Euphrates have been outposted by a U.S. Marine battalion.[47] From this town, one road and the rail line run roughly parallel to the river. Another road and the oil pipeline cut the corner and go directly across the desert to Hadithah. The next population center astride the rail line is Al Fubaymi.

Tarayiyah and Safra

Tarayiyah is on the main road just east of Al Qaim. Satra is farther east along that road, but well north of the rail line.

Obeidi (Al 'Ubaydih)

Obeidi lies in a bend of the river just north of Qaim. Still on the south bank, it was the last city taken by the Marines during Operation Steel Curtain in November 2005. The Marines and accompanying Iraqi army contingents met "strong resistance" there, possibly because the insurgents believed themselves trapped in a cordon.[48] One large anti-armor device was found and exploded beneath the main road through New Obeidi. In another incident, a daisy-chain of explosives was discovered just off the road in suspicious rock mounds.[49] During the Operation, citizens pointed out "weapons stockpiles" and IEDs "hidden in gardens of homes."[51] On 16 November, a Marine squad encountered a hidden explosive as it entered a farmhouse in Obeidi.[51] Insurgents then "raked" survivors and rescuers alike with small arms and rifle-grenade fire.[52] That farmhouse could have been part of a defensive strongpoint matrix protecting an infiltration trail. As of June 2006, New Obeidi has been outposted by Marines.[53]

Mish'al, Al Jurn, An Nahiyah

Mish'al is just north of Obeidi in the same river bend. Al Jurn lies between road and river about halfway between Al Qaim and An Nahiyah. An Nahiyah is on both road and rail line about 40 miles east of the Syrian border.

Ad Hidhriyah and Al 'Awan

These towns are off the main road and on the tiny road paralleling the river. Their residents would undoubtedly have access to boats.

Anah and Fuheimi (Al Fuhaymi)

Anah is a large town on the south bank of the river opposite Rawah. It is on the railroad, but well north of the main highway.

Fuheimi is on both road and rail line between Anah and Hadithah.

Suwihal, Shahma, and Tartasa

These populated areas are off the main highway and on a tiny river road. Though quite diminutive, Suwihal is directly on the rail line. That rail line will not intersect another town until Hawija Arbarr.

Sulaimaniyah and Hadithah (Madithah)

Sulaimaniyah is the next built-up area on the main road to Hadithah. It lies just south of a new dam across the Euphrates. That dam creates Lake al-Qadisiyah. For much of its livelihood, Sulaimaniyah depends on business from the south.

It was in the next town to the south—Hadithah—that, on 3 August 2005, 14 Marines were killed by a huge explosion beneath their armored amphibian. To remove any trace of a buried bomb, the foe had tunneled beneath the road. This is a Lebanese *Hezbollah* technique.[54] On 6 October, the Marines followed IED triggering wires to a mosque. There they found a large buried weapons cache.[55]

Hadithah is also where six Marine snipers were ambushed in the summer of 2005. It was rumored that they had been sent to the same firing position no fewer than five times.[56] That event provided some of the only evidence of *Hezbollah* involvement along the Euphrates. Its perpetrator, *Ansar al-Sunna,* is a known *Hezbollah* affiliate/proxy. *Ansar al-Sunna's* parent—*Ansar al-Islam*—has Iranian backing and *Hezbollah* advisers.[57]

A video of the assault on the sniper team released by a group claiming to be from Ansar al-Sunni *[sic]* shows a team of masked insurgents firing mortars at the sniper position. After the mortar attack, a group of insurgents can be seen swarming up a sandy-colored hill, firing their weapons.[58]
— *The Times* (UK), 12 June 2006

Early on, the Muslim militants had so much control over this town of 90,000 that they had managed to institute *sharia* law.[59] Hadithah has since been the target of several operations: River Blitz (February 2005), New Market (May 2005), Quick Strike (August 2005), and River Gate (October 2005). Then, the Marines began to outpost it. During Operation Red Bull in late December, Kilo Company, 3rd Battalion, 1st Marine Regiment discovered eight communications bay stations and 27 cell phones.[60] A Shiite Iraqi Army unit (probably former militiamen) also guards Hadithah.[61]

Al Haqlaniyah and Hawija Arbarr

Haqlaniyah was part of Operation Quick Strike in August 2005.

Map 4.8: Upper Middle of Conduit
(Source: Courtesy of Univ. of Cal. at Berkeley Lib., "8085/iraq/200k/i38_20.jpg," 1:200,000 Topographic Map, Soviet Union, Sovetskaia Armiia, Generalnyi shtab, 1972-1991)

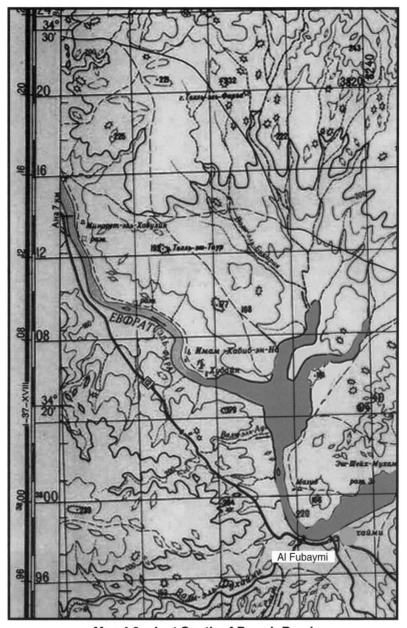

Map 4.9: Just South of Rawah Bend
(Source: Courtesy of Univ. of Cal. at Berkeley Lib., "8085/iraq/200k/i38_20.jpg," 1:200,000 Topographic Map, Soviet Union, Sovetskaia Armiia, Generalnyi shtab, 1972-1991)

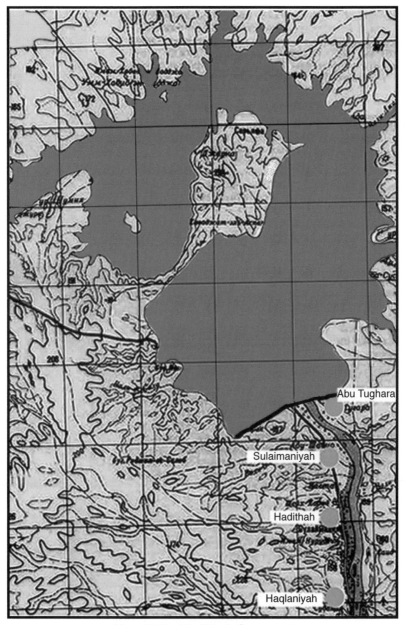

Map 4.10: Hadithah Segment
(Source: Courtesy of Univ. of Cal. at Berkeley Lib., "8085/iraq/200k/i38_20.jpg," 1:200,000 Topographic Map, Soviet Union, Sovetskaia Armiia, Generalnyi shtab, 1972-1991)

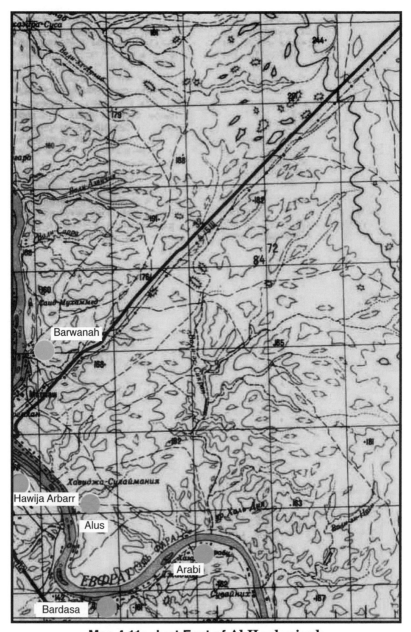

Map 4.11: Just East of Al Haqlaniyah
(Source: Courtesy of Univ. of Cal. at Berkeley Lib., "8085/iraq/200k/i38_20.jpg," 1:200,000 Topographic Map, Soviet Union, Sovetskaia Armiia, Generalnyi shtab, 1972-1991)

The Marines attacked it again in October 2005 during Operation River Gate.[62] Neither time was any find of major significance reported

Hawija Arbarr is on both highway and railroad just south of Al Haqlaniyah. From Hawija Arbarr, the rail line skirts all major population centers for a hundred miles. Its first stop is Ar Ramadi. An all-but-deserted linear terrain feature might be followed by incoming *jihadists*.

Bardasa, Mashhad, Khan al Baghdad, Sahiliya, Mashkan

These are small towns on the main highway between Hawija Arbarr and Hit.

Arabi, Tasiya, Samaniya, Marwaniyah

These are villages on the tiny road that parallels the river between Bardasa and Mashhad.

Zurarq, Ad Darmiyah, Al Qutbiyah, Baziyah, Khadaram

These towns are also on the tiny road along the river between Khan al Baghdad and Sahiliya.

Hit and Khauza

Hit is on the main road but not the rail line. Near it in March 2005, a Marine unit took fire from snipers atop palm trees.[63] During subsequent moves through Hit, U.S. troops have encountered any number of IEDs. They searched the town during Operation River Blitz (February 2005) and Sword (July 2005). During Operation Koa Canyon (January 2006), U.S. Marine and Iraqi Army units searched an area between Hit and a place called Baghdadi (130 kilometers northwest of Baghdad and 43 miles from Hit).[64] Baghdadi and Khan al Baghdad must be the same. During Koa Canyon, Coalition forces discovered a lot of buried ordnance, but they used mine-sweeping equipment (instead of tracking skills) to do it.[65]

Eight days of backbreaking searches through villages and fields along the western Euphrates River valley have yielded thousands of pieces of ordnance as Iraqi Army soldiers and U.S. Marines continue Operation Wadi Aljundi (Koa Canyon) in Iraq's Al Anbar province.

Aimed at isolating insurgents and their weapons, the combined Iraqi and U.S. force began the latest sweep Jan. 15, and have uncovered a staggering amount of weaponry.

The soldiers and Marines are making their way inch-by-inch through caves, fields, wadis, and islands in an attempt to disrupt the insurgents.[66]

— 2nd Marine Div. news release, 23 January 2006

Khauza is a small place on the main road between Hit and Aquba.

Aquba, Abu Tibban, Khan Abu Rayat, al Qutriya, Zangura

Just west of Ramadi, the highway from Ar Rutbah and the Jordanian border enters the area. These towns are all on the lesser road along the river.

Mandau and Ar Ramadi

Mandau is on both road and rail line west of Ramadi. It is the first inhabited area along the rail line for 100 kilometers southeast of Hawija Arbarr. Not much rebel activity has been reported there, possibly because the Coalition lacks the troops to outpost it.

Ar Ramadi lies between the river and Lake Habbaniyah. It has been the scene of off-and-on combat since the U.S. invasion. On 17 November 2005, that fighting took on a new complexion. In what has been likened to a "mini-Tet Offensive," all five outposts of 2-69 Armor in the western part of the city came under ground attack. After all-day reconnaissance, the enemy assault elements came in behind a mortar barrage and beneath machinegun fire from every direction. On 23 August, a truck bomb had rendered a whole platoon of Americans unconscious in one of those outposts.[67]

In November 2005 in northern Ramadi, U.S. soldiers uncovered a weapons cache that spanned "an area several soccer fields in length

. . . hidden among farms and a residential area." In January 2006, Marines discovered another "dump" consisting of more buried caches of weapons.[68] On 12 April, U.S. Marines uncovered another "huge weapons cache" in Ramadi. Subsequently, munitions were found in soccer stadiums and train stations.[69]

On 17 April, the Marines defending Ramadi's Government Center came under the second coordinated assault in nine days.[70] Then, it was revealed that tiny teams of rebels had been firing rockets, mortars, and machineguns at Government Center and other U.S. installations on a "daily" basis and "sometimes several times a day." It was now a city in which *jihadists* moved around freely and engaged any U.S. troops brave enough to venture forth from their bases.[71]

At 400,000 in population, Ramadi is twice the size of Fallujah and more directly astride the region's main thoroughfares. By late May 2006, the situation there had deteriorated so badly that the U.S. military had to dispatch from Kuwait its main reserve fighting force for Iraq—a full 3,500-man armored brigade.[72]

Instead of a Fallujah type assault, the new U.S. contingent and its Iraqi accompaniment planned to cover one neighborhood at a time with company-sized outposts. In the first "Mulaab" neighborhood—where a buried bomb had once lifted an American 60-ton tank well off the ground—they found more IEDs than they could handle. The enemy returned every night to replace those that had been neutralized. Still, Coalition forces managed to occupy an arms-filled soccer stadium and a militant-filled mosque. Their foes' strategy was simple—to create enough chaos that local citizens would have to depend on the insurgency for both security and livelihood.[73]

> Elsewhere in the city [outside of Mulaab], however, insurgents maintain a stranglehold on neighborhoods and institutions.[74]
> — *Chicago Tribune,* 9 July 2006

Ramadi continues to be strategically important to the enemy. The most logical explanation is that it lies astride a major resupply and reinforcement route.

Silariya, Dhibban, and Habbaniyah

These towns are just off the main road between Ar Ramadi and

Al Habbaniyah. Habbaniyah is a larger built-up area just north of a lake of the same name. The narrow strip of land between lake and river constitutes a chokepoint for travel.

South Bank Route Assessment

The rail line to the south and west of the Euphrates skirts many populated areas in Anbar Province. That rail line would make a perfect navigational aid for *jihadist* reinforcements. The main infiltration route into Danang from the south paralleled a rail bed.

Stone-mining operations would provide ready-made underground facilities along any possible transit route. There is a big quarry 1,000 meters southwest of Fallujah, and another 3,000 meters to the west-northwest of town. A large dig exists 1,000 meters west of Habbaniyah, and there are eleven or more along the south bank above Ar Ramadi. Some 1,000 meters to the southeast of Abu Tibban is still another. There are two quarries just north of Hit, and another just north of Anah. (See Maps 4.13 to 4.20.)

While the south bank hypothesis holds some water, it is just as likely that the route starts and ends on the other side of the river.

The Other Possibility─Route Follows the North Bank

During Operation Dagger (June 2005), Marines raided an enemy training facility on the marshy shores of Lake Tharthar, north of Baghdad.[75] That would suggest a lane through the land bridge between the southern end of Lake Tharthar and the eastbound Euphrates. For infiltrators coming in from the north, the lake might serve as a limiting feature for land navigation. If detected on the river road anywhere between Rawah and Hit, increments of fighters could head due east to the lake and then south. Most of the towns discussed next are on the road paralleling the river, but some are inside the above-mentioned land bridge.

Al Rubut (Ar Rabit) and Ish

On the north bank of the Euphrates, Al Rubut is the first town on the main road from Syria into Iraq.

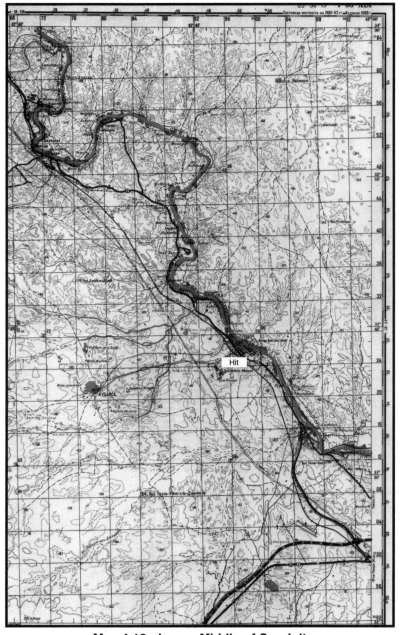

Hit

Map 4.12: Lower Middle of Conduit
(Source: Courtesy of Univ. of Cal. at Berkeley Lib., "8085/iraq/200k/i38_20.jpg," 1:200,000 Topographic Map, Soviet Union, Sovetskaia Armiia, Generalnyi shtab, 1972-1991)

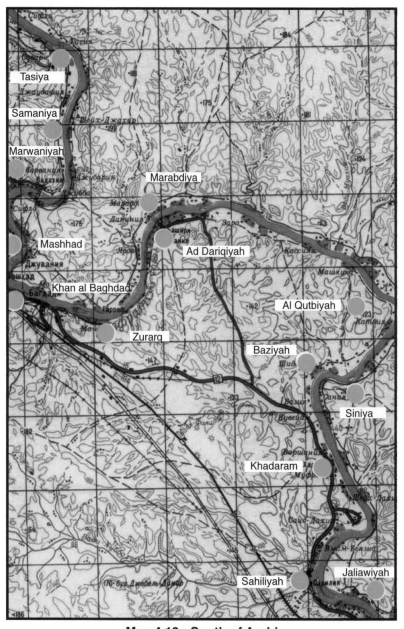

Map 4.13: South of Arabi

(Source: Courtesy of Univ. of Cal. at Berkeley Lib., "8085/iraq/200k/i38_20.jpg," 1:200,000 Topographic Map, Soviet Union, Sovetskaia Armiia, Generalnyi shtab, 1972-1991)

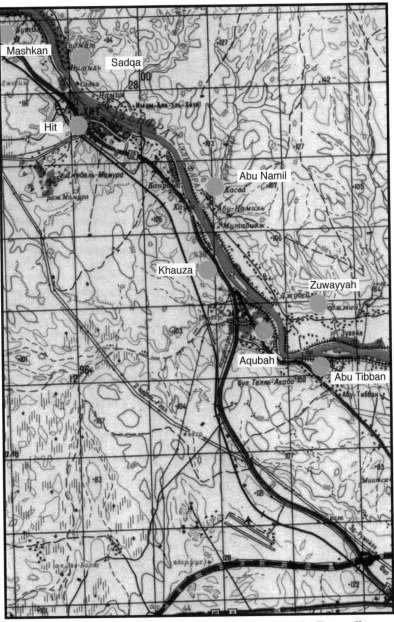

Map 4.14: Just North of Eastern Bend into Ar Ramadi

(Source: Courtesy of Univ. of Cal. at Berkeley Lib., "8085/Iraq/200k/l38_20.jpg." 1:200,000 Topographic Map, Soviet Union, Sovetskaia Armiia, Generalnyi shtab, 1972-1991)

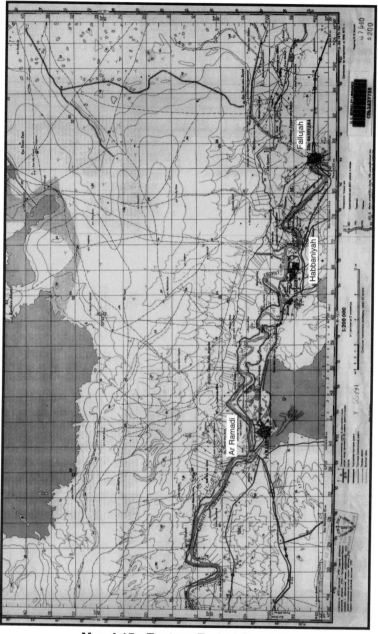

Map 4.15: Eastern End of Conduit
(Source: Courtesy of Univ. at Cal. at Berkeley Lib., "8085/iraq/200k/l38_20.jpg," 1:200,000 Topographic Map, Soviet Union, Sovetskaia Armiia, Generalnyi shtab, 1972-1991)

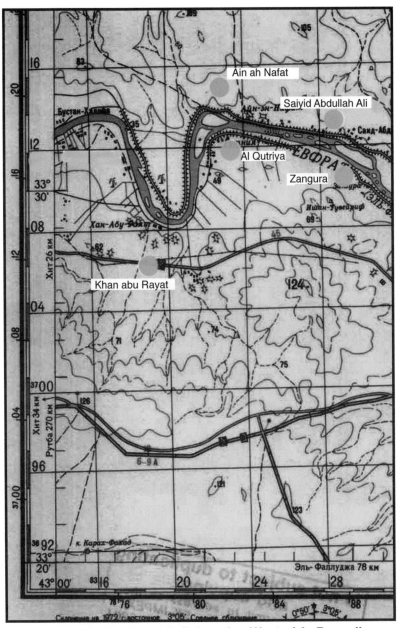

Map 4.16: Road and Rail Junction West of Ar Ramadi
(Source: Courtesy of Univ. of Cal. at Berkeley Lib., "8085/iraq/200k/i38_20.jpg," 1:200,000 Topographic Map, Soviet Union, Sovetskaia Armiia, Generalnyi shtab, 1972-1991)

69

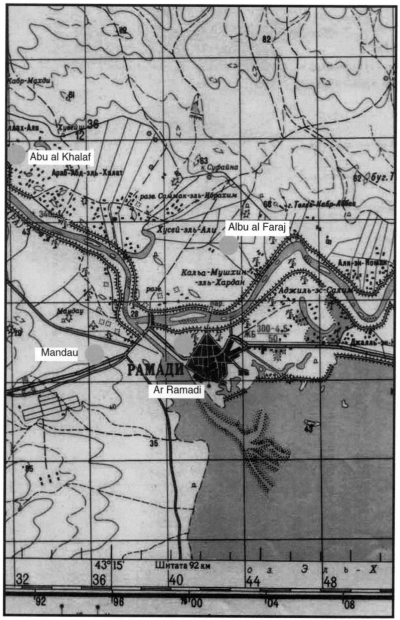

Map 4.17: Ar Ramadi Portion
(Source: Courtesy of Univ. of Cal. at Berkeley Lib., "8085/iraq/200k/i38_20.jpg." 1:200,000 Topographic Map, Soviet Union, Sovetskaia Armiia, Generalnyi shtab, 1972-1991)

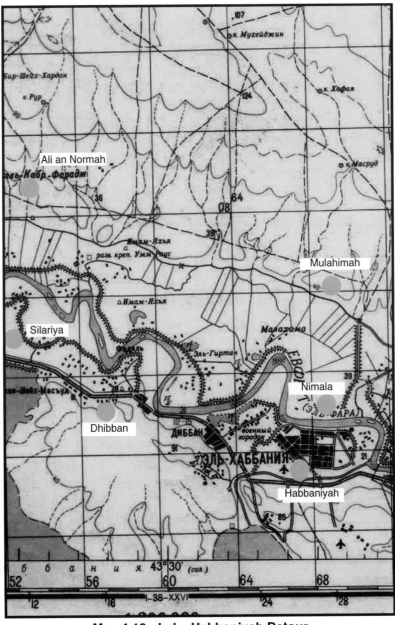

Map 4.18: Lake Habbaniyah Detour

(Source: Courtesy of Univ. of Cal. at Berkeley Lib., "8085/iraq/200k/i38_20.jpg," 1:200,000 Topographic Map, Soviet Union, Sovetskaia Armiia, Generalnyi shtab, 1972-1991)

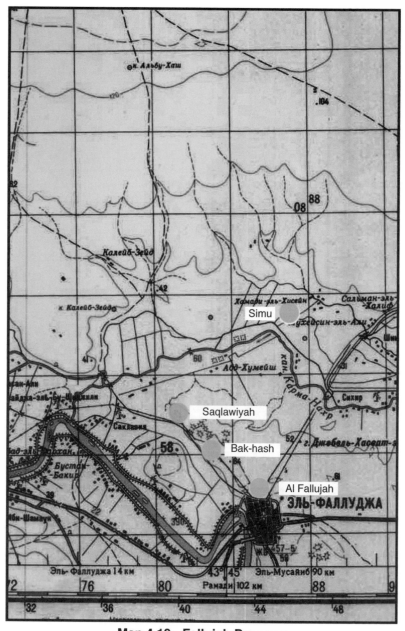

Map 4.19: Fallujah Passage

(Source: Courtesy of Univ. of Cal. at Berkeley Lib., "8085/iraq/200k/i38_20.jpg," 1:200,000 Topographic Map, Soviet Union, Sovetskaia Armiia, Generalnyi shtab, 1972-1991)

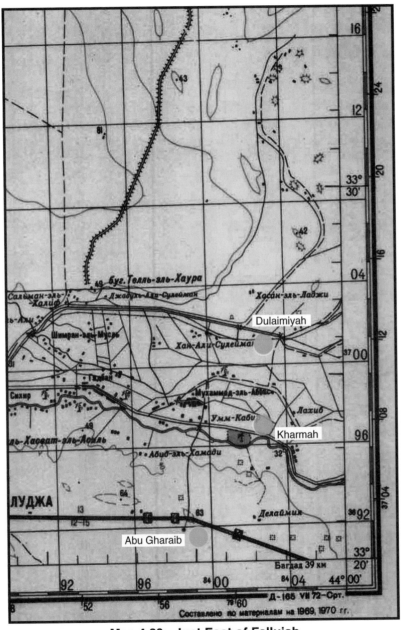

Map 4.20: Just East of Fallujah
(Source: Courtesy of Univ. of Cal. at Berkeley Lib., "8085/iraq/200k/i38_20.jpg," 1:200,000 Topographic Map, Soviet Union, Sovetskaia Armiia, Generalnyi shtab, 1972-1991)

Just north of Al Qaim is a place called Ish.[76] That puts Ish on the opposite bank of the river. "Cave complexes" were found in the vicinity of Ish.[77] That was the first indication that enemy infiltrators might be following the north side of the Euphrates, while using south-side activity as a diversion. Easterners will often follow through on undercontested diversions, so both sides of the river and its center must still be watched.

Dughayman and Rumana (Rammanah)

Dughayman is slightly off the main road and on the north bank of the river. It is south of Rumana.

Rumana is the town across the Euphrates River (to the northwest) from the older, western portion of Obeidi. During Operation Iron Fist in October 2005, Marine attack helicopters fired on several houses in Rumana.[78] Rumana was also searched during Operation Steel Curtain in November.[79]

Rumiyah, Ja'banyah, Al Bubiyah, Ad Dayr, Al Luriyah

These small towns are situated on the main road that roughly parallels the river. The local economy is based, in large part, on farming.

Al Ammari, Shaqaqliyah, Al Bubiyah

These villages are off the main thoroughfare and directly on the river. As such, they would handle a certain amount of boat traffic.

Rawah

Rawah is on the north bank of the Euphrates. In July 2005, a U.S. Stryker Brigade moved in from Mosul to garrison Rawah in one of the most significant maneuvers north of the river. The Marines had only operated on that side of the Euphrates for short periods.

They did so at the Syrian border during Operations Matador and Steel Curtain in May and November. During Operations Quick Strike in August and River Gate in October, they swept through the town of Barwanah just south of Lake Qadisiyah. On Operation Dagger in June, they had inspected the south shore of Lake Thar-thar.[80]

Just east of Rawah (where the river turns south) is a bridge spanning the waterway.

Barwanah, Abu Tughara, and Hadithah Dam

Barwanah is a small town on the east bank of the Euphrates. It is south of Hadithah and east of Haqlaniyah. It was a part of Operation Quick Strike in August 2005. Two months later, the Marines revisited the place during Operation River Gate.[81] Since that time, it and its sister cities (Hadithah and Haqlaniyah) have been heavily worked by 3rd Battalion, 1st Marine Regiment. That battalion has found many caches. They contained "tons of weapons, ammunition, artillery and mortar shells, and IEDs."[82] During the October elections, the people of Barwanah were less jubilant than the residents of the other two cities.[83] During Operation Red Bull at the end of December, half of the battalion's 75 ordnance discoveries were by Lima Company in Barwanah.[84]

Abu Tughara (or what is left of it) is now below the eastern side of Hadithah Dam. During Operation Brand Iron in the spring of 2006, Marine Combat Engineers dug burlap bags of weapons and ammunition from the side of that dam. During this short period, those engineers found over 500 weapons caches throughout the Triad Region.[85]

The Marines were writing a new chapter in their illustrious history. In a 4GW environment, effectively blocking an enemy's resupply/reinforcement routes is one of the few ways to do him harm without creating additional problems for friendly forces.

Alus, Marabdiya, Siniyah, Jaliawiyah, Sadqa, Abu Namil

These six towns are on the road that parallels the east bank of the Euphrates. While most residents live along this conduit of commerce, others live on the riverbank.

Zuwayyah, Ain ah Nafat, Saiyid Abdulla Ali, Abu al Khalaf

Here are more villages on (or near) the road that parallels the east bank of the Euphrates River. For a living, their occupants depend, in large part, on agriculture. The road and river trade also help.

Ali an Normah, Mulahimah, Saqlawiyah, Baq-hash

These places are on the main road from Ar Rutbah to Fallujah. As that roadway winds south, it becomes more heavily populated.

Amiriyat al Fallujah

On 2 December 2005 in the village of Amiriyat al Fallujah (just west of Fallujah), some two dozen Marines assembled for undisclosed reasons (possibly a formation) inside the courtyard of a mill.[86] When one stepped on a buried pressure plate, 10 were killed and 11 wounded by artillery rounds rigged in series.[87] This is the type of thing that can be prevented with mantrackers in the unit. Through their heightened awareness of surface detail, they can often spot a uniformly shaped or slightly discolored patch of ground. They can also guess what kneeprints and digging in the middle of a courtyard might mean.

Fallujah

Fallujah sits astride the main highway from the west and just north of the river. When under assault by the Marines in late 2004, its mosques played an important role in its defensive scheme. Many were found to contain munitions and fighters,[88] and to have connecting underground passageways.[89] A large, well-maintained tunnel network was also found in Fallujah during the assault.[90] These tunnels were steel reinforced, some big enough for bunk beds and trucks.[91] Others connected the larger places of worship.[92] U.S. troops also found subterranean crawlspaces between houses and evidence of movement through the sewers.[93]

During the initial assault on Fallujah, two Chechen snipers killed 15 Marines.[94] In late December 2005, three more Marines were killed there. It was rumored that snipers were again responsible. Since that time, Fallujah has remained a largely destroyed and uninhabitable urban area. Its infrastructure will take a very long time to restore.

Simu and Karmah (Nahiyat al Karmah)

Simu is well north of the Euphrates, but directly in line with a series of rock quarries that lead into Karmah.

Karmah is also quite far from the river. If the infiltration route were to skirt Fallujah to the north and then run eastward into Baghdad, it would pass through Simu, Karmah, and Dayrat al Ri. Through an informant's tip, Marines made a significant discovery on 4 June 2005. In Karmah (50 miles west of Baghdad), they uncovered a huge bunker hewn out of a rock quarry. It had living spaces, kitchen, showers, air conditioning, and a fully stocked armory. The black uniforms, ski masks, compasses, and night vision devices would indicate an operations center that may have doubled as a hidden conduit waystation.[95] A member of 1st Battalion, 6th Marines also remembers an ammunition cache and bunkbeds in caves four to five miles northwest of Karmah. That would put them in the vicinity of Simu.[96] On 12 November 2005, a suicide VBIED (Vehicle-Borne IED) killed a Marine near Karmah.[97] It has since been the site of other bombings.

If, instead, the infiltration route passes through Fallujah, it would next intersect Abu Gharaib. That city has certainly seen enough action to be important to the enemy.

Abu Gharaib

Abu Gharaib lies between Fallujah and Baghdad. On 2 April 2005, the enemy launched a full-blown attack against Abu Gharaib prison.[98] As an old smuggling route had Abu Gharaib as a portal, that attack may have been to do more than just free prisoners.

On 24 March 2006, two large weapons caches were discovered in Abu Gharaib.[99]

77

North Bank Route Assessment

As the Kharmah quarry facility was probably used as an infiltration waystation, the other quarries along the north and east bank of the river instantly attract suspicion. There are three small ones 2000 meters west-northwest of Kharmah (half way to Simu). The other sighting of billeting caves would be in the vicinity of Simu. To the northwest of Simu is the south end of Lake Tharhar (and the camp that was found there).

There is always the possibility of more than one route. Another may closely parallel the north bank of the river in the Fallujah area. A good-sized quarry exists 2,000 meters northwest of Habbaniyah. Across the river from Ar Ramadi are others—two 2,000 meters north-northeast of town, and another 3,000 meters northwest. (See Maps 4.17 through 4.20.)

Discovering the Route's Exact Trace

Four things occur along an Asian-style infiltration route: (1) caches of ordnance, equipment, and food are dug up; (2) underground billeting, medical, and communication facilities are found; (3) in-transit units are spotted; and (4) in-transit units stumble into some opposition. By connecting the dots between any cache, sighting, or firefight along a suspected route, one can arrive at its approximate trace. To determine the precise location of parts of the path, one must send in mantrackers from the side at several different places. Then, by keeping the suspected thoroughfare under satellite surveillance, one could successfully slow the flow of goods and personnel along it without causing the enemy to change its location. That can only be done by sabotage, e.g., accidental detonations, vehicular mishaps, coincidental illumination, curfews, checkpoints, etc. Resorting to the standard U.S. program of bombardment, ambush, and raid will simply cause the enemy to shift his valuable route's footprint.

With satellite-directed Global Positioning System (GPS) devices, the enemy can easily find remote watering holes in trackless desert. Early in the war, U.S. troops captured a GPS device near the Syrian border into which remote locations had been entered. While it is not known what those locations were, they could usefully be retrieved from the mountains of intelligence.

Also indicative of an active infiltration route are enemy booby-traps and snipers. The most dangerous areas should be most closely searched for above- and below-ground waystations.

Additional Evidence of *Hezbollah* Pipeline Management

In May 2006, U.S. officials detected shipments of advanced RPG-29 "Vampir" rocket launchers into Iraq.[100] This hand-held weapon shoots a PG-29V round that has a tandem warhead for penetrating the reactive armor of modern tanks and bunkers. It also shoots a thermobaric, anti-personnel round—the TBG-29V.[101] That FAE-tipped rounds may now be in the hands of the insurgents should have been shock enough. But where they came from, and the route they took, were the real news.

They [the officials] said the weapon system has been smuggled from Syria into Iraq by operatives of the Iranian-sponsored Hizbullah. . . . They said the weapon was used by Hizbullah against the Israeli Army in the late 1990's.[102]
— *World Tribune,* 11 May 2006

79

The Ongoing War in Iraq

- What has happened in Iraq since September 2005?
- How has the enemy's position been strengthened?

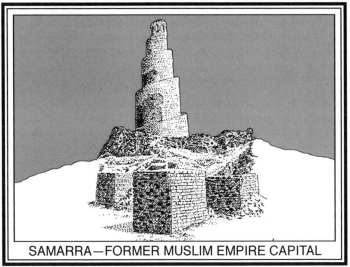

SAMARRA—FORMER MUSLIM EMPIRE CAPITAL

(Source: DA Pam 550-31 [1990], cover)

What the Imported Fighters Now Face in Iraq

However the Sudan-trained fighters are reaching the center of Iraq, they are now part of a quickly escalating civil war. The radical Shiites whom Saddam had so brutally held in check were now in power.

Little-Known History of the Region

The Shiite activist revival in the Middle East did not grow out of the Iranian Revolution of 1979. It began in Najaf, Iraq, in the 1960's. Its first political manifestation was the forerunner to the *Dawa* party that anchors the United Iraqi Alliance (UIA). From that forerunner came Ayatollah Khomeini and his vision of another Muslim empire.[1]

Without any knowledge of this historical anomaly, one could make little sense of the hundreds of daily incidents in Iraq. They all serve a purpose, but that purpose is not readily apparent to a Western occupier. While Sunni proxies of Iran have been helping to keep the Coalition busy around Baghdad, Shiite fundamentalists have been infiltrating the Iraqi army and police units in the

Figure 5.1: British Light Infantryman
(Source: Courtesy of Orion Books, from *World Army Uniforms since 1939*, © 1975, 1980, 1981, 1983 by Blandford Press Ltd., Part II, Plate 38)

south. In British-occupied Basra, the effect on individual freedoms (particularly those of women) has been most dramatic. When the British tried to crack down on police officers with Shiite-militia ties, Iran demanded that the British withdraw from the city.[2] While the British had attempted minimal force (to their absolute credit), they failed to risk the scores of tiny neighborhood outposts that could have collectively won the day. (See Figure 5.1.)

The Parliamentary Elections of 15 December 2005

On 14 December 2005, ABC News reported that a truck full of counterfeit ballots had been intercepted at the Iranian border. Even more telling than the ballots' source was the Iraqi Interior Ministry's response. With former Badr Brigade member—Baqir Jaber—at its head, Iraq's internal security bureau denied the report.[3]

This came as no surprise to those who had been closely watching the developments in Iraq. That Iraqi army and police units were being filled with Shiite militiamen had been reported from any number of reliable sources. The new government's jailers had been caught maltreating prisoners. Death squads were also reported.[4] When former prime minister Allawi alleged widespread civil-rights abuses, ruling party head al-Hakim declared the abuses had been exaggerated to divert attention from the Saddam Hussein trial.[5]

A Civil War in the Making

If Iraq's army and police units are to defeat its insurgency, they will need enough organizational integrity and military expertise to do so. The first prerequisite has been elusive, because both systems have actively recruited local militiamen. The resulting influx of Islamists creates both intelligence bonanza and tactical edge for the insurgents. If a security installation's defenders can't be converted, they will be overrun through an open gate.

While *al-Qaeda* and the Baathists will be blamed, the Coalition itself has provided the biggest spark for civil war. By claiming that the Sunnis alone were responsible for the insurrection and allowing a fundamentalist Shiite party to steal the vote, the Coalition has unwittingly taken sides in an internal dispute.

83

The Civil War's First Subdued Round

In Samarra on 22 February 2006, the upper half of the Askariya Mosque's golden dome was "surgically" removed with explosives. Not since Kitchener "shortened" the silver tower of Mahdi's tomb in Omdurman, had the defacement been more careful. Just after dawn in that mostly Sunni city, a small group of men had somehow gained access to the third most holy Shiite shrine in Iraq. According to the *London Times,* that shrine had been occasionally used as a base by Sunni insurgents.[6] While *"Al-Qaeda in Iraq"* quickly took credit for the attack, its true instigator may never be known. What is known is that Iran's agenda was furthered by the resulting chaos.

The Samarra bombing triggered reprisals so severe that a day-time curfew was imposed on Baghdad and surrounding provinces over the subsequent weekend. During that short period, up to 120 Sunni mosques were attacked, and as many as 1300 people were killed.[7] Behind much of the trouble was Iraq's *Hezbollah*-look-alike, the Mahdi Army. Its leader had been in Beirut at the time of the bombing. In its aftermath, Iraq's security forces contained so many al-Sadrists that Baghdad police vehicles were openly flying Mahdi Army colors. Sunnis would later say that most of those police had done nothing to control the mobs, while others had actually joined in the killing of Sunnis and desecrating of Sunni mosques.[8] Through it all, many Sunni insurgents still regarded al-Sadr as an ally. He had fought with them at Fallujah in the fall of 2004.[9]

Al-Sadr's subsequent statements and itinerary spoke volumes as to what had actually occurred after Samarra.

> ... Muqtada al-Sadr, whose own militia was blamed for many of the attacks on the Sunnis, repeated the appeal [call for unity] Sunday [26 February] ... upon his return from neighboring Iran.
>
> He accused Americans and their coalition for stirring up sectarian unrest and demanded their withdrawal.[10]
> —Associated Press, 27 February 2006

> Our enemies are not only those who hate Shiites ... but also the occupation that allowed ... [extremists] to enter the holy shrine and demolish it. We want the occupation troops to leave our country. This is our main demand.[11]
> — Al-Sadr spokesman, *Newsweek,* 6 March 2006

Might Ayatollah Khamenei and *Sepah* have gotten impatient over America's post-election promise to stay on in Iraq? They have been known to chastise Shiite clerics unto death. To accelerate their occupiers' problems, would they not sacrifice a dome top? Whatever the intention, the Samarra bombing may have ignited a civil war that had been smoldering since the previous fall. If so, America's tacit permission of a fundamentalist Shiite regime played no small part in its outbreak. That regime's death squads and prison excesses may have pushed the conservative segment of the Sunni population over the edge. As the British had done in India, too many American leaders had tried to play one sect off against the other. Hopefully, that's where the comparison ends. (From mid-1947 to mid-1948 in India, Partition violence claimed the lives between one and two million people.[12])

By June 2006, there were reports of Sunnis abandoning Shiite-dominated Basra in droves, and Shiites leaving predominantly Sunni areas in equally large numbers.[13] Though low in intensity, a civil war was definitely in progress.

Al-Sadr Provides Additional Proof of Iran's Method

Iran doesn't care if the new Iraqi government restores order over the short term or not. Until the occupiers leave, it has a way to provide the bare minimum of alternative basic services to the neighborhoods. Iran's new anti-Western axis includes not only established nations and long-standing organizations, but also al-Sadr's group.

> Rising tension between the West and Iran is coinciding with the emergence of a loose anti-Western alliance. . . .
> Centered in Iran, this alignment has hardened in recent months . . . with Tehran shoring up old alliances and strengthening ties with countries (like Syria and Iraq) and with groups (Hizbullah, Hamas, and [Palestinian] Islamic Jihad). . . .
> The alliance includes the Mahdi Army of Moqtada al-Sadr, who in visits to Iran in January and February vowed to come to the defense "by all possible means" of Iran.[14]
> —*Christian Science Monitor,* 20 April 2006

85

There are Sunni movements in the axis, because Ayatollah Khomeini had called for an Islamic revolution by both Shiites and Sunnis. Though radically Shiite, al-Sadr shares the same revolutionary open-mindedness.

There is no Sunni or Shia resistance; there is an Iraqi Islamic resistance.[15]
— Al-Sadr in *Newsweek* interview, 8 May 2006

On 26 March 2006, the Mahdi Army was reported to be again running its own courts. This time, there had been 50 executions as a result of their findings. Soon, al-Sadr's "sectarian hit squads" were suspected of as many as 70 killings a day in Baghdad alone.[16]

In the national legislature, Sadrist lawmakers fill about 30 of the Shiite coalition's 128 seats. This equals the number held by the Supreme Council of the Islamic Revolution of Iraq (SCIRI), though SCIRI is widely believed to be stronger. Before the January 2006 election, Sadrists controlled the ministries of health, transportation, and civil affairs. During that and the May sequel, they were thought to be trying to add those for education and housing. They ended up with the ministries of education, agriculture, health, and transportation.[17] Al-Sadr had a peculiar interest in controlling any or all of the basic services.

[Amatzia] Barram, the Iraq expert in Washington, calls the Sadrist approach brilliant grass-roots politicking, and warns that four years down the road they're likely to have doubled their strength in parliament. . . .
. . . "We are like Hamas," says Mr. Rubaie, the Sadrists political tactician. "We will bear arms and will not compromise our right to resistance, but we also help the people and win elections."[18]
— *Christian Science Monitor,* 30 January 2006

How Iran Can Capitalize on Civil War

Sepah has no fear of an Iraqi civil war. It knows how to suppress other rebel influences when the time comes. It did so in Iran in 1979, and its offspring — *Hezbollah* — did so in Lebanon in the 1980's.

Most Americans now realize that the new Iraqi government's leaders are (with the exception of its president) from three fundamentalist Shiite organizations—the *Dawa* Party, SCIRI, and Muqtada al-Sadr's group. Each has its own militia.[19] Personnel from those militias have been filling up Iraqi army and police units and committing their share of human-rights abuses. On 8 April 2006, a senior Iraqi official acknowledged that an "undeclared civil war had been raging for more than a year." The solution, he said, was for the Iraqi security forces to acquire more power so that the foreign occupiers could leave.[20] His logic was not that of a democracy-oriented public servant. "U.S. officials believe that Iranian intelligence agents have infiltrated the most senior levels of the Iraqi government," according to *Newsweek.*[21]

Then, in late April, a videotape of a still healthy al-Zarqawi surfaced. His reference to the "hated Shiites" was a little too melodramatic to be believable. Obviously intended to reinforce the mistaken belief that the Iraqi insurgency was strictly Sunni, it did little to obscure al-Zarqawi's well-documented cooperation with Iran, *Hezbollah,* and al-Sadr.[22]

The New Islamist Regime Picks Another Prime Minister

Having required al-Sadr's lone vote to be elected—al-Jaafari did little to prevent the Mahdi Army from retaliating for the Samarra mosque bombing. Still, the fledgling parliament was about to enter its fourth month of deadlock. To provide more forceful leadership, its Shiite majority nominated a new prime minister in April 2006. Jawar al-Maliki may be remembered as a coalition builder, but not in the humanitarian sense of the term. He had been the head of the radical *Dawa* party's unconventional warfare (guerrilla) wing.[23] It was a secretive, cell-based network of bombers and assassins that was Saddam Hussein's most feared opposition.[24] The *Dawa* party is the direct descendent of the "Party of Islamic Call" (*Hizb ad-Da'wa al-Islamiya)* that spawned Ayatollah Khomeini. One of Maliki's first acts was to change his first name back to Nuri. Nuri al-Said was the no-nonsense, pro-Western dictator of Iraq in the late 1950's.[25]

One of al-Maliki's first promises was to "integrate" the militias into the armed forces and police.[26] As the Sunni's main complaint had been the infiltration of army and police security elements by Shiite militiamen, al-Maliki cannot be expected to provide much relief. Nabeal Younis, a senior lecturer in public policy at Baghdad University has long worried that the supposedly national army is nothing more than a collection of militias with differing loyalties.[27] On 2 May 2006, hundreds of recruits in restive Anbar Province protested during their graduation ceremony at the prospect of being posted away from home. They said that they had been promised that they would serve only in their hometowns.[28]

A Huge, Quasi-Official Agency Emerges

In April 2006, a large, but obscure, security force was first reported in Iraq. Called the Facilities Protection Services (FPS), it already had 146,000 members. They wore uniforms and were well organized. While the Interior and Defense Ministries denied any affiliation, the al-Sadr controlled Transportation Ministry hired thousands of FPS personnel. One U.S. official warned that the militias were "slowly gaining control of the (state security) apparatus."[29] Another gave the following explanation:

> The FPS has basically become a private army for the ministers. They have no accountability.[30]
> — *Newsweek,* 24 April 2006

Then, the other shoe dropped. The U.S. had created the FPS in late 2003 to protect Iraqi infrastructure. By so doing, it had not only provided the Shiite militias with a back door through which to infiltrate the ministries,[31] but also law-enforcement status. Spread through 27 ministries, the FPS answers to no U.S. or Iraqi government authority.[32]

The "Little Way" of Taking Over a Country

Western leaders think "big." By helping a Third-World nation to adopt the democratic process at the national level, they assume that they will improve the lives of its citizens. Eastern leaders think "small." They know that by tolerating an overtly democratic national government, they can do what they want at the community and individual level without much Western interference. The new Iraqi government is overtly parliamentary, but decidedly pro-Iranian and thus inherently Islamist. It has promised to incorporate Shiite militias into its security forces but has been slow to quell Shiite vigilantism.

While the West has been content to monitor Iraq's legislative milestones, Iraq's infrastructure has been systematically taken over by Islamist elements. The latter has been accomplished—one neighborhood council, police station, medical facility, and private enterprise at a time. First reported in Basra and Karbala, this disturbing trend has now moved north. Behind many of the takeovers is the same apparently immune protagonist—the Mahdi Army. Four councilmen from Baghdad's Hay Somer neighborhood were killed by suspected al-Sadrists in August 2004.[33] There was a police station "coup" by undetermined elements in Ramadi in the summer of 2005.[34] In May 2006, an al-Sadrist nurse at Kadimiyah Hospital in Baghdad announced that he was now in charge.[35] Of note, many of the incidents have been linked by subject matter to the ministries al-Sadr controlled—initially Health, Transportation, and Civil Affairs, but expected to expand to Education and Housing.[36]

> A doctor who ridiculed the idea of this 34-year-old [nurse] appointing himself administrator of the 700-bed hospital was slapped across the face by his new boss, who ordered armed security guards to escort the medic [doctor] from the building.
>
> The expulsion was a brutal warning to other staff who might question the right of the al-Mahdi Army, a Shia militia, to install one of their own to run the hospital.
>
> The same is happening in schools and colleges, the Civil Service and government ministries and leading businesses as Baghdad's middle classes are sacked to make way for militia apparatchiks. . . .
>
> Saddiq al-Medhi, a dentist queuing with his wife and two daughters at the city's airport yesterday, had his clinic hijacked by militiamen. . . .
>
> Head teachers complain that they have been usurped by militia loyalists who do not have the necessary qualifications or experience. . . .
>
> A Baghdad University professor, who is too afraid to give his name, said: "We are all victims of this new thought police. No longer content to intimidate us with violence, these

militias want to control our every move, so they appoint the administrators and managers while dissenters lose their jobs."

Private businesses, particularly those with lucrative government contracts, have seen senior staff replaced by men with militia links. Mustapha al-Ali, 46, who runs a trucking company, showed up at his office in Sadr City last week to find a new "managing director" in his chair accompanied by two gunmen.

Mr. al-Ali had spent months concealing his importation of health equipment for the Health Ministry as that would make his company a target for Sunni insurgents. Now the Shia militia have supplanted him.

"It's no good going to the police to complain, because in my area they daren't cross the Mahdi Army," he said. "The militias are the new rulers."[37]

— *The Times* (UK), 11 May 2006

The Death Squads Continue under the New Regime

To no one's real surprise, the Shiite death squads continued under the al-Maliki regime. On 12 May 2006, U.S. troops rescued seven of the ten hostages that dozens of gunmen (some wearing uniforms) had just take from two Sunni villages northeast of Baghdad. Some of the gunmen were apprehended at the same time. They told police that they came from Baghdad and were members of militia loyal to Muqtada al-Sadr.[38] Two weeks later, U.S. officials admitted that possibly thousands of Mahdi Army gunmen had joined Iraqi police forces.[39]

On 22 May, a Western journalist of Iraqi descent who had just returned from Baghdad made public his findings on PBS's Jim Lehrer News Hour. He said that the Mahdi Army was not in the process of taking over the army and police force but "was the army and police force."[40] He went on to say that Sunnis were being specifically targeted. One could not help but compare these events to what had already happened in Basra and Karbala. They also closely resembled *Sepah's* "counter-competing-insurgency" consolidation campaign of 1979 in Iran and the *Hezbollah's* equivalent in Lebanon. On the same day, al-Maliki admitted the security services had been infiltrated by militias and announced a "special protective force" for Baghdad.[41] He was, in all probability, referring to the FPS.

The events in Iraq were starting to look more and more like *Hezbollah's* 1980's consolidation phase in Lebanon—when it had to forcefully assert its dominance over Syrian-backed *Amal.* They also resembled *Hamas's* ongoing fight to wrest control over Palestine from *al-Fatah.*

A Questionable Document Emerges after Zarqawi's Death

On 9 June 2006, two American bombs ended the perverted life of Abu Musab al-Zarqawi. Subsequently produced by Iraqi officials was an updated *al-Qaeda* war plan. After refuting the obvious (that the insurgency was alive and well), the plan attempted to exonerate Iran. Its inconsistencies in date and detail spoke volumes about the true instigator of the violence and allegiance of the Iraqi government.

A blueprint for trying to start a war between the United States and Iran was among a "huge treasure" of documents found in the hideout of terrorist leader Abu Musab al-Zarqawi, Iraqi officials said Thursday. . . .

The al-Qaida in Iraq document was translated and released by Iraqi National Security Adviser Mouwafak al-Rubaie. There was no way to independently confirm the authenticity of the information attributed to al-Qaida.

Although the office of Prime Minister Nouri al-Maliki said the document was found in al-Zarqawi's hideout following a June 7 airstrike that killed him, U.S. military spokesman Maj. Gen. William Caldwell said the document had in fact been found in a previous raid as part of an ongoing three-week operation to track al-Zarqawi. . . .

The document also said al-Zarqawi planned to try to destroy the relationship between the United States and its Shiite allies in Iraq. . . .

The language contained in the document was different from the vocabulary used by al-Qaida statements posted on the Web. For example, it does not refer to the Americans as "Crusaders" nor use the term "rejectionists" to allude to Shiites.[42]

— Associated Press, 15 June 2006

"It is necessary first to exaggerate the Iranian danger and convince America . . . of the real danger coming from Iran." . . .

Bomb attacks against the West would be blamed on Iran "by planting Iranian Shiite fingerprints and evidence"; declaring ties between Iran and "terrorist groups . . ."; and "disseminating bogus messages" that Iran has WMD [Weapons of Mass Destruction] and "there are attempts by the Iranian intelligence to undertake terrorist operations."[43]

— document excerpts, *Christian Science Monitor*

A Top Field Commander Hints at the Problem

As of the first of June 2006, no amount of dollars, sweat, or blood seemed to be getting the job done in Iraq. The explanation was simple. While secretly fueling the insurrection, Iran had established influence over Iraq's new government. Iran was now openly aiding the pro-government Shiite militias.

U.S.-led forces arrested a regional commander for a pro-government Shiite militia suspected of smuggling surface-to-air missiles and spying for Iran, the U.S. military said on July 7.

Adnan al-Unaybi, leader of the Mehdi Army militia in charge of an area south of Baghdad where two U.S. helicopters were shot down this year, was arrested during an Iraqi-U.S. raid near the town of Hilla, 100 kilometers (62 miles) south of Baghdad on July 6.[44]

— Reuters, 7 July 2006

Because U.S. policy is based on the idea that *al-Qaeda* and the Baathists are solely to blame for the trouble, U.S. military leaders have been hesitant to suggest that Iran might be using Sunni proxies. All the while, no one in Israel doubts that Sunni *Hamas* and Sunni *PIJ* are the direct instruments of Shiite *Hezbollah* and indirect instruments of Shiite *Sepah*.

"They [the Iranians] are using surrogates to conduct terrorist operations in Iraq both against us and against the

Iraqi people," the commander, Gen. George W. Casey Jr.,
told reporters. . . . He said that the Iranian assistance had
increased since January. . . .
    Some training is being carried out in Iran, he said. In
other cases, Hezbollah, the Lebanon-based terrorist group,
is providing weapons and training at Iran's behest.[45]
    — *New York Times*, 23 June 2006

Shortly thereafter, the Head of the Joint Chiefs of Staff confirmed that Iran was fighting a proxy war against the Coalition in
Iraq.[46] While the Sunnis were never mentioned, their connection
was implicit. If the only ones doing any fighting in Iraq are Sunni,
then Iran's proxy must be Sunni. There have been reports of Iranian
soldiers operating inside the Sunni Triangle since the beginning of
the war.[47] In July 2006, several were captured there.[48]

Too Many Coincidences to Ignore

On 16 June 2006, two GIs were kidnapped from their outpost 12
miles south of Baghdad and then brutally murdered.[49] A week later,
Hamas dug a 1000-foot tunnel into a Gaza fort to capture an Israeli
soldier.[50] Fully realizing that neighborhood outposts could turn the
tide of battle, the insurgents were encouraging their poll-conscious
occupiers to pull back into more heavily fortified enclosures, and
then altogether.
    Possibly to take the heat off one or more protegee, the inventor of
kidnap tactics — Lebanese *Hezbollah* — then captured two Israeli soldiers in a cross-border raid on 12 July.[51] After Israel later attacked
as a result of this raid, Iraq's new prime minister — al-Maliki — would
refuse to condemn Hezbollah.[52]
    Three soldiers were similarly abducted by *Hezbollah* right before
the Israeli government decided to pull out of southern Lebanon in
2000.[53] Sadly, America's foreign policy still precludes any discussion
of a mutual instigator of the various kidnappings.

The Civil War Flares Up

In July, there a was a huge spike in the Baghdad continuum of
violence. This spike was so severe that 5000 more American troops

had to be pulled into Iraq's capital city to try to restore order.[54] The long-simmering civil war had reached spontaneous-combustion stage. When U.S. forces entered Sadr City on 7 August to arrest "individuals involved in . . . torture cell activities," Iraq's new prime minister and president got mad.[55] While no one was looking, al-Sadr had become one of the prime minister's biggest fans. In return, al-Maliki may deem the Mahdi Army's alternative legal system as an integral part of his "efforts at national reconciliation."[56]

This and the problems in Gaza and along the Lebanese-Israeli border had provided Iran with a much-needed respite from world attention. Yet, Iran and its hidden sponsors now had the West much less befuddled than before.

Iran's Growing Militancy

- What has transpired in Iran since September 2005?
- In what ways has Iran become more involved in Iraq?

GUARDIANS OF THE PERSIAN EMPIRE

(Source: DA Pam 550-68 [1989], cover)

Iran's Unprecedented Need for Foreign *Baseej*

During the costly Iran-Iraq War, Iran was able to recruit enough *baseej* from its own citizenry. It would need outsiders only to pursue a regional revolution. While U.S. leaders have failed to come to this conclusion, Iran's recent elections make it more likely to be true.

Iran's Slide toward Radical Fundamentalism

On 14 December 2005, President Ahmadinejad of Iran proclaimed that the WWII Holocaust had been a myth. This came just weeks after he had wanted Israel erased from the face of the earth and the Anglo-Saxons defeated.[1]

None of this came as much of a surprise to dedicated Iran watchers. Ayatollah Khamenei had cleverly rigged the presidential election. After Ahmadinejad took office, virtually every Iranian ministerial post was filled by a former leader of Iran's Revolutionary Guard *(Sepah)* or notorious secret police (Ministry of Intelligence and Security [MOIS]).[2] Brig.Gen. Ahmad Kazemi (the new commander of *Sepah* ground forces) and Mostafa Mohammad-Najjar (the new defense minister) had both served with the Iranian contingent in southern Lebanon.[3] (*Sepah* has since demonstrated the advantages of decentralized control to the Iranian army.) (See Figure 6.1.)

Figure 6.1: Enlisted Iranian Tank Commander
(Source: Courtesy of Orion Books, from *World Army Uniforms since 1939*, © 1975, 1980, 1981, 1983 by Blandford Press Ltd., Part II, Plate 118)

Iran Continues to Subvert the Iraqi Peace Process

Through Steven Vincent's courageous journalism in mid-2005, many Americans learned of Iran's oppressive influence over everyday life in Basra. Yet, only a few were aware of a similar situation in Karbala. *Iraq al-Ghad*—an Iraqi independent daily—claims that thousands of Iranian MOIS agents have been given Iraqi citizenship, and that all senior administrative and security posts in Karbala are now under their control.[4] This problem may not be restricted to the Shiite cities. In May 2006, *al-Taji* (another Iraqi newspaper) claimed that 1,577 of the 1,972 *jihadists* arrested over the previous year were Iranians.[5]

As Badr Brigade and Mahdi Army personnel continued to fill Iraq's army and police units in other parts of the country, their hidden mentor kept up the illusion that the insurgency was strictly Sunni in origin. Among its ploys was supplying sophisticated IEDs to Sunni proxies.

Iraqi military forces recently discovered an Iranian-made weapons cache hidden in Tikrit, northwest of the capital Baghdad. Tikrit is the hometown of deposed former Iraqi President Saddam Hussein.

The new Iranian-made weaponry was found hidden in a large well in the west of Tikrit, according to an Iraqi army officer speaking on condition of anonymity.

The discovery appears to confirm repeated U.S. and Iraqi assertions that Iran was sending covert agents and weapons into Iraq to assist militias.

In August 2005 U.S. Defense Secretary Donald Rumsfeld castigated the Iranian government after U.S. forces stopped a truck filled with high-tech explosives entering Iraq from Iran.[6]

— UPI, 12 April 2006

Iran Now Directly Supports *Hamas*

When *Hamas* unexpectedly won the Palestinian election in early 2006, it did not trade its hard-line approach for Western funding. It simply took money from Iran. In early April, the *Hamas*-led government did nothing to stop *Palestinian Islamic Jihad (PIJ)*

97

from launching rockets from Gaza into Israel. Later that month, it defended a *PIJ* suicide bombing inside Israel.[7] But *Hamas* was doing more than just watching. During March, it recruited thousands of fighters for its new army. That army's mission will be "to destroy Israel."[8]

> Hamas sources said a Hamas army was established in 2005 in [the] wake of the Israeli unilateral withdrawal from the Gaza Strip and has formed units in cities throughout the area.
> The sources said thousands of Palestinians have already been recruited into the new military force which has as its mission to destroy Israel and replace it with an Islamic state.
> The army has been based on Hamas's Izzedin Kassam military wing, Middle East Newsline reported. A senior commander in Izzeddin Kassam told the Palestinian newspaper Dunya Al Watan that Hamas has established units in every major city and refugee camp in the Gaza Strip. The commander said thousands of Palestinians have been trained to fight. . . .
> The training was designed to last four months, the commander, identified as Abu Huzaifa, said. . . .
> Abu Hazaifa said Palestinian cadets were taught firearms training, rappeling *[sic]* buildings and outposts, launching Kassam-class short-range missiles, and infiltrating enemy bases. He said the instructors were Hamas fighters who had been trained . . . in such countries as Iran, Lebanon, Sudan and Syria.
> The sources said Hamas has already developed a system to quickly mobilize thousands of fighters. They said the fighters would wage fierce resistance to any Israeli attempt to capture the Gaza Strip.[9]

Diverting Attention from Its Iraqi Involvement

Throughout the spring of 2006, Iran flaunted its plan to build nuclear weapons. While its intent was probably to draw attention away from the subversion of Iraq, its rhetoric merely substantiated that subversion. On 17 April 2006, President Ahmadinejad threatened to use some 40,000 trained suicide bombers if Iran was attacked.[10]

If such a government were planning to extend its revolution to northern Africa, then one must look back into African history to see what tactics and support might be forthcoming from that region. This is the purpose of Part II.

Part Two

"Dark Continent" Lessons

"You will come bragging, but return taken down a peg."
— old Zulu saying

(Source: "Zulu Izaga," collected, translated, and interpreted by Robert Robertson [a missionary], *Natal Colonist* [Durban, South Africa], 1880)

7 Zulu Double-
_____ Envelopment

● Which African tribe has successfully contested the West?

● How could that tribe breach British lines?

REDCOAT WITH SPEAR, SHIELD, AND MASK, 1880

(Source: *Military Uniforms of the World*, by Preben Kannik [Pan Macmillan], © 1968 by Blandford Press; DA Pam 550-74 [1992], p. 193; FM 5-103 [1985], p. 4-19)

The Dark Continent's History Is Long and Complicated

While overly proud Europeans might think "underdeveloped" Africa has no history, they could not be further from the truth. Africa's heritage is as diverse and interesting as it is tragic. But, from a hot fire comes good steel; and through it all, Africa's various peoples have developed a depth of character that has to be seen to be believed. With relation to warfare, a good place to start in the study of these peoples is with the much-vaunted Zulu. To this day, some of their tactical techniques would still work against modern weaponry.

The Zulu Way of Making War

The Zulu tribe migrated to northern Natal in southern Africa from the central-lakes region (Congo) in the fifteenth century. For over 350 years, it remained an obscure group. Then, through the organizational ability and generalship of Dingiswayo (an Abatetwa chief) and Shaka (his successor), they began to abuse their neighbors. After taking over in 1818, Shaka merged the Abatetwa with the Zulu and set off to establish an empire. He revolutionized warfare in South Africa by replacing the throwing spear with a stabbing version, and traditional tactics with radical maneuvers. Armed only with the short, stout "assegai," his warriors could no longer toss their spears and fall back, but instead had to close with their foes.[1] (Over the years, Asians have developed a similar interest in short-range combat. It was through "hugging" and penetration, that Communist armies managed a tie in Korea and victory in Vietnam. That's how they dodge U.S. supporting arms.)

With very little gear and intentionally callused feet, Zulu troops could quickly cover great distances in the approach march. They traveled single file in three separate, but parallel, columns.[2]

Zulu attacks were remarkably sophisticated for their era. They involved frontal feints, double envelopments, and nighttime assaults. (All three are still used by the best light infantrymen in the world—the North Vietnamese, North Koreans, and Chinese.) Below is a brief synopsis of Zulu exploits against Dutch settlers and British regulars. Of particular interest are the circumstances that allowed their "unarmed" assault tactics to work against heavily armed defenders.

> [For 12 years,] King Shaka and his . . . regiments sallied forth across the length and breadth of modern-day Kwa-Zulu-Natal, trampling and dispossessing all rival tribes in their path with the innovative weaponry and battle-strategies. . . . Gone were the throwing-spear and small shield of his forefathers—standard issue during three centuries of inter-clan warfare—replaced by the stabbing-spear and full-length body-shield designed to facilitate Shaka's lethal new concept—encircling his enemy with a horn-shaped pincer movement and engaging in highly effective hand-to-hand combat. . . .
>
> During this consolidation of his Zulu empire, King Sha-

ka established a working relationship with the predominantly British colonists. . . . This situation was to change drastically at the hands of Shaka's co-assassin and successor—his half-brother Dingane. . . .

Seven years into Dingane's reign [1836]—but a thousand kilometres south in the Cape Colony—the Boer people were about . . . to become "Voortrekkers" . . . a nation "going forth" to seek political self-determination [from the British]. . . . The tall ships of their predecessors' emigration from Europe would be replaced by the . . . covered ox-wagon. . . .

Of several wagon trains to embark on the arduous journey into an unknown hinterland, the group led by Piet Retief entered the Kingdom of the Zulu in 1837, and immediately began negotiating with Dingane for land to establish an independent Boer territory. On 6 February 1838—the day scheduled to finalise their agreement—King Dingane had Piet Retief and 101 Voortrekkers put to death at his royal settlement near Ulundi. Dingane's *impis* [regiments] then massacred other groups of would-be settlers camped in the vicinity of Estcourt. The [Boer] survivors . . . headed inland . . . intent on revenge.

Within nine months the Voortrekkers believed themselves capable of defeating Dingane's Zulu hordes [and sallied forth]. . . .

. . . [On 16 December 1838] along the banks of a river near Dundee known to the Zulu as "Peaceful One"—a 15,000-strong *impi* attacked the 460 Voortrekkers . . . and experienced the first failure of their Shaka-devised battle strategies. Traditional weapons, ox-horn formation and unquestioning bravery proved no match for the flintlocks, field artillery and mounted marksmen of the Boers' own unique tactics . . . and the ensuing carnage remains known as "The Battle of Blood River." . . .

While the enthronement in 1840 of King Mpande served to normalise relations between Zulu and Afrikaaner—and maintain a cordial Zulu-British atmosphere—his son and heir-apparent harboured dreams that would impact on Colonial authorities. . . . Prince Cetshwayo ascended to the throne in 1872, but unlike the Shakan era, his expansionist campaign included the harassment—and murder—of pioneer farmers. Six years of resulting British dissatisfaction led to The Ultimatum—a boundary award and list of demands presented to the Zulu on 11 December 1878. . . . When King Cetshwayo failed to respond by the prescribed deadline—New Year's Eve 1878—his silence was interpreted as defiance . . . and the British authorities declared war. . . .

. . . Lord Chelmsford immediately launched a two-pronged assault, and ready-assembled British columns invaded Zululand from the southeast coastal belt and inland from the vicinity of Dundee . . . while Redcoats garrisoned in the northwest mountains around Utrecht were given a "watching brief." The Central Column was the first to engage Cetshwayo's army, but Chelmsford had grossly underestimated his foe. . . .

Unexpectedly employing diversionary tactics [on 22 January 1879], an estimated 15,000 Zulu warriors surprised and successfully split the British force at Isandlwana, near Nquthu, and in a two-hour engagement killed all but 74 of the 1,500-strong invading troop. . . .

Within hours and a mere 15 kilometres due west of Isandlwana, some 4,000 Zulu attacked the Swedish mission station at Rorke's Drift used by the British as a magazine and field hospital. Here, the "Heroic Hundred" earned 11 Victoria Crosses . . . while holding the *impi* at bay for 12 hours. When the Zulu finally retreated, they left behind 500 dead—to the 17 British fatalities.

The [British] regiments invading from the eastern seaboard were also set upon that day, ambushed by 5,000 warriors lying concealed among bushes and gullies. Although their casualty list was high, the 4,000-plus British repelled wave after wave until late afternoon when the Zulu withdrew . . . allowing the column to continue its march. . . .

. . . [T]hese invaders from the coast reached Eshowe the following day, but did not immediately press on towards the Zulu capital of Ulundi. . . . This, in turn, compelled Zulu commanders in the southeast to resort to a new strategy. They laid siege to the British settlement, blocking communication and supply routes for more than two months, until Eshowe was finally relieved after the Battle of Gingingdlovu. . . .

Unlike the Coastal and Central columns, the troops under Captain Moriarty who filed out of the mountainous northwest encountered no enemy action until the second week of March . . . when they were outnumbered and almost annihilated at Ntombe Drift in the vicinity of Paulpietersburg. Surprisingly, the superior-numbered Zulu force withdrew, allowing the British to consolidate . . . only to be defeated [by the Zulus] a fortnight later on the slopes of Hlobane Mountain near Vryheid.

Buoyed by this victory, King Cetshwayo's army sought to press home their perceived advantage . . . but it was the Zulus' turn to underestimate their foe. . . .

Early afternoon on the day after Hlobane, an estimated 25,000 warriors launched themselves against a fortified British position at nearby Kambula. They were repelled again and again . . . eventually taking flight and pursued on horseback until nightfall. Although this crushing defeat proved to be the turning point of the Anglo-Zulu War, Lord Chelmsford . . . called for reinforcements. . . .

Many . . . skirmishes punctuated Lord Chelmsford's determined efforts to converge on the Zulu kingdom's Royal Seat. Soon after the formerly besieged Coastal Column passed through Melmoth, the full might of Britain's war effort was concentrated alongside the Umfolozi River . . . [near] the Zulu capital of Ulundi. Here, on 4 July 1879, the British dealt their enemy the death-blow . . . routing the Zulu army for the last time, capturing Cetshwayo and tearing his realm asunder.[3]

List of Battles

Voortrekker-Zulu
Saailaager, 12 February 1838
Veglaer, 13-15 February 1838
Rensburg Koppie, 17 February 1838
Blood River, 16 December 1838

Anglo-Zulu
Nyezane, 22 January 1879
Isandlwana, 22 January 1879

Fugitives Drift, 22 January 1879
Rorkes Drift, 22 - 23 January 1879
Ntombe, 12 March 1879
Hlobane, 28 March 1879
Kambula, 29 March 1879
Ginginglovu, 2 April 1879
Ulundi, 4 July 1879 [4]

What Happened at Isandlwana (Islandwana)

The above battle synopsis says a large British force was split at Isandlwana but fails to mention it was encamped (deployed in a hasty defense) at the time.[5] As Westerners deem their defensive firepower omnipotent, the under-armed Zulus must have had an exceptional attack plan.

Chelmsford, led an army of 5,000 British and 8,200 African troops into Zululand in three widely dispersed columns. On January 22, while he was absent with a portion of his force seeking out the Zulu, his central column of about 1,800 British and 1,000 Africans camped at the base of a tall crag called Isandhlwana. There it was attacked by some 10,000 Zulu. All but 55 British and 300 Africans were slaughtered. No prisoners were taken.[6]

At the end of the Isandlwana battle, Cetshwayo's half brother and a fourth of the Zulu horde set off for the British supply depot at Rorke's Drift on the Buffalo River.[7] Cetshwayo had said that no Zulu force should attack an entrenched British position (deliberate defense),[8] but his half brother failed to connect that instruction with impromptu fortifications.

The Rorke's Drift Affair

The Battle of Rorkes Drift is portrayed in the film "Zulu." The film was well researched, so various tactical conclusions can be drawn from its panoramic portrayal of the action.

The battle only lasted 12 hours.[9] It started in the early evening, continued all night, and concluded with a dawn assault. In the final stages of the Zulus' approach march, the rhythmic beating of shields sounded to the British like a railroad train. Then, everything went quiet, while separate Zulu contingents closed in on the outpost. They did so through group rushes all along an imaginary line. Those groups swarmed quietly through the sparse vegetation and stopped/disappeared without any apparent signal in each lateral depression in the earth. They were moving to assigned positions in the famed "buffalo-head" maneuver. This is where two groups—the head and loins of the buffalo—approach a quarry from the front. At the last moment, all the warriors in the buffalo's head disperse around both sides of the quarry as if folding horns. Thus, any part of the buffalo's torso is always a feint. While the movie shows the Zulu chief initially sacrificing his men to count British guns, he more probably launched something little used in the West—a probing attack. Suffice it to say that the buffalo's loins continued to demonstrate before the British outpost while the horns enveloped it through feeder creeks.

Of note, the warriors in the frontal diversion got down each time a British rank fired. By dropping to the ground at the command of "fire," they could elude most, if not all, of the bullets. When the Redcoats were allowed to fire at will, the diversionary Zulus hid in the grass. This prevented the British from taking well-aimed shots. (Such tricks may seem unprofessional to a contemporary Western commander. But, they're smarter than what he requires in the assault—moving upright through a steady stream of machinegun bullets.)

Meanwhile, Zulu snipers were crawling around the outpost to the top of a hill. With overhead fire, they would cover the main attack(s)—horn tip penetration(s) at the right and left rear of the objective. It was from those directions that the most determined attacks finally came. (The Chinese were to penetrate U.S. positions this way 70 years later—at the Chosin Reservoir.)

To find the best place for an all-out assault in the rear, the Zulus did some probing. They discovered less resistance where the depot building abutted the perimeter. All the while, their brethren continued the frontal diversion to kept the British from reinforcing the back. After the most dramatic of the frontal feints, the Zulus finally launched their main assault from the rear. The whole idea was to confuse the British as to which of the attacks was real. (When unexpectedly successful in the Orient, demonstrations and probes are often allowed to carry an objective.)

109

The British didn't have smokeless powder in those days. The Zulus must have realized that they could temporarily blind their foes by getting them to fire successive volleys. Thus emerges the probable details of their assault. As long as the assault element went to ground during each fusilade, it could closely approach the British. (While bending forward during an assault is acceptable in the West, getting down and then catching up is not. Still, it would be easy for a lightly clad young American—who was trusted as much as he was "loved"—to do just that. While advancing forward at Stalingrad, Soviet soldiers routinely dropped as if shot so they could pop up again in the same place without being immediately killed.)

As the spear stabbers closed in, the bayonet thrusters took their traditional stance. It was not long before innovation began to trump standardization. As the Zulus came within feet of a adversary who had learned one thing, they simply did another. Many threw their "assegais" as their immediate foe dutifully complied with his limited interpretation of close combat.[10] Though designed for stabbing, the short spear's heavy end made it a lethal projectile at that range. By 1888, Zulu warriors were carrying three short throwing spears and one stabbing spear.

> They carried huge shields of ox-hide on the left arm . . . while on the right they carried two or three throwing assegais [spears] for hurling at the enemy, and a broad-bladed stabbing assegai which they kept for hand-to-hand fighting. In their girdles was slung a club or axe for polishing off purposes.[11]

The Battle of Rorke's Rift was largely fought at night (another attribute of the state-of-the-art Eastern method). Thus, one can conclude that—through common sense—the Zulus had developed refined night-fighting techniques.

The Final Battle at Ulundi

With the Battle of Ulundi, the first Zulu war ended. There would be other revolts until 1906, but nothing to compare with this one. A Western military machine had been successfully stymied by a spear-carrying tribe. It would be another 70 years, before that machine would begin to realize (in Malaysia) that the Zulus had all but compensated for firepower with "woods-smarts" and tactical technique.

Ulundi [the Zulu capital] . . . lay in an amphitheatre of hills. . . . [T]he British advanced in hollow square. Halting within a mile of the kraal [fenced enclosure] this imposing force offered battle. Before them were ranged 30,000 dauntless savages armed with assegais [spears], rifles and oval shields. . . . Lord Chelmsford's object was to draw them on to the square and a score of mounted irregulars were accordingly sent forward. The lure was a success. Enraged at the taunts of this handful of men, the Zulus began to advance. The enemy extended their formation so that they might envelop and crush the square. . . . [T]hey rolled across the plain, chanting their war song. . . . A tempest of lead and iron received them. . . . If for a moment they wavered or fell back it was only to come on once more. . . . But courage was [in] vain against that quadruple line of steel [cannon and three rows of riflemen]. . . . One chief, more daring or skilled than the rest, dashed his warriors upon the right rear angle of the square and threatened a hand-to-hand fight—bayonet against assegai. But the guns were soon at work and rolled them back under a storm of shrapnel. At last, the savage hordes began to waver. . . . Drury-Lowe led his lancers out of the square at a gallop. An ambush checked their charge and emptied many a saddle. Another moment and lance and sabre pierced and rent the black mass. Yet the fight went on until the King's Dragoons and a flying column advanced and drove the stubborn remnant of the enemy into the hills and gave Ulundi to the flame. From this blow, the Zulus, once the masters of South Africa, have never recovered.[12]
— William Maxwell, 1902

At Ulundi, most of the Zulu losses were from charging the British "square" and being unable to deal with the British counterattack.[13] The 17th Lancers burst from within the square and ran them down. That square very probably contained a few overturned wagons as well.

A Later Look at the Zulu Defense

In 1887, Britain annexed Zululand and placed it under the administration of the Governor of Natal. With a few other rebel chiefs, Dinizulu soon launched a campaign to drive all European traders and missionaries from the territory. This campaign enjoyed limited success, and the Zulus soon got the chance to show what they knew about defensive tactics. (Again, their actions look more like what one might expect in modern-day Afghanistan.)

In the summer of 1888, the Governor of Natal appealed to Capetown for military aid. General Smyth mustered an army of two thousand British troops and left for Zululand with his aide-de-camp, Captain Baden-Powell.

They soon found that Dinizulu was entrenched atop a forbidding mountain called the Ceza. General Smyth moved his headquarters to within a few miles of the rebel stronghold and prepared to attack. He put Baden-Powell in command of an advance column of British troops and [non-rebel] Zulu warriors.

As B-P and his men climbed a ridge leading to the Ceza, they saw several rebel warriors scrambling into the caves of an opposite ridge. B-P's men hit the ground, taking cover behind clumps of bushes and boulders. Bursts of gunfire echoed from the caves across the way, and bullets zinged off rocks and sent up spurts of earth. B-P ordered his men to spread out and attack the rebels from either side. Racing from boulder to boulder, then diving for cover again, firing constantly at the dark enemy caves, the men gradually closed in on the outnumbered rebels. Suddenly the enemy fire ceased and several warriors emerged from the caves with their arms held high above their heads. . . .

That night, B-P led his advance column deeper into the Ceza bush, to the very foot of Dinizulu's mountain stronghold. At daybreak his men stormed the mountain, racing up its steep slopes across boulders and ravines until they reached the network of small wooden huts and hastily built stone forts at the summit. But most of the huts had been burned. The forts were empty. The mountain was deserted.

During the night, Dinizulu had escaped with his followers across the frontier into the Transvaal Republic. Yet he realized now that further resistance was futile. A few days later he returned to Zululand and surrendered peacefully to British authorities.[14]

What has just been described is a strongpoint matrix, complete with bombproof shelters and hidden escape routes. From the standpoint of tactical evolution, that is more advanced than the linear defense that U.S. forces use. The "state-of-the-art" strongpoint defense (without escape routes) is generally thought to have been pioneered by the Germans in 1917. Thus, one must expect modern-day Africans to have a natural feel for both offense and defense at short range.

The Zulus remained quiet until a half-hearted attempt to regain lost lands in 1906. Though again defeated by the British, they had put the world on notice that commonsense maneuver can often compensate for a complete absence of firepower.

Zulu Tactics in Perspective

For all but the most professional of U.S. infantrymen, what happened in Africa over 100 years ago has no impact on modern warfare. However, light-infantry tactics are, by definition, timeless. They have more to do with surprise than technology. Thus, the maneuvers with which stabbing spears trumped rifled barrels still have utility under similar circumstances. In today's world, the "horns of the buffalo" maneuver remains nothing short of brilliant. The center of an Asian formation will sometimes fall back to create an impromptu "firesack." And an Asian force will double-envelop during a meeting engagement. But nowhere in Asian tactics is the combination of both ploys. That the most contested part of the buffalo dropped to the ground while less contested parts continued to move forward is also noteworthy. The Zulus' greatest accomplishment, however, was in how they were able to capitalize on the idiosyncrasies of British weaponry to cross the last few yards. While U.S. arms manufacturers would never admit it, all U.S. weapons have limitations. Those limitations vary from tiny design flaws to predictable employment modes.

Any GI who deems African tactics outmoded is in for a rude awakening. He or she is reminded that, within the Western World, only the Germans and Finns have fully embraced 3rd-Generation warfare. However, as early as 1900, part of the African population already had—the Boers.

Boer Stalking
Attack

- Why were the Boers so successful against the British?
- What was their final approach to a British position like?

BOER SHARPSHOOTER, 1900

(Source: *Military Uniforms of the World*, by Preben Kannik [Pan Macmillan], © 1968 by Blandford Press; FM 5-103 [1985], p. 4-19)

The Colonization of Southern Africa

Shortly after the Dutch East India Company established a ship-provisioning station at the Cape of Good Hope in 1652, Dutch farmers ("boers") began to arrive. Great Britain occupied the area in 1806 and annexed it nine years later. Between 1836 and 1840, about 4,000 Boers departed the British enclave for the northeast on the "Great Trek."[1] (See Figure 8.1.) Some went to Natal; others, toward the Vaal River. It was the latter who were massacred by the Zulus and got their revenge at Blood River. Behind tightly chained wagons, they could handle many times their number.[2]

The Boers then established three communities—one in Natal; one north of the Vaal (in what would become the Transvaal Republic); and one south of the Vaal (in what would become the Orange Free State). Britain annexed Natal in 1842, cutting off the Boers' access to the sea. After recognizing the sovereignty of the other Boer lands for 25 years, Britain annexed the Transvaal in 1877. In December 1880, the Transvaal's residents took up arms in the "First War of Independence." When the British were humiliated at Majuba, they granted the Transvaal "full internal independence" with a few hidden conditions. (See Map 8.1.) Here are the events leading up to the British embarrassment:

> British forces were marched northwest from Port Natal-Durban to Newcastle, from where they first attempted, on 28 January 1881, to invade Boer territory at Laing's Nek, in the vicinity of Volksrust. This attack failed, as did the

Figure 8.1: Ox and Cart of the "Great Trek"
(Source: DA Pam 550-93 [1981], p. 1)

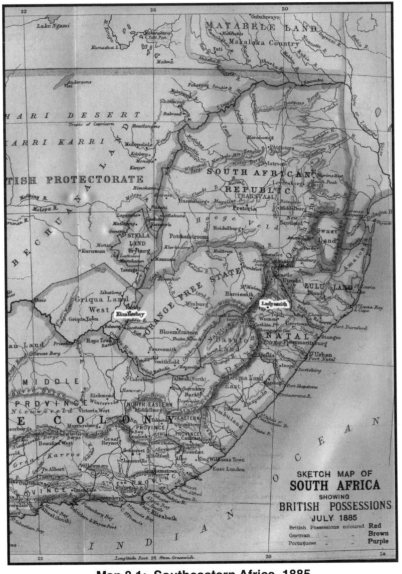

Map 8.1: Southeastern Africa, 1885
(Source: Courtesy of General Libraries, University of Texas at Austin, from their website for map designator "south_africa_1885.jpg")

second incursion, ten days later on the nearby Schuinshoogte ridge. The shortcomings of scarlet uniform, gleaming white helmet and conspicuous fighting formation saw the tide turn irrevocably against the British on the morning of 27 February 1881, on verdant slopes at the Battle of Majuba.

General Colley had led his troops up this "Mountain of Doves" during the night, only to be killed as the Boer soldiers who climbed to an even higher position at daybreak put the British to flight. An armistice was signed a few days later at the foot of "Majuba," followed by a peace treaty in Newcastle.

The subsequent Pretoria Convention . . . was never wholly acceptable to the fiercely independent Afrikaaner, and their discontent simmered.[3]

When a British "coup-fomenting" raid on Johannesburg failed in 1896, the stage was set for the "Anglo-Boer War."[4] As all-out conflict loomed, the Boer Republics acquired the world's best rifles and artillery pieces from Germany. Though virtually devoid of military training, their "citizen soldiers" were well mounted, excellent woodsmen, and good shots.

The Anglo-Boer War

The Aglo-Boer War was fought between British colonial forces and Dutch settlers between 1899 and 1902. Its final spark occurred over Bechuanaland—the vast area to west of the Transvaal and north of Cape Colony. Though primarily inhabited by African tribes, many Boer settlers had moved there. The British feared that the Transvaal government might try to take over Bechuanaland, so they sent in an army of four thousand men. That army subsequently occupied the rail junction of Mafeking at the Transvaal border. (See Map 8.2.) Meanwhile, British reinforcements, including Baden-Powell's regiment, stood by in Cape Colony and Natal.[5] Baden-Powell had, for his chief scout, an American tracker by the name of Frederick Burnham.[6] (See Figure 8.2.) On 5 October 1899, two Boer contingents converged on Mafeking and Natal.

The immediate support of *kommando* fighters from the

Orange Free State gave the Boer two fronts from which to threaten the northern triangle of Natal. They invaded, occupied Newcastle on 15 October, and pushed southeast for five days before clashing with British regiments on Talana Hill near Dundee.

Uniforms now daubed with khaki-brown paint, the "Redcoats" drove their enemy from this strategic high ground, but at great cost. The following day, 21 October, a

Map 8.2: Area between Kimberley and Mafeking, 1887
(Source: Courtesy of General Libraries, University of Texas at Austin, from their website for map designator "british_bechuanaland_1887.jpg")

British victory at Elandslaagte, south of Glencoe, freed the rail corridor for survivors of Talana Hill to escape farther south . . . to Ladysmith. . . .

When Boer patrols from the Orange Free State were spotted crossing the Drakensberg Mountains into Natal near Winterton, the British dispatched a camouflaged, armoured reconnaissance train from Estcourt. . . .

On 15 November 1899, Boer guerillas [sic] ambushed and derailed the train, killing a number of British soldiers [and capturing young Winston Churchill]. . . .

Ten days before Christmas 1899, Sir Redvers Buller's first attempt to cross the Thukela River near Colenso failed dismally, and the number of brigade hospitals . . . bore testimony to its outcome. . . .

Figure 8.2: Chief Tracker Burnham As Drawn by Baden-Powell
(Source: Courtesy of Paladin Press, from *Tactical Tracking Operations*, © 1998, by David Scott-Donelan, p. 6)

History regards Buller's next foray—in late January 1900—as the most bloody and futile of all his attempts to relieve the beleaguered town . . . with 500 fatalities in hilly terrain around Winterton. This was the desperate Battle of Spioenkop . . . from which the Boer emerged relatively unscathed. . . .

When Buller's regiments again failed to breach enemy lines—within a fortnight of Spioenkop, at the Battle of Vaalkrans—Britain launched the most concerted offensive ever seen in the Southern Hemisphere. . . .

From the first dawn attack on 21 February 1900, blood was spilled for six days in a series of punishing encounters on the hills surrounding Ladysmith. Collectively known as the Battle of Thukela Heights, these hard-fought victories were ultimately crowned with British re-occupation of the town by nightfall on the 26th. . . .

. . . British troops set about recapturing Dundee which they finally accomplished after penetrating Boer defences on 13 May. A week later they experienced a minor setback at Scheeper's Nek, south of Vryheid, when a company of Bethune's Mounted Infantry surprised a congregation of Boer folk and Swaziland policemen at prayer. The church-goers forced the British to withdraw after a short, sharp engagement.

General Buller's regiments captured Botha's Pass, west of Newcastle, and advanced into the Orange Free State within a month of relieving Dundee, and later broke through into the Transvaal Boer Republic a little farther north at Allemans Nek in the Volksrust area. . . .

On 24 September 1900, Boer commandos heading east towards the coast were stopped in their tracks at Fort Prospect, near Babanango, by a vastly outnumbered British garrison. . . .

. . . [I]t was at Italeni—only a short distance away but more than a year later—where the second Boer invasion of Natal came to a standstill.

Sporadic fighting continued [unabated] for eight-and-a-half months . . . in northern Natal, the Cape Colony and within the two Boer republics . . . until [the] signing of the Peace Treaty in Vereeniging on 31 May 1902.[7]

List of Major Battles

First War of Independence
Laing's Nek, 28 January 1881
Schuinshoogte, 8 February 1881
Majuba, 27 February 1881

Anglo-Boer, 1899 -1902
Talana, 20 October 1899
Elangslaagte, 21 October 1899
Nicholson's Nek, 30 October 1899
Siege of Ladysmith, 2 November 1899 - 28 February 1900
Armoured Train Incident, 15 November 1899
Willow Grange, 23 November 1899
Colenso, 15 December 1899
Platrand, 6 January 1900
Spionkop, 24 January 1900
Vaalkrantz, 5 February 1900
Thukela Heights, 12 -27 February 1900
Helpmekaar, 13 May 1900
Scheepersnek, 20 May 1900
Botha's Pass, 8 June 1900
Lancaster Hill, 11-12 December 1900
Blood River Poort, 17 September 1901
Italeni, 26 September 1901
Holkrans, 6 May 1902 [8]

The Ill-Advised Plan to Bottle Up the British Garrisons

The Boers had hoped—through a series of rapid victories—to force the British into a quick settlement. As such, they tried to isolate or destroy all British forces already in Natal and the Cape Colony. In Natal, they encircled Kimberley and Mafeking. (See Map 8.2.) Then, they went after Ladysmith and Dundee. In the end, all they had accomplished were long and ineffective sieges of Kimberley, Mafeking, and Ladysmith.[9] A major assault was finally launched against the latter, but it was beaten back by the British. The Boers never made a concerted effort to take Durban, the eastcoast seaport.[10] In Cape Colony, they failed to seize all the vital rail junctions. These oversights were to prove their undoing. Through it all, the British had gained time to muster and land a sizable reinforcing army.[11]

The Boer Combatant

Despite the Durban oversight, the Boers knew what was strategically important and what wasn't. Instead of just killing soldiers, they went after transportation hubs and supply trains.

Like some "billy yanks" and "johnny rebs" in the American Civil War, Boer troops elected their officers. They were allowed other democratic processes as well. Battlefield "decisions" were made by *krygsraads,* or war councils—a process by which the men chose a course of action by vote. Further, "[Boer] men . . . could elect to go on leave . . . when they chose—with or without permission."[12] While Western leaders might scoff at so little discipline, they must remember that the Boers gave a larger and better equipped adversary all it could handle for almost three years. Though "steeped in tradition," that adversary would go on to lose millions at the Somme and other WWI battlefields. The question Western leaders should have been asking since 1918 is this: "Are there tactics that lend themselves to more individual skill and less control?" Or conversely, can too much unit discipline result in unnecessary casualties?

The Boers were not infantrymen per se, but while dismounted they were good enough hunters to easily sneak up on (and often past) a British sentry. That they were loosely controlled gave them more confidence and initiative. As this chapter will show, those qualities were further harnessed by a form of maneuver that required no signals. The Boers became so good at short-range infiltration, that they may have partially inspired WWI German Stormtrooper technique.

The Boer Offense

The Boers could best be described as an army of self-sufficient snipers. While dismounted, each had the stalking ability of an expert hunter. Yet, their unit tactics were largely predicated upon what highly skilled individuals can accomplish collectively. There

123

is little evidence of any subordinate-element "maneuver" at the company, platoon, or squad level. In every encounter, there was simply an encircling swarm of opportunistic Boers. As Western leaders are generally more comfortable with the well-choreographed/dogged approach to war, the Boers may have actually contributed to the evolution of modern infantry tactics. They proved that a lone infiltrator can generate more surprise than a larger contingent. For many types of strategic targets, his singular efforts can accomplish more than a fully supported battalion. It risks fewer lives and causes less collateral damage. There is a lesson here for anyone who would hope to win a 4th-Generation war. In modern terminology, the Boer way of attacking an objective might be called "individual swarm" tactics.

The Boer Defense

At Magersfontein in December 1899, the Boers attempted to block the British advance on Kimberley. They dug their trenches at the bases of small hills, instead of their tops. These trenches allowed "defenders to stand upright and fire over the breastworks while concealed by camouflage fashioned from branches and grass." The Boers partially roofed some trenches to provide protection from artillery fire.[13] (Prior to this time, Western armies had relegated most trenching to offensive siege operations. After this time, most Eastern armies have defended in a way similar to that described above.) At Magersfontein, much of the attackers' preparatory bombardment landed—without much effect—on the hilltops. After decimating the assaulting British with rifle fire, some of the Boers worked around the British flank (possibly to acquire more targets).[14] Such a maneuver without any better reason resembles the encirclement that East Asians attempt during chance contact. In Africa, it may draw its inspiration from the Horns of the Buffalo. The only link may be both culture's respect for the combat potential of the individual.

At Colenso three days later, the Boers tried to stop the British drive on Ladysmith. Their defense was so innovative as possibly to inspire the Eastern post-WWII norm. To fully appreciate it, one must first have a feel for the terrain in which it was applied. At Colenso, the Tulega River formed a "V" with flat land in its middle and hills at its rear. Far behind the "V" was Ladysmith. "There were tier upon tier of rust-coloured kopjes [rocky hills or buttes], sweeping up from the tree-lined bed of the Tulega River to culminate in the peak of Bulwana. Beyond Bulwana was Ladysmith."[15] At Colenso, the British were stopped in their tracks by a hail of rifle fire from the front and both flanks. In effect, the Boers had established a band of strongpoints and drawn the British into an intervening "firesack." As is often done by Asian armies, those strongpoints were nothing more than the intermittently occupied portions of a zigzag trench. Because that trench was partially roofed, the strongpoints could be secretly moved. When the British finally entered the primary recess to that network, they were "marooned in the open within a few hundred yards of the enemy's [hidden] trenches, which enfiladed them on three sides."[16] "[T]he Boers' . . . [force was in] a thin line of slit-trenches and gun positions zig-zagging across hill and plain."[17] As before, those trenches were predominantly at the base of hills, and the hilltops were empty.[18] Thus, most of the British preparatory naval gunfire did no good.

In barren terrain, the Boer trenches were the width of a man at the surface and a little wider below (to provide shelling protection). They were just deep enough for a man to stand up and comfortably fire his rifle. From 100 yards away across level ground, the trench itself was completely invisible.[19]

For the Boers, Colenso was more than just a delaying operation. They had drawn the British into a trap and were in search of full surrender. While a few Boers offered terms under a flag of truce, others crept up on the British command group through a gully.[20] When they finally appeared, the British commander had no choice but to give up. A strongpoint matrix of sorts was again encountered along the Tulega River in February 1900.[21]

As the British drew closer to Ladysmith, the Boers had a different plan in mind. Whereas they had used a river to block withdrawal at Colenso, they would now use waterways to block an advance.

Dig trenches in the tall grass along the river banks. Camouflage the trenches with stones. Scatter the soil behind, where it would be invisible. Dig dummy trenches on the skyline, where the British would expect them. Arm them with dummy guns, made of tree-trunks and corrugated iron. Dig away the stones in the river to destroy (or conceal) the drifts [fords].[22]

Boer Guerrilla Tactics

Badly outnumbered, the Boers were eventually forced to resort to less conventional tactics. Highly mobile "commandos" (mounted Boer contingents) would make lightning attacks at the rear of British formations and then disappear into the veld.[23] It was then that the true guerrilla phase began. De Wet was the most successful of the guerrilla commanders. Having superior scouts, he had no trouble eluding the 50,000 British soldiers sent after him. As do most guerrillas, he simply moved backwards.

Though technically part of a group, Boer fighters were used to operating alone. As such, they easily transitioned into guerrillas. Their tactical maneuvers became an abbreviated version of what they had done earlier. Still, they had some limitations.

Deprived of their artillery, Boer guerrillas lacked the assault technique to penetrate barbed-wire-enclosed blockhouses.[24] Kitchener's scorched-earth, civilian-internment, and blockhouse-chain strategies soon brought the rebels to bay.

Summary of Boer Tactics

The Boers initially outnumbered the British and scored impressive victories in all areas adjacent to their lands. Then, to stave off defeat, they resorted to guerrilla warfare. The British would eventually require 450,000 men to quash a force of irregulars that never exceeded 60,000.[25]

For the first time, the British had machineguns.[26] The Boers had smoke-free Mauser repeating rifles that were accurate from over 1,000 yards. Their individual marksmen "thought for themselves" and always shot from behind cover, according to Winston Churchill.[27] The Boers were therefore almost impossible to spot. They became one of the Western World's first "unseen forces." As such, they could not be confronted by traditional volley fire or hand-to-hand combat. When things were not going well as expected, they simply rode off, ready to fight when conditions improved. In effect, they had denied the British the opportunity to strike a decisive blow.[28]

The Boer way of fighting would have a major effect on African guerrilla methods and worldwide conventional warfare. The Boers are most famous for their short-range "infiltration tactics"—sneaking between enemy holes during the first stage of an assault. In essence, they were practicing 3rd-Generation small-unit tactics (bypassing tiny enemy strongpoints) some 18 years before the German Army pioneered many of the concepts and procedures of squad-level Maneuver Warfare.

In *The Defense of Duffers Drift*, a Boer War veteran offers a series of fictionalized accounts of enemy attacks upon an increasingly fortified river crossing. (See Figure 8.3.) In the first, the Boers have a local farmer guide them into position. Then, they surround the British camp on all three dry sides, crawl in on it through dense cover, locate its sentries, shoot those sentries at the first alarm, and rush into its tented area.[29] As the first shot rang out at the crack of dawn and the camp was swarming with Boers within seconds, the Boers must have spent most of the night sneaking up on the camp. In 2nd-Generation tactics (attacking enemy strongpoints), the assault force almost never bypasses a wide-awake sentry.

In the second fictionalized account, the Boers did not rush the camp but instead fired from hidden positions on all three sides. Only after the British surrendered, did they notice a Boer behind every bush and ant hill for 100 meters. This is a tactic for which Asians are famous. When well-aimed shots are taken from behind a rock, stump, or mound by soldiers directly opposite each other, there is little chance of fratricide.

The next three accounts depict long-range Boer shelling. In the sixth and last, several of the Boers succeed in sneaking into the British position. As with the first two vignettes, all of the infiltration occurs after dark. To this day, night fighting is the norm only in the Eastern World.

Cross Pollination between Afrikaner and Other African

The Zulus and the Boers intermittently fought and helped each other. This led to the sharing of tactical techniques—some of the best on the African continent at that time.

Figure 8.3: Terrain around Duffer's Drift
(Source: FMFRP 12-33, p. 8)

In 1840, Panda, a brother of Dingaan [Dingane], led a revolution and, with the help of Boer commandos (Afrikaner yeomanry) made himself king.[30]

Several hundred heavily armed Boer adventurers took sides in this [a later Zulu] civil war [in 1883-84] and helped Chief Dinizulu of the Usutu tribe gain power over neighboring tribes.[31]

During the Aglo-Boer War, there were 100,000 blacks (of various tribes) "fighting" on the British side and 50,000 on the Boer side. They were primarily used as trench diggers, runners, wagon drivers, and farm laborers. But, at the siege of Mafeking, the British reputedly had 1,000 blacks under arms.[32] After the Anglo-Boer War, other Africans would hear of the inherent weaknesses in the Western way of war. The Zulus were not quite finished with their former adversaries.

Zulu antipathy towards both British and Boer remained at low intensity throughout the war . . . with one notable exception. Three-and-a-half weeks before the Peace Treaty was signed, Zulu warriors launched a surprise attack against Boer folk gathered on Zuinguin Mountain between Vryheid and Paulpietersburg . . . killing 56 at the Battle of Holkrans. . . .

Anti-settler feelings among the Zulu resurfaced in the Greytown district four years after the Anglo-Boer War, when Colonial authorities suspended the powers of Chief Bambatha for "tax evasion." He rebelled . . . and convinced a number of fellow traditional leaders in the region to follow suit. Fearing for the lives of local Whites, a police column entered the area to bring to safety three women and a child. During their return journey on 4 April 1906, four policemen—plus a trooper and his dog—were killed by the Zulu at Ambush Rock. The British Army was sent in . . . and Chief Bambatha, along with his followers, were trapped and killed in the Mome Gorge. This effectively put . . . [an end] to the rebellion that ultimately [had] claimed some three-and-a-half thousand lives. . . .

Ironically, the rebellious chief shared his Greytown

roots with the birthplace of Boer Commandant-General Louis Botha, who led the second invasion of Natal [with a crushing victory at Blood River Poort] and went on to become the first Prime Minister of the Union of South Africa in 1910.[33]

Just north of the Transvaal was another British Protectorate—Matabeleland. Within it lived the Matabele Tribe, an offshoot of the Zulus. When their rebellion was crushed by the British in 1896, they forfeited most of their military power. Yet, some of their descendents would become some of the best guerrilla fighters in the world. They would join the Selous Scouts in what was to become Rhodesia.[34] But before that story must necessarily come South Africa's journey into the modern age.

South African Reconnaissance

● How tactically sophisticated were the communist rebels?

● In what ways could they detect a South African patrol?

SOUTH AFRICAN "RECON COMMANDO," 1974

(Source: *Uniforms of the Elite Forces*, illustrations by Michael Chappell [Cassell PLC], ©1982 by Blandford Press Ltd., Plate 23, No. 68; FM 5-103 (June 1985), p. 4-19)

First Two-Thirds of the 20th Century in Southern Africa

After defeating the Boers in 1902, the British incorporated both Boer republics into the Union of South Africa. This Union (subsequently called "South Africa") operated under a policy of apartheid—the separate development of the races. In turn, South Africa occupied the German colony of South-West Africa during WWI. It was administered as a League of Nations' mandate until 1946 and then unofficially annexed. During the mid-1960's, the U.N. demanded independence for the territory and renamed it "Namibia." That independence would not be realized until 1989.

In 1923, the British government additionally annexed both Northern and Southern Rhodesia from their own South Africa Company. In the southern part of Rhodesia, a constitution was formulated in 1961 that favored white leaders. Three years later, those leaders unilaterally declared independence from Britain (without British approval) and became "Rhodesia."[1] The northern part of Rhodesia was voluntarily given its freedom and became "Zambia" the same year.[2]

In 1960, the Union of South Africa was allowed to leave the British Commonwealth and declared a free republic.[3] From 1960 to 1966, the British also granted independence to "Tanzania" (formerly the combination of Tanganyika and Zanzibar) and to "Botswana" (formerly Bechuanaland). The two Portuguese colonies of "Angola" and "Mozambique" would not follow suit until 1975. (See Map 9.1.)

Filling the British Void

Southern Africa's subsequent guerrilla conflagrations can be interpreted in two ways. Either they were popular uprisings against colonial oppression, or they were orchestrated steps in communist expansion. Those who most closely watched the rebels (the Rhodesian and South African militaries) became convinced of the latter. Much of the South Africans' evidence is offered below. If they are correct, the current flood of Chinese into Sudan,[4] Nigeria,[5] Eritrea, Djibouti, Somaliland,[6] and in other places within Africa becomes more worrisome. If *al-Qaeda, Sepah / Hezbollah,* and the Chinese have been cooperating on the subjugation of Africa, then what has been happening elsewhere takes on new meaning.

Whatever the degree of communist involvement in southern Africa's guerrilla wars, one thing is certain. Most of the insurgents were following either the Maoist (start in the countryside) or the Soviet (start in the city) method. In Maoist uprisings, the rural peasants are mobilized. In Marxist-Leninist uprisings, the urban workers are the prime movers.[7] Thus, it must be assumed that all African *jihadists* understand one or the other method. It must further be assumed that all know something about Chinese or Russian small-unit infantry tactics.

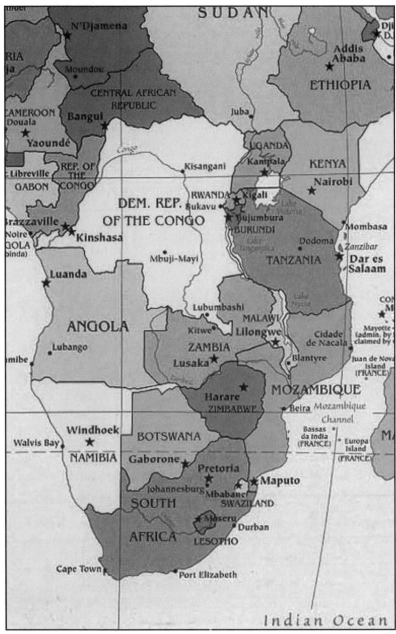

Map 9.1: The Continuing Struggle for Southern Africa
(Source: Courtesy of General Libraries, University of Texas at Austin, from their website for map designator "africa_pol_2003.pdf")

All That Occurred before 1977 in the Union of South Africa

After inspiring unrest in South Africa's black townships, the PAC (Pan African Congress) and ANC (African National Congress of South Africa) were both banned by its government in 1960.[8] PAC had split off from ANC in 1958. PAC's military wing—POQO (African acronym)—preferred to attack people rather than inanimate objects. In 1961, MK *(Umkhonto we Sizwe,* ANC's military wing) damaged a number of government buildings with explosives. This attack and MK's preparation for it was orchestrated by the illegal SACP (South African Communist Party). MK personnel were sent for guerrilla training to Algeria, Egypt, Ethiopia, and Tanzania. A few were even sent to Peking.[9] The plan was for a "people's war" with explosives against police, railway, and power facilities. The externally (foreign) trained guerrillas would lead that war and be called "cadres."[10] In 1968, POQO became APLA (Azanian People's Liberation Army).[11]

The Namibian Issue

Namibia is the coastal nation just northwest of the Union of South Africa. (See Map 9.1.) There are also two ways of interpreting Namibian history—the South African way and the British/U.N. way. In 1946, the U.N. refused to allow South Africa to annex South West Africa. In turn, South Africa refused to place the territory under U.N. trusteeship. In 1961, the U.N. General Assembly demanded that South Africa terminate its League of Nations mandate and plan for the territory's independence. In 1966, SWAPO (Southwest Africa's People's Organization) launched an armed struggle against the South African occupation. Two years later, South West Africa was renamed Namibia by the U.N. General Assembly. In 1972, that same august body recognized SWAPO as the "sole legitimate representative" of Namibia's people.[12]

The South Africans, on the other hand, viewed SWAPO as armed insurgents bent on fomenting violence in their protectorate. As such, they went after the SWAPO base camps. (See Figure 9.1.) This brought them into armed conflict with the countries and organizations that harbored them. The South Africans soon came to see their struggle as one against a larger and more nebulous foe—communist expansionism.

South African Operations in Angola and Namibia

By 1966, Soviet-backed SWAPO guerrillas were operating against the Portuguese occupiers of Angola from rear base areas in Zambia. At that time, UNITA (National Union for the Total Liberation of Angola) was allied with SWAPO and also fighting the Portuguese.[13] (See Map 9.2.)

By early 1974, South African Reconnaissance (SA Recce) personnel were operating covertly in southern Angola to curtail SWAPO infiltration from Zambia. To do so, they relied heavily on their man-tracking skills.[14] Their government had determined that its armed forces could best defend the nation by becoming counterinsurgency experts.

Figure 9.1: South African Patrol Leader in Namibia, 1978
(Source: Courtesy of Orion Books, from *World Army Uniforms since 1939*, © 1975, 1980, 1981, 1983 by Blandford Press Ltd., Part II, Plate 96)

Two other guerrilla outfits in Angola—then MPLA (People's Movement for the Liberation of Angola) and FNLA (National Front for the Liberation of Angola)—had also been fighting the Portu-

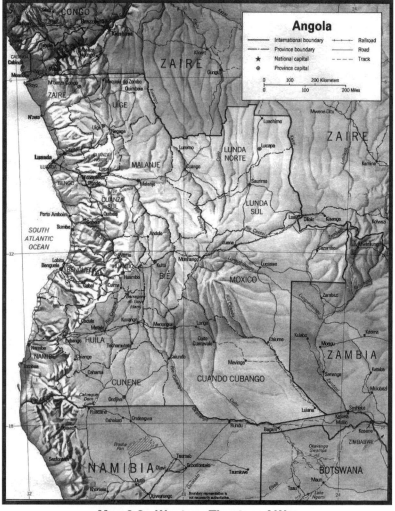

Map 9.2: Western Theater of War

(Source: Courtesy of General Libraries, University of Texas at Austin, from their website for map designator "angola_rel90.pdf")

guese.[15] Both were communist affiliated, but only one was blatantly Marxist—the MPLA. It had possessed Soviet backing since 1961.[16] Though not formed until 1974, the FNLA would initially have Chinese instructors. It was only later that Zaire and the U.S. would assume/share that support.[17]

As FRELIMO (Front for the Liberation of Mozambique) had done in East Africa, MPLA took over the Angolan government after the Portuguese departure in 1975. It immediately adopted a Soviet style of government and accepted more Soviet aid. UNITA had been the first movement to accept the Portuguese cease-fire and became the MPLA's only local opposition.[18] As such, it became a South African surrogate and was given SA Recce trainers.[19] This did little good, and the MPLA was soon able to drive UNITA away from the Angolan capital of Luanda.

In November 1975, Fidel Castro began to reinforce MPLA's military wing with between 15,000 and 20,000 Cuban regulars.[20] The only country in the region strong enough to contest a Cuban expeditionary force was South Africa. It sent in motorized "battlegroups." By December 1975, those South African battlegroups with UNITA (and some FNLA) ground attachments proliferated in the central part of Angola.[21]

Meanwhile at the northern end of Angola, the American CIA had been preparing FNLA and Mobutu's Zaireans (through wherewithal and training) to open up another front.[22] The first FNLA drive was in November on Quifangondo, a fishing village north of Luanda. Though supported by South African artillery fire, it failed miserably. Before long, most of the FNLA units and their Zairean attachments were chased back into Zaire.[23] At that point, the SA Recce teams had little choice but to form small guerrilla bands to work behind MPLA lines.[24] All the while, the South Africans had been trying to keep the extent of their role in the Angolan War secret.[25] Soon the secret was out, and political pressure from the West forced the South African battlegroups to withdraw in early 1976. As they left, the Soviet-backed MPLA and Cubans moved back in. To prevent any further interference from the West, the Soviets positioned a small amphibious landing force just off the West African coast in January 1976.[26]

In the aftermath of the South African withdrawal, MPLA and SWAPO declared themselves allies.[27] That meant that SWAPO could direct all of its attention to Namibia, and that SA Recce would now have to raid SWAPO bases just inside Angola.[28] Soon, SA Special

Forces started to form a unit from FNLA and UNITA refugees who had once been soldiers. What resulted was a counterguerrilla force called 32-Battalion. It was initially able to keep the principal SWAPO and FAPLA (People's Armed Forces for Liberation of Angola—MPLA's military wing) encampments away from the Namibian border.[29] Then SWAPO initiated a series of forward bases only 15 kilometers back.

> Normally, they site them anything from a hundred to eight hundred meters north of a chana [grassy area]. Invariably a tall tree, for use as an observation post, was in the immediate vicinity.
> The forward bases were constructed Soviet-style for all-around defense with a system involving an extensive network of trenches supported by bunkers well-roofed to enable the inhabitants to survive preliminary bombardments, and with a command post in the center.[30]

To counter the forward-deployed base camps, 32-Battalion decided to out-guerrilla the guerrilla by sending platoons into Angola without any support from Namibia. A few conventional assaults were also tried. On one occasion in October 1977, an SA Recce team single-handedly assaulted a small SWAPO base during a 32-Battalion offensive. From the fresh and unhurried spoor of a base-circumnavigating security patrol, the Recce team could tell that it still had the element of surprise in its favor.[31]

By the late 1970's, the Recces, 32-Battalion, and UNITA were teaming up to attack the FAPLA bases near the border. Then, to counter the Cuban threat, South Africa again sent in armored columns.[32] Finally, SA Special Forces and Recce teams tried to interdict—at various chokepoints—SWAPO's supply lines to the coast.[33] What happened next in this theater of war will have to wait until the end of this chapter. First, there is some catching up to do on events in the east.

Anti-SWAPO Strikes into Zambia

From 1976 to 1978, the South Africans also went after SWAPO bases in Zambia. The attack on one of the two camps at Shatotwa was particularly lethal. It blocked all avenues of escape with machinegun fire and mines. Within the sister base was discovered a Soviet adviser.[34]

Meanwhile, much had been happening along the east coast of Africa. Again, there was overwhelming evidence of communist instigation.

The Early Raid into Tanzania

For years, Pretoria had also been resisting the subversion of Africa's southeastern coast. Dar-es-Salaam had become the transshipment point for ordnance going to almost every liberation movement in the region.[35] Near that Tanzanian seaport were several enemy training facilities.

> FRELIMO, like half a dozen other liberation movements including the ANC, were well ensconced in Tanzania. FRELIMO's main camp was at Mbeya where training was undertaken by Cuban and Red Chinese instructors. Others were at Tunduru, Nashingwea, Lindi, and on the island of Zanzibar.[36]

As a communist takeover was clearly afoot, the South Africans allied with the Portuguese. In 1972, SA Recce raided Dar-es-Salaam from a South African submarine.[37]

South African Assistance to the Portuguese in East Africa

War had come to the other Portuguese colony of Mozambique in 1964 with FRELIMO guerrillas infiltrating southward out of Tanzania. (See Map 9.3.) Handcuffed by an obsessive aversion to casualties, the Portuguese were no match for them. Their large and totally predictable formations were easily damaged by opportunistic guerrilla groups. (See Figure 9.2.) As the Portuguese began to falter in 1972, the Rhodesians and SA Recce tried to help them by stepping up their operations inside Mozambique.[38]

> FRELIMO knew they were safe after ambushing a [Portuguese] convoy, because unlike the . . . Rhodesians,

139

the Portuguese rarely mounted follow-ups, so they liberally sprinkled the surrounding bush with booby traps and anti-personnel mines to make sure they [the Portuguese] stayed on the roads.

[By comparison] Rhodesian foot patrols operated in the Mozambique bush for spells of up to fourteen days at a time . . . with scant resupplies. . . .

The size of a normal Rhodesian patrol was four men. . . . The Rhodesians astonished the Portuguese by even considering operating in "hot" areas on foot and in small numbers. They [the Portuguese] refused to do it themselves. . . .

The Rhodesians had often tried . . . to engender a spirit of aggression in their Portuguese allies.[39]

Figure 9.2: Portuguese "Armored" Trooper, 1973
(Source: Courtesy of Orion Books, from *World Army Uniforms since 1939*, © 1975, 1980, 1981, 1983 by Blandford Press Ltd., Part II, Plate 63)

With the Portuguese expeditionary force demoralized and falling apart, it was finally agreed during talks in Lusaka, Zambia, in September 1974 that Portugal would hand over the governing of

Map 9.3: Eastern Theater of War
(Source: Courtesy of General Libraries, University of Texas at Austin, from their website for map designator "mozambique_rel95.pdf")

Mozambique to FRELIMO.[40] Portugal had been spending 50% of its gross national budget on its African wars and had a 23% inflation rate.[41] According to a regional historian, FRELIMO moved quickly to create a Stalinist, one-party society. It nationalized most, if not all, of the private property without compensation. It relocated whole tribes to communal villages. And it established a chain of "reeducation centers" for anyone who didn't want to cooperate.[42] As many as 75,000 people may have died in those centers.[43]

Like the South Africans had in Angola, the Rhodesians sponsored some local opposition to FRELIMO. It was called RENAMO (Mozambique National Resistance) and regularly operated from bases inside Rhodesia. As RENAMO would go on to fight FRELIMO until 1992 (well after Rhodesia's demise),[44] one suspects their sponsorship may have reverted for a while to South Africa. A regional historian has proof of RENAMO personnel and equipment being ferried by South African transport planes and trucks from Zimbabwe to new camps within that country's borders.[45]

The Communist Pincers on Rhodesia

While Chinese-backed ZANLA (Zimbabwe African National Liberation Army) attacked eastern Rhodesia from Mozambique, Soviet-backed ZIPRA (Zimbabwe's People's Revolutionary Army) attacked western Rhodesia from Botswana. By the early 1970's, the Soviets and Chinese were beginning to vie for southern Africa, though their proxies (local militias) still cooperated. While ZANLA had Chinese advisers,[46] FRELIMO and ZIPRA had Soviet advisers.[47] ZANLA was organized as a purely guerrilla army, whereas the others (after the Portuguese defeat) became more conventional in nature. FRELIMO was primarily prepared to defend Mozambique's borders against Rhodesian incursion. Whenever a Rhodesian helicopter overflew a FRELIMO camp, it took RPG fire from below. During any ground assault, FRELIMO defenders fought doggedly from their trenches.[48] Then, after conferring with Soviet advisers in late 1979, the president of Mozambique sent FRELIMO troops into Rhodesia in support of ZANLA. He concurrently tried to usurp control over elements of that organizaton.[49]

Meanwhile, through ZIPRA in Botswana, the Soviets had been trying to create armored columns to preempt ZANLA and roll right into Salisbury.[50] ZIPRA had its rear base areas in Zambia. As such, it tried deploying guerrilla bands to southern Matabeleland (northern Rhodesia), but they were often in contention with ZANLA counterparts.[51]

Allied with ZIPRA was ANC and its military wing, MK. It was MK that had been rebelling in South Africa since 1962, and it was MK that was helping to raid Rhodesia from ZIPRA's Zambian base camps. In 1967, the South Africans sent "riot police" and helicopters to help stem this infiltration.[52] As Rhodesia started to go under in 1979, the South Africans also sent SA Recce teams into Zambia. Those teams dropped bridges, mined roads, mounted ambushes, and generally monitored the entire frontier with Rhodesia.[53] Their efforts would complement Rhodesian SAS's (Special Air Service) interdiction of the Chinese-built Tan-Zam railroad.[54] All subsequent "SAS" references will be to the Rhodesian variety.

South African Help for Rhodesia

ZANLA's people were being trained in Tanzania. From Dar-es-Salaam, cadres were shipped down Mozambique's coast and then trucked (or walked) overland to the Rhodesian frontier.[55] Late in the war, ZANLA set its sights on southern Matabeleland—where the boundaries of South Africa, Rhodesia, and Mozambique all meet. In October 1977, the Selous Scouts relinquished the responsibility for stopping infiltration through this sector to SAS.[56] SAS would have the help of South Africa's "A" Group, 1-Reconnaissance Commando (15 white and 40 black special operators).[57] With secret "observers" on this front since 1976,[58] the South Africans would now assume a more direct role in the fighting.

As SAS and SA Recce teams began to enter Mozambique, FRE-LIMO's forces did what they could to stop them. Among its tools was the natural tracking ability of the indigenous population. To sneak up on someone in Africa, a Western maneuver element must first realize it is leaving telltale sign and probably being followed.

> FRELIMO, under the tutelage of Soviet and East German military advisers . . . , based units at all sidings along the line of rail and whenever these cadres heard aircraft sounds, they began patrolling predesignated sectors . . . looking for infiltrators' spoor [evidence of passage].[59]

143

Among the SA Recce missions was interdicting the road to Mapai in Mozambique. On one such raid, a Recce team was backtracking to obliterate its trail when it noticed something strange. While crossing a rail line, the point element had seen nothing. Then, the "tail-end-charlie" noticed a human silhouette on the horizon between the tracks. As that visage drew closer, it was seen to be carrying a RPD light machinegun and its partner, a RPG. To make matters worse, the hard-to-see visitors were only the lead element of a much larger patrol.[60] While this may have been a "chance meeting," it may also have been a case of "special operators being followed." On a subsequent operation, a SA Recce Team picked up a FRELIMO tail near the same rail line and had trouble shaking it. They spent a whole day on the run and then just barely survived an ambush.[61] That rail line paralleled the South African border and provided an excellent "observation lane" through the heavy vegetation. Very probably, FRELIMO had established outposts all along it to watch for trespassers. At each outpost were trackers and stalkers whose job it was to guess the trespassers' destination and arrange for an appropriate welcome. Whenever a FRELIMO battalion suspected an enemy reconnaissance team was around, it subdivided into tiny groups and widely dispersed as individual ambushes.[62]

Though followed and cornered, an SA Recce team was almost impossible to capture. One such team simply hid in the bushes until dark and then exfiltrated the FRELIMO encirclement.[63] It was this degree of individual skill that allowed 50 operators to dominate a vast area behind enemy lines. Soon, all military strategy, tactics, and skill would give way to political expediency. The British (probably with U.S. and U.N. approval) had pressured the Rhodesians into stopping all offensive operations.[64]

Rhodesia Becomes Zimbabwe

Like the Union of South Africa, Rhodesia had at one time been a part of the British Commonwealth. To regain British acknowledgment as a sovereign nation, the Rhodesians agreed to a general election in 1980. Then, to the utter surprise of the West, Mugabe—the head of ZANLA's parent political party—won the election. As promised, he immediately installed a Marxist regime. Mugabe was no ordinary freedom fighter. He had attended the Nanking Military Academy in China.[65]

Zimbabwe was to briefly regain British Commonwealth status. But in 2002, it was suspended from that Commonwealth. A year later, it officially abandoned the alliance.[66] Though Zimbabwe has little, if any, petroleum reserves, it is still heavily courted by China.

How the South Africans Interpret the ZANLA Method

As FRELIMO had before the Portuguese departure, ZANLA followed the Maoist method.[67] The two worked well together and often ran joint operations from FRELIMO bases.[68]

Mao [Tse tung] emphasized the importance of working in the rural areas. His famed dictum decreed that guerrillas must move amongst the peasants in the way a fish moves through water. . . . The first rural targets, he preached, should be [seized] by the stealth of the guerrilla and the politicisation of the people—the towns would then fall like the proverbial ripe plums.[69]

As such, Rhodesia's transitional elections were improperly influenced by ZANLA.

Some 7,000 guerrillas had gone to ground in the tribal areas on the orders of ZANLA commander, Rex Nhongo. He told them to ignore the cease-fire, hide their weapons, and persuade the people to vote for ZANU P/F (Zimbabwe African National Union Patriotic Front) (Verrier, *The Road to Zimbabwe,* 86). . . .

When ZANLA first infiltrated its political commissars into the Rhodesian tribal areas in 1972, they embraced the . . . methods of the [communist] Orient to politicise the tribesmen. On entering villages, they selected people for execution. . . . Their objective was to rid communities of their leadership and destroy the *bourgeois*.

Executions were conducted in an exemplary [local] fashion. . . . ZANLA's reign of terror has had few parallels in recent African history.

Not surprisingly, it took little persuasion to get villagers

145

to set up informer networks, report on the activities of the security forces, feed and look after incoming guerrillas, and spy and report on [unseemly] reports of their fellows. . . .
After Lancaster House [the cease-fire conference], . . . [ZANLA] guerrillas were able to live openly amongst the villagers without fear of attack by the Security Forces. . . . [T]he unsophisticated tribesmen took this as a signal the guerrillas had "won." . . .
So when ZANLA guerrillas insisted that ZANU P/F would win the independence election and announced that their first task afterwards would be to open the ballot boxes and identify those who had voted against them with the help of a special machine imported from Romania, the villagers believed them. They also accepted that those who voted against ZANU P/F would afterwards be put up against walls by ZANLA and shot (Sutton-Price, *Zimbabwe,* 63).
. . . Britain's quaint idea of stationing British bobbies in uniform at polling stations to ensure fair play, was at the least naive. . . .
An admission that ZANU P/F used its notorious political commissars to intimidate the indigenous people into voting for them came during Granada Television's *End of Empire* series when Edison Zvobgo said: ". . . [W]e had a very large army left (outside the assembly points), who remained as political commissars . . . simply to ensure that we would win the election (Flower, *Serving Secretly,* 255-256)." . . .
So much for the democratic process, African style.[70]
—Peter Stiff, renown South African historian

It was at this point in history that most of Rhodesia's famed Selous Scouts joined the South African Reconnaissance Regiment. There were other elements being supported by the Chinese in that region. One was the PAC.[71] ANC (from which PAC split off) had originally been supported by the Chinese but had switched over to the Soviets.[72] In 1978, several ANC and MK leaders flew to Hanoi in North Vietnam for instruction from General Giap.[73] Soon, MK was running some of its operations against South Africa out of Mozambique.[74]

In 1981, "SA 6-Recce 6" (former Selous Scouts) went after an ANC/MK facility in Matola.[75] Similar raids by other SA Recce teams would continue against ANC/MK targets in Mozambique and Zambia until 1987. Meanwhile, the west-coast theater of war was again heating up.

The Angolan Conflict Persists throughout the 1980's

By the end of 1980, UNITA had captured the ex-Portuguese airbase at Mavinga in southeastern Angola. Mavinga would now function as a forward logistics base through which supplies could be flown in from Zaire and Namibia. For two years, MPLA launched drives against Mavinga from its regional bastion at Cuito Cuanavale.[76] While none of these drives were successful, SWAPO had established a number of bases in southeastern Angola from which it could more easily attack Namibia. It was SA Recce's job to do something about those bases. As MPLA's support of SWAPO became more apparent, the South Africans began to target related parts of the Angolan infrastructure. In November 1981, SA Recce went after the oil installations in Luanda harbor.[77]

Soon, larger elements of the South African Armed Forces were going after SWAPO bases and their FAPLA affiliates inside Angola. Some major clashes between South African and FAPLA motorized columns resulted. To the north, UNITA took this opportunity to expand its sphere of influence.[78] Soon U.S. support for the South African offensive began to wane, and a U.N. sponsored international agreement forced its cessation.

In early 1985, the MPLA/Soviet/Cuban alliance reoccupied the strongholds in south central Angola that the South Africans had been forced to vacate by the Lusaka Accord of 1984. (There were a number of Lusaka Accords.) To consolidate the gain, the Soviets sent in large quantities of military hardware. The billion-dollar aid package included MIG-23 fighters and HIND helicopter gunships. It also brought FAPLA's total of tanks to 550.[79]

In August of that year, FAPLA assembled a force of twenty brigades for a renewed push against UNITA in southeastern Angola. The force included a SWAPO semi-conventional brigade and five MK (ANC) battalions.[80] Soon, they were being cut down by 32 Battalion's air-bursting multi-rocket barrages and South African night-strike aircraft. Among their casualties (according to UNITA intelligence) were 19 Soviets and 116 Cubans.[81] Then, a Soviet general took over all MPLA forces. Backing him up were 3,000 So-

147

viet and East German advisers and 45,000 Cuban ground troops.[82] FAPLA's new mission was conventionally to overwhelm all UNITA bases in southeastern Angola. General Shaganovitch commenced his new offensive in June 1986. Through a series of spoiling attacks, Battalion 32, SA Recce, and UNITA were able to slow the advance. Finally, South African air, artillery, and motorized infantry joined into the fight. On 29 September 1987, President Botha directed his armed forces to help with a UNITA counteroffensive.[83] The fighting raged until peace talks were re-initiated in the summer of 1988.

> After . . . American-brokered talks between South Africa, Cuba, and Angola [MPLA], the Brazzaville Protocol was finally signed by those parties on 13 December 1988 and ratified at the U.N. . . . . It agreed to a disengagement of the SADF [Defense Forces] from Angola, a phased withdrawal of Cuban forces from Angola and the . . . U.N.-supervised independence elections to take place in SWA/Namibia, and the withdrawal of the SADF [from Namibia] in 1989.[84]

"Peace" Finally Comes to South Africa As Well

The 1990's brought a political end to apartheid in South Africa and ushered in black majority rule. President de Klerk held out the hand of reconciliation to ANC in 1990, promising an election on 27 April 1994. ANC agreed to talk, but PAC/APLA continued to fight from its bases in the northern Transkei region, hoping to acquire more land before the elections.[85] Again, to the West's surprise, ANC won the election.[86]

That Didn't Stop Angolan Retribution

At this point in history, the record gets a little fuzzy. It's clear that the U.S. and South Africa had been supporting UNITA.[87] That support may have even included Stinger missiles.[88] What is unclear is which organization refused to stop fighting. BBC News claims that UNITA declined a peace deal that would have allowed elections in 1991 and kept fighting for another three years.[89] The U.N. sent peacekeepers into Angola in 1994, but they were forced (by renewed fighting) to leave in 1999. When UNITA leader Savimbi was finally killed in 2002, his army agreed to a lasting cease fire.[90] By then, the action had already shifted to the northern end of Angola where a former adversary of the MPLA had been deposed and his deposer supported by Angolan troops. That possible expansion of MPLA interests will be the subject of chapter 11. Here is the time line of events.

> 1989—[MPLA leader] Dos Santos and UNITA leader . . . Savimbi agree to cease-fire, which collapses soon afterwards and guerrilla activity resumes. . . .
> 1991 April—MPLA drops Marxism-Leninism in favour of social democracy.
> 1991 May—Dos Santos and Savimbi sign peace deal in Lisbon which results in a new multiparty constitution.
> 1992 September—Presidential and parliamentary polls [are] certified by U.N. monitors as generally free and fair. Dos Santos gains more votes than Savimbi, who rejects results and resumes guerrilla war.
> 1993—U.N. imposes sanctions against UNITA. The U.S. acknowledges the MPLA.
> 1994—[MPLA] government and UNITA sign Lusaka Protocol peace accord.
> 1995—Dos Santos and Savimbi meet, confirm commitment to peace. First of 7,000 U.N. peacekeepers arrive.
> 1996—Dos Santos and Savimbi agree to form unity government and join forces into national army.
> 1997 April—Unified government inaugurated, with Savimbi declining post in unity government and failing to attend inauguration ceremony.
> 1997 May—Tension mounts, with few UNITA troops having integrated into army.
> 1998—Full-scale fighting resumes. U.N. plane shot down. Angola intervenes in civil war in Democratic Republic of Congo on the side of [new] President Laurent-Desire Kabila.[91]
>
> — BBC News, *Country Profile,* 8 December 2005

One cannot leave the 20th Century without closely examining Rhodesia's last few years. Of particular interest would be any military miscalculation. Rhodesia had perhaps the best guerrilla fighters the West has ever produced, but those guerrilla fighters had never heard of 4GW.

10

Selous Scout
_____ Infiltration

- How did the Selous Scouts operate?
- What were their tactical techniques?

RHODESIAN "SELOUS SCOUT," 1974

(Source: *Uniforms of the Elite Forces,* illustrations by Michael Chappell [Cassell PLC], ©1982 by Blandford Press Ltd., Plate 23, No. 69; FM 5-103 (June 1985), p. 4-19)

An Amazing Record

Established in 1973, "the Selous Scouts . . . were officially credited . . . for being directly or indirectly responsible for 68% of all the insurgents killed within Rhodesia during the course of the war [until 1980]. Losses suffered by Selous Scouts amounted to less than forty."[1] Most of the "indirect" kills were from targets referred to the Rhodesian Light Infantry. (See Map 10.1.)

One cannot draw too many conclusions—one way or the other—from such a statistic. Most wars—to include guerrilla wars—are decided by which side runs short of strategic assets. The average foot soldier has little strategic value and can easily be replaced. Thus, a unit's kill ratio is not a good measure of its success. Those who make "killing" their primary objective have fallen victim to a cruel paradox of war. History records any number of cases in which the winning side has had more casualties. Still, war is an unfortunate business, and the killing of foot soldiers to get at an enemy's strategic assets or to defend one's own is acceptable behavior. As long as the fewest possible are killed, that behavior remains "moral."[2] Of course, that further assumes that the war was "just" to begin with.[3] Under no circumstances can "hand-raising" combatants or "collaborating" civilians be killed.

The 68% figure for the Selous Scouts is a little shocking, but there were mitigating circumstances. Officially, the Selous Scouts were trackers. The only time a Western army had previously beaten a Maoist insurgency was in the early 1950's in Malaysia. After each Malay terrorist incident, the British would dispatch a tiny team of mantrackers to ambush its perpetrators. That way, only "terrorists" were harmed. Because the mantracking approach has already defeated guerrillas, it is more "moral" than its electronics/firepower equivalent. That equivalent—the U.S. way of war—has yet to work against Eastern insurgents.

> They [the Selous Scouts] work in remote parts of Rhodesia hunting down terrorist spoor and leading the infantry in for the kill if the invading group is too big for the small two or three man teams to handle on their own.[4]
> — *Armed Forces Journal,* May 1977

It was because of the Selous Scouts' proficiency at close combat that their foes so often accused them of atrocity. As will soon be demonstrated, many of those foes practiced what—in the West—would be considered unconscionable behavior. Thus, their accusations must be taken with a grain of salt. Within the Scouts, a few isolated excesses may have occurred, but there is no evidence of widespread atrocity. The Selous Scouts were simply the best counterguerrilla force the West has produced. If anything, they should be commended for their aversion to supporting arms. Sadly, the Scouts may have accomplished more through the destruction of enemy facilities and materiel alone. All the killing helped to turn world opinion against their government. Those who would devise 4GW tactics for America should be aware of the trade-off.

152

The Selous Scouts gained the most notoriety from their August 1976 raid on the Nyadzonya/Pungwe guerrilla base camp in Mozambique. In guerrilla wars, training facilities are among the most important targets, strategically. Sneaking far behind enemy lines to enter a camp containing 70 times one's number requires

Map 10.1: What Was Formerly Rhodesia

a fairly lethal exit strategy.[5] Anything less would mean certain suicide. Though many unarmed ZANLA trainees were lost in this incident, history will probably not record it as a massacre. The intent to kill as many trainees as possible may have been somewhat misguided. And, a few Scouts may have gotten a little carried away during the final sweep. However, in the heat of battle, those kinds of things happen to the most disciplined of armies. At least, the Scouts were chivalrous enough to face their foes eye-to-eye. That's better than indiscriminate, standoff bombardment.

> This operation involved a raid on a large ZANLA base 60 miles inside of Mozambique by a Scouts column comprising ten trucks and four armored cars, again disguised as FRELIMO vehicles. The Scouts in the first four vehicles were also dressed in FRELIMO uniforms. They cut the telephone lines leading to the town where the terrorist base was located, then drove straight into the camp. They then opened fire on the unsuspecting insurgent terrorists drilling on the parade ground, killing at least 1,028. Fourteen important ZANLA insurgents were captured and taken back to Rhodesia for interrogation. On their way out of Mozambique, the raiding party blew up the Pungwe Bridge to prevent any pursuit and returned to Rhodesia safely. In a separate action, the covering team deployed to block the column's escape, ambushed a Land Rover whose six occupants were found to be senior ZANLA officers; all six were killed.[6]

Because of the Rhodesian government's apartheid policy, Selous tactics may be ignored at a time when they might prove most useful. Those tactics can be easily purged of unnecessary killing. The Scouts had a tiny, semi-autonomous organization. As such, it made its own policies. One of those policies was to join four blacks for every white and to give them equal opportunity in all things.[7] Another was to do something that most Western units would never do—fight its foes "man to man" instead of through standoff firepower. Where the hearts and the minds of an indigenous population are at stake, the close-combat approach is far more productive than wasting infrastructure and bystanders. At least, the Scouts got within feet of their kill zones to verify their targets; the users/programmers of smart bombs don't.

Unlike the Rhodesian Army, the Selous Scouts were forced—by their size and mission—to learn and respect the diverse cultures and customs of the region.[8]

Each member of the Selous Scouts, down to the lowest ranking White soldier, speaks at least one African language—necessary for communication with their Black comrades-in-arms with whom they work in the closest possible context as equals.[9]

The rest of this chapter will be dedicated to the ways in which African insurgents fought, and Selous Scouts countered.

A Brief Glimpse into Rhodesia's Future

In 1980, Rhodesia became Zimbabwe, and the Selous Scout Regiment became the Zimbabwe Parachute Regiment.[10]   It was then that most of the Scouts went to South Africa to join No. 5 Recce Commando.[11]   "The . . . British-supervised election [had] brought Robert Mugabe and his ZANLA to power."[12]   It had been ZANLA and ZIPRA that the Selous Scouts had been primarily fighting. Both organizations sent some of their best recruits to Russia, China, and Cuba for training.[13]

Toward the end of the war, the Rhodesian security forces faced an almost insurmountable problem. The rebels became deeply entrenched in tribal groups, instead of withdrawing to uninhabited areas where they could be tracked, or inhabited areas where they could be informed upon.[14]   In other words, the rebels created the equivalent of "secure base areas" within the indigenous population itself. Below is what is believed to be a fairly accurate description of how they did it.

ZANLA's Way of Instilling Loyalty

Because of ZANLA's links to the new Zimbabwe government, one must try to be objective in the assessment of its methods. It is clear that the insurgents became entrenched in the tribal society. Through "pseudo-operations" (the forming of fake rebel gangs), the

155

Selous Scouts succeeded in infiltrating the society through which ZANLA swam. Thus, they certainly had the means to acquire accurate "human" intelligence on ZANLA's methods. Nations that depend solely upon electronic intelligence are in no position to criticize the Scout method, for they can only guess at interpersonal relationships. What is to follow may sound impossible and barbaric to Westerners, but such things have happened all too often in African history. They still happen today at the border between Sudan and the DRC. The European colonialists had grown rich while their African neighbors suffered. ZANLA promised a redistribution of wealth and woe to anyone who didn't want to cooperate. There is a lesson here for those who would push national democracy without first having some semblance of local freedom.

> The ZANLA commissars . . . promised the tribesmen, that in return for their support, when ZANLA came to power all the good things belonging to the white men would be theirs. . . .
>
> The commissars would conclude these meetings by giving clear warnings as to what would happen to the villagers collectively, family units or individual persons, should anyone decide to become a "sellout" by reporting their presence to the authorities. . . .
>
> The people would then be invited to tell the commissars who the stooges and puppets of the government were. . . . They were also collectively ordered to indicate the families of serving soldiers and policemen. . . .
>
> Sometimes a man, a wife, a mother or a father, or a whole family would be pushed to the front by the crowd and would be publicly put to death by the commissars. . . . Sometimes the insurgent commissars, wishing to bind the tribesmen to them by a pact of blood, would order the villagers to kill the sellouts or stooges themselves. . . .
>
> Afterwards . . . the commissars would select and nominate various members of the population . . . to act as contact men and "policemen."
>
> The contact men and policemen played a vital role in the insurgent network and a chain of these men was gradually created until they stretched from inside Mozambique to the farthermost reaches of the operational area. . . .

By order of the insurgents, it became and was the duty of every person in the Tribal Trust Land concerned to pass every scrap of information relating to the security forces to the local contact man. . . .

In addition to collating intelligence, the contact men were responsible for the selection of bases and the collection and provision of food for the insurgents. They were also responsible for the transmission of letters and message between detachments and sections, and arranging and setting up security procedures for meetings between various groups. . . .

The policemen worked with and under the contact men and were responsible for maintaining the insurgents' system of law and order. They could not, however, discipline or punish anyone themselves. Any suspected sellout . . . would be taken by them to the local insurgent leader.

The contact men and policemen were later supplemented, as the war progressed, by the *mujiba* system. . . . Although too young to fight they [the children] could still act as ears and eyes, or as messengers or go-betweens with the civil population. . . .

And so, by these methods, Mao Tse Tung's dictum that to be successful, a guerrilla must move through the population as a fish does through water, was satisfied by ZANLA.[15]

ZANLA's Abilities and Techniques

Woods dwellers can frequently do things that their urban counterparts can't. In this spirit, the following quote from the Selous Scouts commander is offered.

[T]he average African has phenomenal physical endurance and possesses an almost uncanny ability to move and see at night. . . . [H]is sense of direction is . . . incredible. On the darkest of nights he has the unerring ability to return to base without the aid of a compass. In addition, his powers of memory and his keen sense of observation . . . made a deep impression on me.[16]

It was not long before ZANLA insurgents were routinely obliterating their tracks after each attack.[17] Instead of forming a defensive circle each night, they slept in a straight line, head to toe, almost touching each other.[18] This formation is normally associated with the Orient. It enables defenders to quickly alert each other and fire in almost any direction without risk of fratricide.[19]

In urban combat, ZANLA fighters liked to hide in the upper floors of buildings. Two Selous Scouts found this out the hard way during a raid on a purported ZANLA arms depot inside Mozambique. While searching an upstairs, open-air hallway, one was shot by an unseen gunman to his front. A few minutes later and a little farther along the hall, his buddy was shot by someone overhead or to his rear.[20] In these kinds of instances, the assailant is often firing through a tiny loophole in wall or ceiling.

Selous Scout Training

The Selous Scouts' motto was *Pamwe Chete* ("all together" in the native Shona dialect). This is much like the U.S. Marine motto—Gung Ho ("working together" in Chinese). Both imply the harnessing of collective wisdom at the lowest levels of the organization. Rhodesia had been a British possession, so its organizations were more apt to be hierarchical and "top-down." The Selous Scouts may have gotten the "bottom-up" approach from the *krygsraads* (war councils) of the Boers, or from the communal thought process of their Maoist adversaries. However they got it, it worked. Any American commander who wishes to have more self-sufficient squads should try something different—allowing each company's NCOs to collectively refine their own techniques.

The counterinsurgency squad must be able to stalk an elusive enemy through difficult terrain and remain self-reliant in case of trouble. That takes more than just physical endurance. It takes resourcefulness under pressure. The British disguised small units as enemy bands in Malaya and Kenya in the 1950's,[21] but the Selous Scouts made this practice into an art.

Instead of the "boot camp" way in which Western recruits hang-ups are adjusted, the fledgling Selous Scouts were simply made to live off the land for 18 days.[22] The experience so challenged their individuality that they became instantly trainable as team players.

First and foremost, the new Selous Scout had to master a wide variety of survival skills. Included were the following: (1) improvising game traps for food; (2) navigation by natural means such as the sun and stars; (3) purifying or filtering stagnant water; (4) building a shelter for protection from the elements; and (5) fire making with a bow and drill. In addition to survival, he learned how to improvise on patrol: e.g., (1) rig an impromptu antenna, (2) build a boobytrap, or (3) make a hide site out of natural camouflage.[23] He also received instruction in compass-assisted navigation, camouflage, foraging, mantracking, and stalking.[24]

Unlike many U.S. military organizations, the Selous Scouts did not consider themselves "the best in the world." In fact, their first commander detested the word "elite." He encouraged his people to keep privilege and rank in perspective.

> We do not consider ourselves an elite group of men, nor do we think we are of the highest calibre. It could cause the men to imagine themselves better than they really are and this could in turn lead to recklessness. We are simply just trackers out to do a job.[25]
> —Maj. Reid-Daly (former Light Infantry Sgt.Maj.)

The lesson to be learned here is one that successful special operations units find obvious, but conventional military commanders can never grasp. Small, close-knit . . . units function best when run in an egalitarian manner [with no special privileges for rank].[26]

Hunter/Killer Teams

Early in the war, the Rhodesian insurgents fled to the lightly populated Zambesi Valley. Like the British had in Malaysia, the Selous Scouts first sent tiny teams of trackers out in a "hunter/killer" role. Soon, their quarries started taking refuge in the villages of more populated areas. It was then that a new, and quite daring, Selous Scout procedure was born. On one occasion, a tracking team crept unseen into a village during a ZANLA rally, eased their way to the front of an enthralled crowd, and shot the speaker. As the crowd and ZANLA bodyguards broke for cover, the Selous Scouts quietly slipped back into the night. They were later to learn that the speaker had been the local ZANLA commander.[27]

159

Two-Man "Reconnaissance" Teams

Selous Scout leaders next realized that their people were well enough trained to survive as two-man reconnaissance teams. Within weeks, there was no target within "Dakota" aircraft range that was immune from attack. The pair of Scouts had only to free-fall parachute into its vicinity during hours of darkness, accomplish their mission, and walk out to a helicopter extraction site.[28]

Selous "Pseudo-Operations"

In law enforcement, the best way to stop organized crime is through undercover agents. Toward the end of the war, the Selous Scouts simply applied this axiom to Maoist revolution. They entered the rebel network as fake gangs. To do so, the Europeans among them simply "blackened up."

> Though the cover mission for the Selous Scouts remained the tracking of terrorists, in reality the unit was [became] a pseudo-terrorist unit, using turned terrorists and Black soldiers from the Rhodesian African Rifles [see Figure 10.1], as well as White soldiers in black face make-up from the Rhodesian SAS, Rhodesian Light Infantry, and other units. These pseudo groups would infiltrate terrorist areas of operation, passing themselves off as terrorists and attempting to subvert the terrorist infrastructure.[29]

This unusual approach to counterguerrilla warfare had been successfully tried by the British in Malaysia. While Westernized sweeps and cordons had trouble surprising anyone, it was a way to take the fight to an elusive enemy.

> [M]ost modern guerilla [sic] tactics, Muslim or otherwise, take their inspiration from . . . communist insurgency doctrine. This means a rigorous attention to internal security, with highly compartmentalized, autonomous cell structures, extensive use of codes and signals, and barbaric recruitment and enforcement mechanisms.
>
> As a result, terrorist groups are extremely difficult to crack. No one cell knows what another is doing or even who

its members are, and only a few . . . have any contact with any higher authority. Within an area, the terrorists can quickly identify and eliminate potential adversaries while subduing that part of the local population not sympathetic with terror and threats of terror.

The only way to learn anything about these cells . . . is to get inside them. . . .

The Scouts . . . perfected the "pseudo team" counter-insurgency concept. . . . [G]roups of fake or "pseudo" terrorists would enter an area and attempt to gain acceptance within the actual insurgent network.

Having made contact and identified the guerrilla group, the infiltrators would then call in a strike force of . . . Rho-

Figure 10.1: Private, Rhodesian African Rifles, 1976
(Source: Courtesy of Orion Books, from *World Army Uniforms since 1939*, © 1975, 1980, 1981, 1983 by Blandford Press Ltd., Part II, Plate 99)

desian Light Infantry. . . . The [Selous] Scouts would . . .
arrange to be elsewhere when the attack came. In later
meetings with insurgents, they might detail their harrow-
ing escape. . . . Properly conducted, the pseudo team could
remain uncompromised. . . .

The key to the Scouts' success was the extensive reliance
on turned, or "tame" insurgents. A constant inflow of these
insurgent recruits kept the intelligence on guerrilla security
procedures up-to-date. At its zenith, turned insurgents
comprised over 50 percent of the Scouts' fighting force. The
rest were the best soldiers, black and white, from various
components of the Rhodesian military.

How did they recruit from this pool of seemingly fanatic,
dedicated guerillas [sic]? Retired Lt. Col. Ron Reid-Daly,
a former commander of the Selous Scouts and author of
"Pamwe Chete . . . ," put it this way:

"It was simple and direct. He [the terrorist] had the
option of being handed over to the police, after which he
would be prosecuted for . . . offenses related to terrorism. If
found guilty he would be hanged. He could, however, change
sides and work with the security forces against his former
comrades. After a short period of intensive contemplation,
the capture elected to change sides. He was immediately
given back his weapon, but unknown to him, its firing pin
had been removed. The fact that he had been given a weapon
astonished . . . him. [I]t was a shrewdly calculated move
designed to sow the seeds of trust. . . .

According to Col. Reid-Daly, despite their vaunted
fanaticism, insurgents were relatively easy to turn. They
generally lived a tough, hand-to-mouth existence and were
acutely aware that while they were putting their lives on
the line every day, their leaders were often living in lush
accommodations, far removed from any danger, traveling in
high diplomatic circles and pilfering the money and supplies
intended for them.

Many of the turned insurgents went on to become some
of the Scouts' most loyal and decorated soldiers. That the
Scouts' formula is an effective counter-insurgency technique is beyond question. Their successes speak for themselves.[30]

— *Defense Watch,* 17 September 2003

Of course, these psuedo-teams would have been in great danger from Rhodesian forces had not certain precautions been taken.

So successfully did the Selous Scouts pass themselves off as terrorists that they were frequently in more danger from Rhodesian security forces than from real terrorists. As a result, when a Selous Scouts pseudo team was working an area, it [the area] was "frozen" and declared off limits to any other security forces operations.[31]

A Selous Contribution to 4th Generation Warfare

The most ingenious part of the Selous method was routinely turning former foe into trusted companion. In a religious context, this is not too different from "loving one's enemy." It gave the Scouts a unique source of real-time intelligence. It also countered their natural tendency to dehumanize their opposition.

Constantly adding turned terrorists, the Scouts kept abreast of current terrorist terminology, identification procedures, and operations; often they were better informed about ter- rorist procedures than the terrorists themselves.[32]

Selous Intelligence Gathering

The Scouts soon realized that technology could not produce the type of intelligence they required.

The Scouts were very successful in gathering intelligence, at least in part from captured diaries and letters. . . . Due to the fragmented nature of their operations, guerrillas rarely have ready access to communications equipment. As a result, they may rely on written communication, leaving much open to capture. Few guerrillas are sophisticated enough to use ciphers, either, so often captured communica- tions are "in the clear." Many politically inspired guerrillas are actually encouraged to keep diaries documenting their political development, and these also frequently include valuable intelligence information. Third World insurgents are generally much less security conscious than organized military forces about documents; hence, captured written material can be an excellent intelligence source, especially for order of battle data.[33]

Selous Tricks

Because guerrillas think of themselves as aggressors, they are often too complacent in their "safe" areas. That's where the Selous Scouts liked to strike. This eroded not only strategic assets, but also guerrilla resolve.

The Selous Scouts' training and operational doctrine inculcated audacity. At various times, for example, White Selous Scouts posed as the "prisoners" of Black Selous Scout "terrorists," and were escorted into terrorist strongholds, where White prisoners were highly prized. At the appropriate moment, the Selous Scouts turned their weapons on the terrorists, wreaking havoc from within. The classic example of audacity was the Selous Scouts raid on the large ZANLA terrorist camp at Nyadzonya Pungwe in August 1976. Using Unimogs and Ferrets [vehicles] painted in FRELIMO camouflage, eighty-four [actually fifty-four] Selous Scouts penetrated Mozambique and drove directly into a large terrorist camp. . . .

. . . [T]he Scouts had a psychologically debilitating effect quite out of proportion to their numbers. It was not uncommon, for example, for two groups of terrorists to begin shooting at each other out of fear that the other group was the Selous Scouts.

. . . [T]errorists, who rely heavily on fear as a weapon, can themselves be rendered psychologically impotent . . . when they become the prey of an enemy who appears, hits hard, and then vanishes.[34]

The Scouts liked undercover "sting" operations. On several occasions, black Selous Scout "terrorists" walked right into enemy camps with white Selous Scout "hostages." Then, some high-ranking

ZIPRA officers got arrested by Scouts posing as Botswana Defense Force personnel. To be accepted by terrorist groups, the Scouts would even stage fake attacks on farms, or fake hits on Special Branch informers.[35]

Selous Combat Techniques

Even when caught in a "near ambush," East Asian soldiers will drop to the ground and crawl off. In dense brush, the Selous Scouts had a different counterambush technique.

Scouts were trained, when under fire from ambush, immediately to direct short bursts of fire at all likely places of concealment for ambushers within their arc of fire. The effectiveness of this maneuver could only be appreciated after seeing a well-drilled stick of Selous Scouts quickly sterilize 360 degrees of an ambush site. Fire discipline was important in this drill, but the Scouts had it.[36]

Sadly, this was called "drake shooting." To quickly establish fire superiority, the Scouts would need prearranged sectors of fire. Each patrol member was given a separate arc (as on a compass) to watch. When ambushed, he would quickly analyze that arc for potential cover and pump two rounds into each location. Upon entering a contested room, Russian soldiers did the same thing in Stalingrad.

He would look at the base of large trees, rocks, and thickets, and "double-tap" two shots into each place. In the case of trees, he would be trained to fire right into them at almost ground level, as bullets fired from modern high-velocity weapons can easily and completely penetrate a tree.[37]

Out-of-Country Operations

Bordering Rhodesia on the west was Botswana and on the east was Mozambique. It was from those countries that ZIPRA and ZANLA launched many of their raids. As a result, the Selous Scouts routinely entered their border areas.

165

During those out-of-country escapades, the Scouts kidnapped ZIPRA officials no fewer than four times from their headquarters in Botswana, raided ten or more ZANLA camps (one in Zambia and the others in Mozambique), emptied out a ZIPRA prisoner of war camp in Zambia, and blew up a suitcase bomb factory in Botswana.[38] (See Figure 10.2.)

More on the Nyadzonya/Pungwe Raid

At the time of this raid, Mozambique was being governed by FRELIMO. FRELIMO was a Marxist-Leninist political/military movement that declared Mozambique independent from Portugal in 1975. It would go on to "win" multiparty elections in 1994.

Figure 10.2: Selous Scout NCO, 1978
(Source: Courtesy of Orion Books, from *World Army Uniforms since 1939*, © 1975, 1980, 1981, 1983 by Blandford Press Ltd., Part II, Plate 98)

To get at this ZANLA training camp in 1976, 54 Selous Scouts would have to sneak through a 30-kilometer-wide band of FRELIMO strongpoints that ran all along the Rhodesian border. They would enter this band over an old smuggler trail and exit it along a zigzag swath of prospector-cut brush. The entry route would take them through a manned border post and a heavily garrisoned town—Vila de Manica. After the raid, it would be FRELIMO who would try to annihilate the raiding party.

The day of the attack would be Monday, 9 August, with most of the approach march (drive) occurring during the night before. Both routes had been reconnoitered by foot patrol. During the first of these patrols, it was discovered that the eight FRELIMO guards at the tiny border post on the smuggler trail went home to a nearby village every evening. After dark on 8 August, a small patrol cut all the telephone lines between that part of the border and Vila de Manica. Then, a column of 14 FRELIMO-camouflaged vehicles, each mounting an automatic weapon from 7.62 mm to 20 mm in projectile size, departed for Mozambique. The convoy crossed over the border through the now-empty outpost about midnight.[39]

> The column, rolling along easily in the bright moonlight, showed only their parking lights so vehicles could keep their convoy distances. The . . . calamity . . . struck.
> . . . One moment the Ferret [armored car] was trundling along the road and the next it was upside down in the riverbed. . . .
> "Blast it [blow it up]," I ordered tersely. . . .
> . . . I looked at the map and realised we were in trouble. They couldn't blast the car, for it was too close to Vila de Manica. If they set off an explosion, the FRELIMO would come running from everywhere. . . .
> The [Selous] column came rumbling through the town, following where possible a back-street route. . . . [T]he column . . . actually passed within a metre or so of a sentry box where the FRELIMO guard was fast asleep. . . .
> Once they were safely out of town, the telephone-line-snipping drill was repeated and telephone communications to Chimoio, the main FRELIMO base in the Manica Province, were rendered useless. Then, to discourage any thought of a morning follow-up, a booby trap was set up across the road.

At 03h30, well on time, they reached an area some kilometres past the Pugwe Bridge, where they pulled off the road into the bush. The men . . . readied to move out again at first light. . . .

According to our intelligence, a resupply column of FRELIMO vehicles from Chimoio went to the insurgent base each Monday morning, about muster time. The plan was to wait until they came, tag on behind and, hopefully, follow them into the base. . . .

The FRELIMO troops had not materialised by 07h00. As waiting any longer would have made the column late, Rob decided to press on and play the situation by ear. . . .

. . . They were on the last stretch to the base, ten, maybe 13 kilometers to go.

Three kilometers farther on, the convoy dipped into a dried-up bed of a stream. . . . , an ideal ambush site.

[T]wo Unimogs [half-ton trucks] . . . plus the closed-in Unimog carrying the explosives, left the column to take up ambush positions. . . .

. . . [S]omeone had to cover the rear to ensure the column was safe from surprise attack. . . .

At 08h30 the head of the column reached the entrance to the camp.

There were six ZANLA guards at the gate. Normally, they would have been accompanied by two FRELIMO soldiers. . . .

The two FRELIMO soldiers had . . . left their posts and returned to their barracks.

This was fortunate for us, for when the inexperienced ZANLA guards hesitated about lifting the boom, Sergeant Guerreiro, his balaclava [floppy hat] pulled well down over his [blackened] face, screamed a torrent of abusive Portuguese at them. . . .

. . . The infantry vehicles paused briefly to drop off the 81-millimeter mortar teams just inside the camp, while the Ferrets hived off to cover the insurgents' anticipated escape routes towards the Nyadzonya River. The Unimogs carried on slowly. . . .

The parade ground suddenly opened up in front of them, and there were few men in the column that did not gasp in amazement at the sight that greeted them. . .

A short distance away from them, as the Unimogs formed into line just off the parade ground, was the largest single concentration of insurgents mustered that would ever be seen by any member of the Rhodesian security forces, throughout the entire war. . . .

Some were carrying weapons but the majority were, thankfully, carrying only practice guns carved from wood.

In a matter of minutes, a surging, milling crowd of several thousand [ZANLA] insurgents surrounded the vehicles in column. . . .

Rob Warraker [the raid leader] realized it had to be plan B [open fire instead of calling senior officials forward to presumably capture], and it had to be plan B quickly. They were at grave risk of being swamped. . . .

A sustained but controlled rate of fire was maintained until all movement on the parade ground ceased.

While this had been going on a certain amount of return fire had been directed at the column from the buildings in the camp, and by the time Rob gave the order to cease firing, five men . . . had sustained minor wounds.

A sweep in accordance with the overall plan then took place and the Scouts moved through the entire camp complex. Sergeant Andy Balaam's mortars gave supporting fire, which concentrated on pre-registered escape routes, which were now packed with fleeing survivors.

The three Ferret scout cars, which had been positioned as cut-offs at the main insurgent escape route down to the Nyhadzonya River as shown in the camp orders, wrought a terrible slaughter. . . .

Unfortunately, both for ourselves and for the wounded insurgent inmates of the hospital whom we had hoped to capture and take back with us to Rhodesia, a chance tracer ignited the thatch of the huge building. This went up like dry tinder and all the patients . . . were quickly burned to death. . . .

. . . Many hundreds [of guerrillas] tried to escape across the river. . . . [O]ver 200 insurgents were drowned while trying to cross to the comparative safety of the far bank. Many more that were attempting to hide in the reeds lining the riverbank were shot during the sweep afterwards.

During the course of the attack 14 prisoners were captured and a vast quantity of documents collected from the
camp buildings, before they were fired.[40]
— Reid-Daly, in *Pamwe Chete*

The place had been categorized as "ZANLA's main logistics base
for infiltration into Eastern [Rhodesia]." It was, as such, a legitimate
strategic target. All but the guards' weapons and ammunition had
been presupposed to be in base armories.[41] Those in the hospital
were veterans of fighting in Rhodesia and thus had an intelligence
value.[42]

On the way out, the Selous column encountered FRELIMO resistance at the Pungwe Bridge. It fought its way over that bridge
and destroyed it. By 3:30 P.M., it had left the Tete road and was
making fairly good time along a prospector "trace" toward Rhodesia.
Then, to everyone's surprise, they crested a hill and saw a FRE-
LIMO-garrisoned village astride that trace. First, the Scouts tried
to bluff their way through. Then, at the sight of mortars being set
up on a nearby ridge, they opened fire, summoned air support, and
headed cross-country for home. After spending the next 22 hours
cutting, winching, digging, and pulling their way toward the border,
they finally crossed the last river into Rhodesia under an ineffectual
FRELIMO mortar barrage.[43] Two days later, Sergeants Guerreiro
and Holdt came straggling across as well. Over-engrossed in the
"winkling out and killing of insurgents hiding in the reeds" at the
Nyadzonya River's bank, they had missed movement.[44]

The ZANLA Account of the Battle

Found among the tons of documents recovered at Chimoio on
a subsequent raid into Mozambique was the official ZANLA report
on the attack by the Selous Scouts on the Pungwe/Nyadzonya base,
dated 19 August 1976. It sets the casualty totals at 1,028 killed,
309 wounded, and 1,000 missing.[45] The ZANLA report also makes
clear that Pungwe/Nyadzonya was a guerrilla base (as opposed to
a refugee camp). Here is a little more of what the report said:

Monday, the 9th August 1976 was declared a [base]
holiday. . . .

Soon after the parade (approx. 8.10 am) the Red Guards took up their positions on the football ground. . . . The total number of people at Nyadzonya on this day was 5,250. . . .

. . . As indicated on the attached map, trenches were dug all around the camp, but a trench without the gun for protection is just as useless. . . .

About 50 FRELIMO soldiers were stationed at Nyadzonya for security purposes. . . .

. . . The attitude of the comrades is much deeper than before. . . . Keeping them in bases often referred to [disguised] as "Refugee Camps" keeps on robbing them of their moral[e] and their desire to concentrate fully on Revolutionary matters. The idea of keeping them unarmed and thereby making them easy targets is most unpalatable.[46]

— ZANLA Report of the Incident, 19 August 1976

Another source shows the document to contain proof of 3,544 male comrades, 387 female comrades, 707 Red Guards, eight administrators, and 604 ordinary tribesmen present at the time of the raid.[47] The term "comrade" was applied to guerrilla fighter and the term "Red Guard" to expert guerrilla fighter (possibly trained by the Chinese).[48] The "ordinary tribesmen" may have been day laborers.[49] The raid had obviously been on a guerrilla base camp, but—for whatever reason—the U.N. was slow to admit it. A news photo shows some of the dead wearing ammunition belts in a mass grave.[50]

A Telling Battle Right before the End

In September 1979, Rhodesian forces (to include Selous Scouts) again attacked a ZANLA complex near Chimoio. It was more carefully laid out than Nyadzonya had been. Its defense involved Soviet/Chinese ordnance and tactics. While it had a plan for temporary occupants to escape, it also had one for permanent personnel to fight.

The complex was huge and consisted of five separate camps, each heavily defended by heavy armaments and anti-aircraft weapons. The emplacements were hewn into the rock outcrops on top of high ground in the area.

171

The most prominent feature was nicknamed Monte Cassino. . . . [It] was a large, almost bald *kopje* [hill]. . . .

It was late in the afternoon when the [Rhodesian motorized] column reached the insurgent base. . . .

For the whole of the first night, the entrenched main column was subjected to harassing RPG-7 and 57-millimetre fire from the base of the Monte Cassino feature. There was also effective and accurate mortaring. . . .

[The next day] the insurgents entrenched on Monte Cassino had an energetic time running from the trenches to their bunkers every time mortar fire was called or when the air force made an appearance. While this was going on, the infantry of the Armoured Car Regiment . . . tried to do their own thing by attacking the main position of Monte Cassino. . . . [A]s they were half-way up the hill, the guns on Ack-Ack Hill opened up on them with great accuracy, pinning them down on the steep slope. I arranged a stonk [barrage] by 81-millimetre mortars and 25-pounders, under cover of which they were able to withdraw. . . .

Peter Stanton had meanwhile returned to base camp with his capture and reported to Colonel Tufty Bate of the Rhodesian Light Infantry. . . . He told Tufty that there was a company of highly trained artillery personnel on the top of Monte Cassino, and, at the time of the attack [on the overall complex] there could have been from 4,000 to 10,000 insurgents within its environs. He confirmed that Soviet advisers had sited the heavy weapons and that a large number of insurgents who had been trained in Tanzania and Red China had recently arrived. . . .

It was decided to mount another attack on Monte Cassino at 10h00 [on the third day]. . . .

. . . The enemy had abandoned the place. . . .

. . . There was nothing to indicate that the terrorists had withdrawn in confusion. To the contrary, everything pointed to a relatively orderly withdrawal.

The camp had an extensive trench system, which laced all over the base, linking large numbers of bunkers. Anti-aircraft positions were in abundance. . . .

Huge stocks of canned food, medical supplies, ammunition and military equipment were also found.[51]

A Pair of Ominous Developments

By late 1979, Robert Mugabe and the Zimbabwe African National Union (ZANU), parent of Chinese-backed ZANLA, had won the elections.

For possibly the first time in African history, insurgents were being called "terrorists." A "terrorist" is someone who does not follow the established norms of civilized behavior. To defeat him, there will always be those who will feel fully justified in violating the Geneva Conventions.

To make matters worse, the opposition had set its own precedent. While Chinese-sponsored guerrillas hadn't fared too well on the battlefield, they had easily subverted the democratic process. Within the Third World, politics would no longer be the alternative to war.

There have been any number of "freedom movements" within Africa since the 1950's. It might be interesting to see how many others were able to successfully combine politics with war, and what was their preferred form of government. Any kind of a trend would suggest one or more, 4GW-proficient sponsors with a similar form of government.

11 __ African-Style Guerrilla Warfare

- What is the history of guerrilla warfare in Africa?
- How does it differ from the East Asian variety?

AFRICAN REBELS ARE "WOODS-WISE"

(Source: DA Pam 550-74 [1992], p. xxix)

The Best Known of the African Rebellions

Most notorious of the African revolts were the Mau-Mau Insurrection of the 1950's in Kenya and the Simba Rebellion of the 1960's in the Congo. Through the magic of Hollywood, both now evoke images of atrocity.

The Mau-Mau Episode

The Mau-Mau militant African nationalist movement sprang

175

Figure 11.1: Mau-Mau Leader, 1952
(Source: Courtesy of Orion Books, from *World Army Uniforms since 1939*, © 1975, 1980, 1981, 1983 by Blandford Press Ltd., Part II, Plate 106)

from the Kikuyu people of Kenya. As much of the labor force on European farms, the Kikuyus had unsuccessfully voiced grievances since the 1920's and 1930's. Then, the Mau-Mau movement got involved. (See Figure 11.1.) It advocated violent resistance to British domination and opposed the presence of European settlers and their ownership of land. After attributing a campaign of sabotage and assassination to Mau-Mau terrorists in October 1952, the British Kenya government declared a state of emergency and began four years of military operations against Kikuyu rebels. By the end of 1956, more than 11,000 rebels had been killed and 20,000 others put into detention camps (where they were encouraged to abandon any nationalistic aspirations).[1] Despite the government's actions, Kikuyu resistance spearheaded the Kenyan independence movement. Jomo Kenyatta, who had been jailed as a Mau-Mau leader in 1953, became prime minister of an independent Kenya 10 years later.[2]

When the main opposition party went into "voluntary liquidation" in 1964,[3] Kenya became a one-party republic and Kenyatta its first president under a new constitutional amendment. As president, he headed a strong central government. Successive constitutional amendments increased his authority. He had the power to arrest political opponents and detain them without trial but used it infrequently. To forestall any tribally based opposition, Kenyatta appointed members of different ethnic groups to his government. However, he relied most heavily on his fellow Kikuyu. He rejected socialist calls for the nationalization of property and instead preached a doctrine of personal and entrepreneurial effort, symbolized by his slogan *Harambee,* or "Pulling Together." Under his pro-Western leadership, Kenya went on to become one of the most stable and economically dynamic of the African countries.[4]

Despite the likeness of Kenyatta's motto to a famous Chinese epithet ("gung ho"), Kenya's Mau-Mau uprising appears to have been self-generated and nationalistic in purpose. The seeds and product of the revolt in the Congo would not be so clear-cut.

The Simba Disruption

The Congo gained its independence from Belgium in 1960. With that independence came internal wars. The Simba uprising was, by far, the worst. The Simba (Swahili word for "lion") revolt began as a reaction to misrule by the new government, but quickly spread. By 1964, the Congolese National Army—with Mobutu as its chief of staff—had suffered many defeats, and the Simba rebels controlled almost half of the country. In August of that year, the rebels seized the provincial capital of Stanleyville and its 500 Western residents. This evoked a joint Belgian-American rescue operation that, in turn, permitted the Congolese National Army to regain the upper hand elsewhere.[5] (See Figure 11.2.)

The capture of Stanleyville dealt a devastating blow to the eastern rebellion. Demoralization quickly set in among the Simbas and their resistance was reduced to isolated pockets by the end of the year. Unfortunately, Prime Minister Moïse Tshombe's popularity within the Congo and his prestige throughout Africa were severely damaged by the Belgo-American operation against Stanleyville. In 1965, Mobutu seized power with United States backing. It may have been no coincidence that the Stanleyville operation had been entitled "Red Dragon."[6] The Chinese had already made their presence known in other parts of Africa. The Simbas may have been somehow supported by them.

Figure 11.2: Colonial Paratrooper

(Source: Courtesy of Orion Books, from *World Army Uniforms since 1939*, © 1975, 1980, 1981, 1983 by Blandford Press Ltd., Part II, Plate 132)

The Varied Causes of the Older Rebellions

While the Mau-Mau movement was trying to free its people of colonial rule, the Simba evolution was more like a power grab. There is no definitive proof that either had a hidden instigator. Both pale in barbarity to the genocides that would later rock Rwanda, Darfur, and elsewhere. The rest of this chapter will be dedicated to more recent rebellions that were obviously instigated by foreign powers in search of Africa's natural resources or spiritual assimilation.

The Definite Pattern with More Recent Revolts

The European nations had colonized Africa for centuries. They did so for its natural resources. Then in the 1960's, most of those European nations granted independence to their African colonies. This set off a worldwide stampede for those same natural resources—the oil, in particular. Western consumer nations curried African favor through economic aid while their communist counterparts resorted to more devious persuasion. The extent of that persuasion is shocking. According to the CIA, the following nations had Marxist regimes: (1) Mozambique from 1975 to 1989; (2) Namibia, 1990 onward; and (3) the Republic of the Congo, 1960-1990.[7] BBC News confirms that Angola's new government was also Marxist in 1975.[8] It even had "people's tribunals" and "labor camps."[9] To this day, the upper half of Angola's flag has a yellow star on a red background, and its lower half has a "hammer and sickle."[10] From chapter 10, it is clear that the Rhodesians would have readily added Zimbabwe to the list.

The governments of Tanzania and Zambia were decidedly Marxist as well. "President Nyerere had progressively transformed Tanganyika into a one party . . . Socialist state following . . . independence from Britain in 1961."[11] As Tanzania's new president, he issued an official declaration of "socialism" in 1967. In 1977, the "Party of the Revolution" became Tanzania's only legal political party.[12] To complete the picture, the Tanzanian "People's Army" was thoroughly equipped with Chinese MIG-19 aircraft and T-62 tanks.[13] Meanwhile, Zambia was nationalizing private enterprise and seizing land for agricultural reform. In 1972, it too became a one-party state.[14] Both nations allowed communist-backed rebel groups to operate from their territory. In fact, Dar-es-Salaam became the main port of entry for the re-export of "liberation movement" weapons throughout southern Africa.[15] It was linked to Zambia in 1975 by a 2,000-kilometer railroad that 25,000 Chinese laborers helped to build.[16] Though intentionally hidden from view, that railroad had a non-too-subtle purpose. That purpose was to transport trainees and wherewithal to the inland guerrilla bases. From Zambia, they could be easily fed into the Angolan and Rhodesian meat grinders.[17]

> This influence soon became sinister. During the early years of Red Chinese aid programmes, it was common for them to conceal their projects behind high fences or hedges. The Chinese aid workers either assumed or were given powers to arrest or eject strangers straying into these areas.[18]

The South African ANC was supported by the Chinese initially (and its PAC offshoot stayed that way).[19] Then, ANC withdrew its cadres from the Chinese training camps to follow the Soviet model.[20] Some of those camps may have been in Angola. Many of ANC's MK fighters were prepared there,[21] and the National Front for the Liberation of Angola (FNLA) is known to have had Chinese instructors.[22] However, most of the Chinese camps were in Tanzania. ANC, FRELIMO, ZANLA, and half a dozen other independence movements received fighters who had been instructed by the Chinese in Tanzania.[23] And it is known that the Chinese had taken over the Soviet training/equipping of the Tanzanian Army.[24]

Not all of the freedom movements used the same style of guerrilla warfare. ANC and FRELIMO had initially used the Maoist style. As soon as the Portuguese left Mozambique, the FRELIMO regime switched for self-defense to more conventional Soviet tactics. By the late 1970's, ZANLA was the only guerrilla movement still using the Maoist method, while ANC and ZIPRA preferred the Soviet.[25]

Paradoxically, the style of war did not always match the source of support. When the communist powers started to vie for the same real estate after their split in the mid-1960's, the various movements took what they could get from either. ZANLA had Chinese support,[26] while ANC and ZIPRA had Soviet.[27] SWAPO was backed by the Soviets as well.[28] As early as 1964, selected FRELIMO cadres were being sent for advance military training to special warfare schools behind the Iron Curtain.[29] As FRELIMO had done in Mozambique,[30] MPLA set up a Soviet style government and accepted Soviet assistance as soon as the Portuguese left Angola.[31]

180

To further confuse an already cloudy situation, ZANLA was closely allied with FRELIMO, while ANC was cooperating with ZIPRA. For a short while in Zambia, a few FRELIMO and ZIPRA contingents even came to blows. Thus, the ever-changing web of support and allegiance was often difficult to track. In 1979, Soviet advisers were spotted helping artillerymen to defend a ZANLA base.[32] The same year, Chinese instructors were seen at a FRELIMO collective farm.[33] Both ZANLA and ZIPRA sent people to China for training.[34] When the Soviet Union finally collapsed in 1989, the Chinese almost certainly took over all Soviet interests in southern Africa. It is not too hard to figure out why.

What Would Occur within the DRC Was No Coincidence

The Republic of the Congo is one of Africa's biggest sources of oil with 267,100 barrels a day in production and 93.5 million more below ground. Its principal export partner is China.[35] Its neighbor—the DRC (formerly Zaire)—possesses an established oil reserve of 1.54 billion barrels and a natural-gas reservoir of 104.8 billion cubic meters.[36]

Through a small expeditionary force and FNLA, Zaire's long-time dictator—Mobutu—initially fought the Soviet-backed MPLA in Angola.[37] In 1998, Mobutu was toppled by a Laurent-Kabila-led rebellion. A year later, the new Kabila regime was itself challenged by a Rwanda-and Uganda-backed insurrection. To preserve that regime, several other countries intervened militarily. Those countries were Zimbabwe, Angola, Namibia, Chad, and Sudan,[38] with Zimbabwe's troops engaged from 1998 to 2002.[39] Because three of those countries were formerly Marxist and one fundamentalist Muslim, one suspects more than just a local feud. The Chinese have had 4000 military personnel in Sudan since 2000 and gave Angola a two-billlion-dollar line of credit in 2005.[40]

From Map 1.2 and Figure 11.3, it is fairly obvious what has been happening. The Rhodesians and South Africans may have been wrong about apartheid, but they were right about the extent of communist subversion. Less apparent in those years was the inevitable alliance between Iran and China. Like China, Iran has a revolutionary government. That means both promote regional growth through insurrection.

The Petroleum and Religion Statistics Tell the Story

As is statistically apparent from Figure 11.3, China is continuing to pursue its own and former Soviet oil and mineral interests in southern Africa. It has even made a "deal" with petroleum-deficient Zimbabwe.[41] Meanwhile, the fundamentalist Muslims are trying to bring *sharia* law to the rest of the continent. According to Map 1.2, only north and east Africa are predominantly Muslim. So, both factions have been active in the other equatorial nations. Most disturbing is that they appear to be cooperating.

China has now become the world's second largest consumer of oil and is struggling to find ample supplies.[42] To fuel its expanding economy and military, it will need that resource from Africa. At present, the U.S. buys oil from Nigeria, Angola, Algeria, and Chad. China, on the other hand, buys oil from Sudan, Angola, Chad, and the Republic of the Congo.[43] It has exploration contracts with several other countries, including Kenya.[44]

As was shown in the Introduction, *al-Qaeda* has been using Somalia as a harbor site for years. It is generally credited with the U.S. embassy bombings in Tanzania and Kenya.[45] Those countries are predominantly Muslim and strategically located, so they are *al-Qaeda's* principal targets in the region. Since an Israeli airliner was almost shot down in Mombasa in 2003,[46] Muslim unrest has steadily increased in Kenya's capital.

For all other Muslim countries north of the equator (with the possible exception of partially Christian Ethiopia), *Sepah / Hezbollah* (in conjunction with the Muslim Brotherhood) has been spreading *sharia* and ostensibly recreating the Old Muslim Empire. One of their newest targets is Chad. Though a Sudanese ally during the DRC intervention of 1998, Chad has been warming up to the West of late. Its president comes from the same ethnic background as the Darfur rebel SLA. On 13 April 2006 Sudan-based insurgents attacked his capital.[47] Led by Bashir Outman, United Front for Democratic Change (FUDC) troops fought their way the 450 miles from their Darfur base camps to the outskirts of N'djamena. The group's very name speaks volumes, because Sudan has been its silent backer.[48] Chad is the fourth largest oil producer in Africa, with only Nigeria, Libya, and Sudan generating more. In Sudan and Nigeria, there has obviously been a joint effort between Iran and China.

As of March 2006, Iran was helping Nigeria to upgrade its

Petroleum Statistics for Various African Countries from CIA World Factbook

	Oil production (barrels/day)	Gas Production (cubic meters)	Oil Reserves (barrels)	Gas Reserves (cubic meters)
Chinese Targets (petroleum-rich, south of the equator)				
Angola	1.6 million	530 million	25 billion	79.57 billion
Mozambique	none	60 million	none	63.71 billion
Democratic Republic of the Congo	22,000	1.108 billion	1.538 billion	104.8 billion
Republic of the Congo	267,100	none	93.5 million	495.5 million
Namibia	none	none	none	31.15 billion
South Africa	216,700	1.8 billion	7.84 million	14.16 billion
Zambia	130	none	none	none
Zimbabwe	n/a	n/a	n/a	n/a
Sepah/Hezbollah Targets (predominantly Muslim, north of the equator, base for Middle East operations)				
Chad	225,000	none	none	none
Sudan	401,300	none	1.6 billion	99.11 billion
Nations on Mediterranean or Red Sea	n/a	n/a	n/a	n/a
Nigeria	2.451 million	15.68 billion	36 billion	4.007 trillion
Al-Qaeda Targets (predominantly Muslim, south of the equator, base for Saudi Peninsula operations)				
Somalia	none	none	none	2.832 billion
Kenya	none	none	none	none
Tanzania	none	none	none	11.33 billion

Figure 11.3: Current Oil and *Sharia* Targets

army.[49] Two months later, China signed four new oil contracts with Nigeria.[50] In Sudan, Khartoum's refinery is jointly owned by the Sudanese government and the China National Petroleum Corporation.[51] The thread of oil must bind together a Chinese/Iranian/Muslim Brotherhood/*al-Qaeda* coalition of sorts. If it does, then China must be reconsidered a possible instigator of regional trouble.

By 18 April, attacks by Muslim militants had cut Nigeria's daily oil production in half—to 1.1 million barrels per day.[52] The Movement for the Emancipation of the Niger Delta (MEND) is behind much of the violence in the Nigerian port areas. As of 7 June, one U.S. oil executive had been killed, three dozen oil workers from the U.S. and other countries kidnapped, and two pipelines bombed—triggering an international increase in the price of oil.[53] As Nigeria is

Figure 11.4: Nigerian Soldier
(Source: Courtesy of Orion Books, from *World Army Uniforms since 1939*, © 1975, 1980, 1981, 1983 by Blandford Press Ltd., Part II, Plate 90)

the fifth largest source of U.S. oil imports,[54] it is of immense strategic significance in the War on Terror. (See Figure 11.4.) MEND is largely non-Muslim in make-up, but it is still funded by Muslims. That makes it a possible Muslim proxy. It also has a Muslim leader—the currently jailed Alhaji Mujahid Dokubo Asari. Asari is an outspoken admirer of Osama bin Laden, but *al-Qaeda* may not be solely responsible for the *sharia* movement in Nigeria's north. Iran and *Hezbollah* have shown more interest in West Africa.

> MEND emerged independent of either the Wahhabi Shari'ah movement in northern Nigeria or the Nigerian Taliban that first appeared in Yobe state in December 2003. . . . Its members are mainly Catholics, though Asari is an exception and maybe there are . . . more Muslims. . . . [A] possible link with al-Qaeda might be the former Bayelsa state governor, Depriye Alamieyeseigha, MEND's main financial supporter, who is . . . suspected of . . . smuggling arms and of enjoying close links with Osama bin Laden.[55]
> — Project for the Research of Islamist Movements

Oil is not Africa's only natural resource. The continent also has diamonds and over half of the world's supply of some very important defense industry metals—namely, platinum, vanadium, chrome, and manganese.[56] With China quickly becoming an industrial giant, those natural resources have recently attracted more attention. But then, China has been interested in Africa for over 40 years.

Several Nations Have Ostensibly Abandoned Marxism

In the early 1990's, the constitutions of four countries were amended to allow multiparty politics: Mozambique (1990),[57] Angola (1991),[58] Tanzania (1992),[59] and Zambia (1992).[60]

Angola only agreed to "social democracy." Its opposition party was so unhappy with the 1992 elections that it resumed fighting.[61] In Tanzania's multi-party elections in 1995, the ruling party won despite international observer observations of voting irregularities.[62] Zambia's elections in 1991 brought an end to one-party rule, but the subsequent vote in 1996 saw blatant harassment of opposition parties. In the Zambian election of 2001, three parties filed a legal petition challenging the election of the ruling party candidate.[63]

In Zimbabwe, there has been no such democratic agreement—phony or otherwise. Mugabe has dominated its political system since independence in 1980. Ignoring international condemnation, he rigged the 2002 presidential election to insure his re-election.[64] In Angola, Savimbi's death in 2002 ended UNITA's insurgency and strengthened the MPLA's hold on power. Dos Santos has pledged to hold legislative elections in 2006.[65] Namibia has been governed by SWAPO since achieving its independence in 1990. Pohamba was elected president in November 2004 in a landslide victory replacing Nojuma who led the country during its first 14 years of "self-rule."[66]

Thus, South Africa and Mozambique are the region's only apparent successes, and Chapter 15 will bring that into question. Might the new colonizer of southern Africa have appeased the West with pseudo-democracy? Peace has its benefits, but at what cost in human rights? In a 4th-Generation world war, the side with Africa's strategic resources will have a much better chance.

What Was Once Rhodesia Is No Longer a Viable Nation

As of May 2006, Zimbabwe was reeling from a 1,042% inflation rate and going through a veritable "economic meltdown."[67] To counter the economic crisis, the Zimbabwe army seized many of the private farms, banks, and railways.[68] The problem was simply the shortcomings of a Marxist regime.

In June, the prestigious *Financial Times* reported that Mugabe's government was being kept afloat by China. Its aid included everything from natural-resource harvesting to military technology.[69] Zimbabwe has platinum, but no oil. Still, it is surrounded by oil producing countries and thus strategically situated.[70]

China was fully supporting Mugabe's ZANU long before Rhodesia's demise in late 1979.[71] While the new leader talked a good game, his legacy was not all sweetness and light. Near the town of Bulawayo in southwest Zimbabwe, there are indications of a 25-year-old massacre involving 20,000 people. More recently, a local TV ad showed a car crash and warned viewers not to commit suicide by voting against ZANU P/F in the elections. Roman Catholic Archbishop Pius Nicube has risked everything to be Mugabe's most vocal, resident detractor. The most recent Maoist land reform has been a disaster. An entire neighborhood was bulldozed, leaving 700,000 people homeless. As many as one third of Zimbabwe's citizens may have already fled the country. The rest face an uncertain future.[72] According to the 2006 World Health Report, Zimbabwean men can now expect to live only to age 37, and Zimbabwean women only to age 34 (the shortest lifespan in the world).[73] Ongoing events in this particular nation provide a glaring example of what Chinese regional assistance can accomplish.

Central Africa's Troubles Have Dual Causes

With a partially Muslim population and huge petroleum reserves, Central Africa is under attack from two directions. In Nigeria, China's state-controlled China National Offshore Oil Corporation has been buying up huge oil block allocations.[74]

In 1999, Alhaji Ahmed Sani became the governor of Nigeria's Zamfara state. He quickly introduced *sharia* law. Eleven more of Nigeria's northern states (all with Muslim majorities) soon followed suit.[75] Then, there was a slaughter. Nigeria, with a population of 130 million, is roughly divided between a predominantly Muslim north and mainly Christian south.[76]

> Militant Muslims have used Shariah . . . to force their brand of Islam on non-Muslims. This has resulted in a wave of . . . attacks against Christians. . . .
> More than 10,000 Christians have been killed since 1999 in Nigeria.[77]

In May 2006, Nigeria's parliament narrowly averted a constitutional amendment that would have allowed its president more than two terms in office. "Chad, Uganda, and Zimbabwe are [just] a few of the countries where leaders have amended the constitution to remove the limits to their power and tenure."[78]

Oil Is Also an Issue in Sudan

Sudan's oil fields are in western Kordofan State and not far from Darfur. Several reliable sources say that oil is to blame for its 20-year civil war in the south.[79] Though loosely established by the

CPA, the precise demarcation in oil-rich Abyei province has yet to be agreed upon by NCP and SPLM. As of 1 June 2006, the SPLM had additionally asked for its own refinery.[80]

Sudan's largest existing oil refinery is on the outskirts of Khartoum. "The facility . . . was built using Chinese know-how, and today it operates . . . using Chinese labor."[81] China not only runs Sudan's oil industry, it owns the controlling interest.[82] To fully fathom Sudan's convoluted history, one must keep this in mind.

> Darfur is actually Sudanese President Omar Hassan al Bashir's second genocidal campaign against the people he rules. The first was waged against the Christian and animist peoples of south and central Sudan.
>
> From the early 1990's to 2002, more than 2 million people . . . perished and 5 million were displaced in an area centered on what is known as Block 5. . . . Block 5 is an area designated for oil exploration.
>
> CNPC [state-run China National Petroleum Corporation] owns 40% — the largest single share — of the Greater Nile Petroleum Operating Co., a consortium that dominates Sudan's oil fields. . . . It also owns the concessions for Block 6, an oil field partly located in southern Darfur. . . .
>
> China is Sudan's largest supplier of arms. . . . Khartoum uses Chinese-made tanks, aircraft, helicopters and other weapons to clear civilians and rebels from oil-fields rich in petroleum.[83]
>
> — *Investor's Business Daily* (Los Angeles), 2 May 2005

Sudan's principal proxy in Darfur is the *janjaweed*. The tactics of Arab raiders should not be taken lightly.

12 _____ **Muslim Raids**

● How do militant Muslims raid opposing villages in Africa?

● Which nations have recently given them support?

MANY OF SUDAN'S *JANJAWEED* OWNED CAMELS

(Source: FM 90-3 [1982], p. 2-5)

Sudanese Paramilitary Groups

Since 1983, the Sudanese government has increasingly relied on local militias to oppose the SPLA in the south. Those militias were given arms and ammunition and usually allowed to operate independently of the Sudanese army.[1] Their tactics too often consisted of raiding non-Muslim villages.

Some of the most devastating raids and acts of banditry against the [southern Sudanese] civilian population were perpetrated by the militias known as *murahalin,* formed among the Rizeiqat, Rufaa al Huj, Misiriyah, and other groups, all members of the cattle-raising Baqqara Arab nomad tribes in Darfur and Kurdufan. These Arab communities traditionally competed for pasture land with the Dinka [tribe]. . . . According to Amnesty International, the raids carried out by the *murahalin* were accompanied by the killing of tens of thousands of civilians; the abduction of women and children, who were forced into slavery; the looting of cattle and other livestock; and the burning of houses and grain supplies. . . .

The Rizeiqat *murahalin* were responsible for one of the worst atrocities of the war when . . . more than 1,000 unarmed Dinka were massacred. The tactics of the Misiriyah *murahalin* were similar to those of the Rizeiqat; their ambushes of refugees and attacks on villagers . . . were among the most murderous. . . . The [Sudanese] government armed the Rufaa al Huj as a militia in 1986. . . .

The government also armed as militias a number of southern [Sudanese] non-Arab tribes opposed to the SPLA. In 1985, members of the Mundari in Al Istiwai . . . were recruited. . . . In Bahr al Ghazal, the government formed a militia [from the people] . . . around [the town of] Waw, and established a training base for it there. . . .

In October 1989, the Bashir government promulgated the Popular Defense Act . . . to give legitimacy to the militias as auxiliaries of the SPAF (Sudanese People's Armed Forces). . . . [It also] established a new paramilitary body, the Popular Defense Forces (PDF), to promote the political objectives of the government and the NIF. This action, did not, however result in the disappearance of the existing militias.[2]

— Hdqts. Dept. of the Army, 1992

Since 2005, there has also been a Chinese military presence in the Waw (Wau) area.[3]

The *Janjaweed*

There are 7,000 African Union (AU) peacekeepers in Darfur. (See Map 12.1.) Yet, Sudan has continued to use "militias drawn

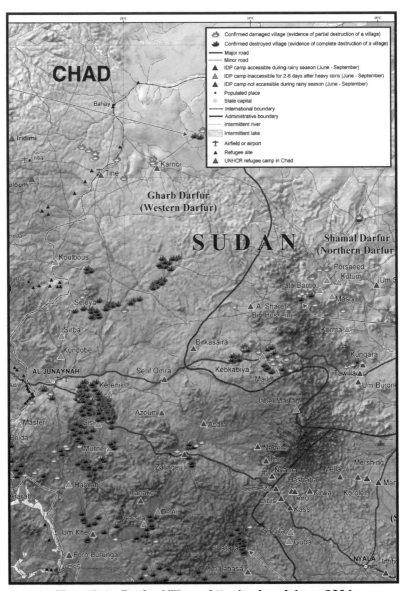

Map 12.1: Darfur Village Attacks As of June 2004

(Source: Courtesy of DigitalGlobe and USAID from University of Texas at Austin website for map designator "darfur_villages_0621_2004.pdf," © 2004 by DigitalGlobe, Inc.)

from Arab tribes" or *janjaweed* to contest the separatist movement by the predominantly black SLA.[4] Since 2003, the *janjaweed* have plundered and burned scores of non-Muslim villages in an effort to deprive the rebels of local-base-area support. In the process, they have displaced and starved the local population during a record drought and thus committed genocide.

In three years since Darfur exploded, tens of thousands of people have died and 2.5 million more have been displaced. An Arab militia known as the *janjaweed* has done most of the killing. With help from the Sudanese army, it has mounted deadly raids against villages and refugee camps alike. The U.N. wants its own peacekeeping force to take over from that of the AU, but Sudan secretly opposes the idea.[5]

> Khartoum says it will stop U.N. peacekeepers from working in Sudan, despite the threat of sanctions.[6]
> — *Time Magazine,* 8 May 2006

Despite strong Sudanese opposition, a draft resolution was finally introduced to the U.N. on 18 August to accept all AU peacekeeping responsibilities in Darfur. Without Sudanese consent, such a transfer of authority is unlikely to occur. According to Associated Press, "President Omar Bashir has warned that Sudan's army would fight any U.N. forces sent to Darfur."[7]

Janjaweed Tactics

Not many specifics have been reported on *janjaweed* tactics. The raiders arrive by horseback, and often with a small, motorized Sudanese army backup. Then they ride around the village,[8] send in a thrust, and call on the Sudanese air force to handle any unexpected resistance.

The *janjaweed* can undoubtedly fight dismounted as well. When their great grandfathers attacked the British company that was Kitchener's desert feint in 1898, they did so in much the same way that Zulus or Boers would have. First, they positioned snipers atop the locally occurring piles of rock to provide overhead covering fire. Then, they sneaked their assault force to within 100 yards of the objective under cover of darkness. Of note, the members of that assault force moved forward from bush to bush a few at a time, instead of all together. As soon as one came within view of a British sentry, he would draw and hold a bead with his rifle sight on that sentry.[9] At the first sound of alarm, the sentry would lose his life, and British commander would lose his ability to determine the direction of attack.

The British of that era had a fairly clever defensive strategy. They would build a man-high barrier of thorn bushes all the way around their position. This barrier would not only temporarily deter mass assault, but also obscure the encampment from view. Of course, the wily Africans were not deterred for long by such a scheme. A few strong-armed warriors simply threw burning spears into the tinder-dry ring.[10] The ensuing conflagration then obscured most of the assault force over the most dangerous last few yards.

Individual initiative and common sense had once again trumped unit hierarchy and arms technology. What most Western military leaders still fail to realize is that their way of operating routinely violates common sense at the squad level and discourages any initiative by the individual soldier. Until they fix this problem, America may never win another war. Part III discusses what realistically can be done now to curtail Muslim and Chinese expansionism in Africa and the Middle East.

Part Three

Grasping the Viper by the Tail

"When a shooting war is on, regulations [doctrinal procedures]
are for use in the absence of brains."
— anonymous U.S. general at WWII onset

(Source: *Men of the Tundra*, by Muktuk Marston [New York: October House, 1969] , p. 45)

13

Slowing the Flow of African Fighters

- What is Africa's most dangerous current conflict?
- How can the flow of African *jihadists* to Iraq be lessened?

INSURGENTS MUST BE TRACKED AND ARRESTED

(Source: FM 90-5 [1982], p. 5-4)

The Most Complex of All 4GW Environments

How to solve Africa's chronic thirst, hunger, disease, corruption, and feuding has confounded Western thinkers for centuries. Those who now deem those problems "endemic to the region" are at risk of another Rwanda-like sin of omission. Perhaps, the problem lies not with God's original people but in how the Western mind operates. A detailed image can be more accurately portrayed with little dots than with broad brush strokes. Radical Muslims and Communist Chinese do not suffer from the "big-picture" syndrome. Nor do they worry about individual safety and human rights. They have the people to flood a region and feed off its misery. Thus, whatever is done to slow the flow of African fighters must attack this problem at its source—the utter destitution that makes a hefty recruiting bonus impossible to refuse. (See Figure 13.1.)

The Islamic Extremists' Plan

In November 2001, a twenty-year old document was discovered in Switzerland. It revealed a top-secret plan by the Muslim Brotherhood to launch a program of "cultural invasion" and eventual

Figure 13.1: Arab Militiaman
(Source: Courtesy of Orion Books, from *World Army Uniforms since 1939,* © 1975, 1980, 1981, 1983 by Blandford Press Ltd., Part II, Plate 124)

conquest of the West. As the Muslim Brotherhood has been linked to *al-Qaeda's* inception, the plan generated a certain amount of interest. Among its objectives were the following:

• Networking and coordinating actions between like-minded Islamist organizations;
• Avoiding open alliances with known terrorist organizations and individuals to maintain the appearance of "moderation";
• Infiltrating and taking over existing Muslim organizations to realign them towards the Muslim Brotherhood's collective goals;
• Using deception to mask the intended goals of Islamist actions, as long as it doesn't conflict with shari'a law;
• Avoiding social conflicts with Westerners locally, nationally or globally, that might damage the long-term ability to expand the Islamist powerbase in the West or provoke a lash back [backlash] against Muslims; . . .
• *Building extensive social networks of schools, hospitals and charitable organizations dedicated to Islamist ideals* . . . ;
• Involving ideologically committed Muslims in democratically elected institutions on all levels in the West [or Western-occupied nations], including government, NGOs, private organizations and labor unions; . . .
• Drafting Islamic constitutions, laws and policies for eventual implementation [italics added].[1]

Whether the Muslim Brotherhood is actively pursuing such a scheme is not important. At issue is the "quasi-humanitarian" method it shares with *Sepah, Hezbollah,* and *Hamas.* Their plan is to provide basic services after sabotaging those of Western-aligned agencies. It is also to work through and subvert the democratic process. The Egyptian parliamentary elections in 2005 saw the Muslim Brotherhood winning 20% of the available legislative seats. That comprised the largest opposition party bloc. About the same time, its Palestinian affiliate—*Hamas*—gained control of the Palestinian Authority. It did so by securing 74 of 132 seats in the Palestinian Legislative Council elections.[2] Regardless of how the elections turn out, all Muslim extremist organizations need fighters to sabotage the legitimate providers of basic services.

199

More *Baseej* for Iran's Iraqi Proxies

The Muslim Brotherhood would like to cover the entire region with Islamic states, and does not particularly care if all are Sunni. It has been actively pursing that goal since WWII. Local militiamen make good revolutionary small-unit leaders. (See Figure 13.1.) Some Arab militias are blocking revolts in Sudan. Others (those listed in Chapter 1) are fomenting revolts all along the Red Sea and Mediterranean. All are good sources of bottom-echelon management. To put any number of ordinary *jihadists* on the payroll, the Muslim Brotherhood has only to enter Africa's urban slums and drought-stricken countryside.

"The military co-operation of the Muslim Brotherhood and Hizbullah [go] back to the 1980's." Their "closeness" has recently been confirmed by Sheikh Bilal, an aide to Hassan Nasrallah.[3] To support Iran's revolutionary initiative in Iraq, the Muslim Brotherhood has been recruiting both types of Islamists across the length and breadth of North Africa.

To operate effectively in equatorial Africa, Muslim proxies need not contain followers of Islam. Nor do they need much recruiting help. One wonders how proxies that never leave the African continent might still be helping Iran.

Iran's Other Interest in Africa

Besides the projection of Islamism, Iran has a strategic goal in Africa that is not be easy to spot amidst the mad scramble for oil. That goal is the acquisition of weapons-grade uranium. According to a U.N. report of 18 July 2006, Tanzanian officials intercepted a huge shipment of smuggled uranium 238 in the autumn of 2005. Bound for smelting in Kazakhstan and delivery to Bandar Abbas, Iran, the high-quality ore had come from the famous Shinkolobwe mine in Katanga Province, DRC. (See Figure 13.2.) It was hidden in containers of another mineral and then transported by road through Zambia. While the Shinkolobwe mine had been officially closed since 1961, U.N. investigators found evidence of recent, illegal excavation. Since 1999, North Korea has been implicated in attempts to reopen the mine.[4] Iran's nuclear ambitions be behind much of the rebel activity in Katanga Province.

More Fighters for Sudan's African Proxies

As demonstrated in Chapters 1 and 2, the Muslim Brotherhood runs Sudan. It has patterned Sudan's government after the one in Tehran. As such, that government operates in much the same way. To derail the SPLA, it has resorted to the LRA.

By early 2006, the notorious Lord's Resistance Army had expanded its operations to the west. It was killing U.N. soldiers in the Garamba Park area near the border between the DRC and Sudan.[5] (See Map 13.1.) In the first Chapter, it was shown that the LRA—though perversely Christian—has been supported by the Khartoum government

As of January 2006, another terrorist outfit—the Democratic Front for the Liberation of Rwanda (DFLR)—was still operating

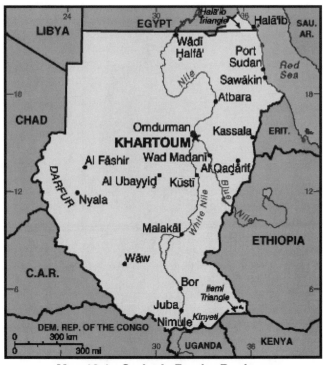

Map 13.1: Sudan's Border Regions
(Source: Courtesy of General Libraries, University of Texas at Austin, from their website for map designator "sudan_sm05.(gif)")

inside the DRC.[6] The DFLR was the perpetrator of Rwanda's genocide in 1994. Because Sudan intervened to save the DRC from a Rwandan army invasion in 1998, one could reasonably conclude that Sudan is also allied with that army's initial quarry—the DFLR. The DFLR is not Muslim, but then neither is the LRA.

The LRA's History

The Ugandan army has been trying to crush the LRA rebellion for almost 20 years.[7] In 1999, Sudan promised to stop aiding the LRA if Uganda would stop supplying the SPLA. In 2003, Sudan allowed Ugandan troops across its border to attack LRA camps. Yet, to this day, well-respected sources confirm that the LRA (led by Joseph

Figure 13.2: Congolese Paratrooper
(Source: Courtesy of Orion Books, from *Uniforms of Elite Forces*, © 1982 by Blandford Press Ltd., Plate 32, No. 95)

Kony) continues to operate from bases in southern Sudan and receive support from the Sudanese government.[8] In theory, the LRA seeks to overthrow the Ugandan government. Like *Hezbollah* in Southern Lebanon and al-Sadr's Mahdi Army in Iraq, it does so through an unholy combination of ruining governmental basic services and providing its own. It targets local government officials/facilities, international aid workers/convoys, Catholic missionaries/churches,[9] medical workers/clinics, and Dinka (SPLA) fighters/camps.[10]

Of late, the LRA has expanded its operations to the west. The Lusaka Accord of 1999 lists the LRA as one of the six irregular "armed groups" operating inside the Democratic Republic of the Congo. The why of it is not quite clear. It may have done so to embrace more Acholi tribesmen, or to do the bidding of a powerful supporter.

> The LRA was founded in 1986 as the successor to the ethnic Acholi-dominated Holy Spirit Movement. LRA leader Joseph Kony has called for the overthrow of the Ugandan Government. . . . He claims to have supernatural powers and to receive messages from spirits, which he uses to formulate the LRA's strategy. . . .
>
> . . . Since the early 1990's, the LRA has kidnapped 20,000 Ugandan children, mostly ethnic Acholi, to replenish its ranks. . . . The LRA forces kidnapped children and adult civilians to become soldiers, porters, and "wives" for LRA leaders. The LRA prefers to attack internally displaced persons camps and other civilian targets, avoiding direct engagement with the Ugandan military. Victims of LRA attacks sometimes have their hands, fingers, ears, noses, or other extremities cut off. [The] LRA has stepped up its activities since early 2002 when the Ugandan army, with the Sudanese Government's permission, attacked LRA positions inside Sudan. Since then, the number of internally displaced [persons] has doubled to 1.4 million, and the LRA has pushed deep into non-Acholi areas where it had never previously operated.[11]
>
> — U.S. State Dept., 2004

As recently as 30 May 2006, the head of the SPLM (and now First Vice President of Sudan) accused the Sudanese Army of fueling instability in southern Sudan by helping the LRA.[12]

203

LRA Tactics

The LRA uses captured children as expendable soldiers.[13] To get enough soldiers, it routinely attacks schools.[14] As such, its assaults are rudimentary—everyone runs forward on line while those few who are armed fire their weapons.[15] Behind them are the handlers who will kill any who falter. The LRA's offensives are mostly aimed at villages. They are punitive in nature but also gather supplies and slaves. Below is a rare description of such an attack plan.

Rebels of the Lord's Resistance Army (LRA) attacked a camp for internally displaced persons (IDPs) in war-ravaged northern Uganda on 16 May 2004, killing scores of people and abducting others. A group of rebels attacked Pagak displaced people's camp in three prongs: one attacked the camp, a second one attacked the soldiers guarding it, and the third one concentrated on the patrol units. The group that attacked the camp set ablaze dozens of grass-thatched huts to create confusion, then looted food and abducted people whom they forced to carry their loot for a distance before they killed them along with their babies.[16]
— *CIA World Factbook,* 10 January 2006

Sudan's Link to Rwanda's Mass-Murderers

As of February 2006, the LRA had linked up with *Interahamwe* rebels around the Bunia area of the DRC.[17] *Interahamwe* is affiliated with the DFLR—the perpetrators of Rwanda's gruesome genocide.

In 2003, the Rwandan Government was still aggressively pursuing the DFLR. The Army for the Liberation of Rwanda (ALIR)—a rebel force of former soldiers and supporters of the previous government—had orchestrated the genocide in 1994. As of 2004, the DFLR was still in the DRC and employing terrorist tactics. Its predecessor—the ALIR—once constituted the Armed Forces of Rwanda (FAR) and was sometimes called *Interahamwe*.[18] In actuality, *Interahamwe* was FAR's civilian militia. Rwanda is only 4.6% Muslim,[19] so Sudan may see it as an impediment to its strategic goals.

FAR was the army of the ethnic Hutu-dominated Rwandan regime that carried out the genocide of 500,000 or more Tutsis and regime opponents in 1994. The Interahamwe was the civilian militia force that carried out much of the killing. The groups merged and recruited additional fighters after they were forced from Rwanda into the Democratic Republic of Congo (DRC; then Zaire) in 1994. They became known as the Army for the Liberation of Rwanda (ALIR), which is the armed branch of the PALIR or Party for the Liberation of Rwanda. In 2001, ALIR—while not formally disbanded—was supplanted by the Democratic Front for the Liberation of Rwanda (FDLR) [DFLR]. . . .

ALIR sought to topple Rwanda's Tutsi-dominated government, reinstitute Hutu domination, and possibly, complete the genocide. . . . In the 1998-2002 Congolese war, the ALIR/FDLR was allied with Kinshasa against the Rwandan invaders. . . .

. . . Exact strength is unknown, but several thousand FDLR guerrillas operate in eastern DRC close to the Rwandan border. . . .

The Government of the Democratic Republic of the Congo provided training, arms, and supplies to ALIR forces to combat Rwandan armed forces that invaded the DRC in 1998 but halted that support in 2002.[20]

— U.S. State Dept., 2004

The War in the Congo Is Far from Over

Rwanda and Uganda entered Zaire in 1996 to eliminate the Hutu *Interahamwe* that had caused the Rwandan genocide. After Mobutu fled, they installed Laurent Kabila as President. When Kabila supposedly forged ties with the *Interahamwe,* Uganda and Rwanda invaded again two years later. This triggered what became known as Africa's first world war. No fewer than eight African neighbors took part. (See Map 13.2.) Kabila became as corrupt as his predecessor and was killed by a bodyguard in 2001. One year after his son—Joseph—assumed power, South Africa (that had realized the role that the DRC could play in its "plan for African rebirth") convinced Joseph and other combatants to sign a peace deal. Groups that had previously been killing each other were integrated into a national army. Some have since reverted back to their prior endeavors. Others have created problems within the army. DRC security forces have now been accused of so much raping, killing, and torture that the U.N. peacekeeping mission is considering an end to its cooperation with them. Without far fewer human-rights abuses, fair elections will not be possible. According to Van Woudenberg of Human Rights Watch, "[The] Congo isn't magically going to become a democracy."[21] In the July 2006 election, Kabila did fairly well in the Eastern provinces, but less well in the provinces near his capital.[22]

The turmoil in the DRC has killed 4 million people since 1998, making it the world's most lethal conflict since WWII. Despite the peace deal that removed foreign armies three years ago, the suffering continues. Rebel holdouts are still active in the east. They have been running murderous raids on villages in Katanga Province. The

Map 13.2: New Target in the Region
(Source: Courtesy of General Libraries, University of Texas at Austin, from their website for map designator "congodemrep_sm05.gif")

DRC army has also been executing people and razing villages. Such methods are like those in Darfur, so the largest U.N. peacekeeping force in the world already has its hands full in the DRC.[23]

[U]nchecked tribal, rebel, and militia fighting continues unabated in the northeastern region of the Democratic Republic of the Congo, drawing in the neighboring states of Burundi, Rwanda and Uganda; the U.N. Organization Mission in the Democratic Republic of the Congo (MONUC) has maintained over 14,000 peacekeepers in the region since 1999; thousands of Ituri refugees from the Congo continue to flee the fighting primarily into Uganda . . . ; in 2005, DROC [DRC] and Rwanda established a border verification mechanism to address accusations of Rwandan military supporting Congolese rebels and the DROC providing rebel Rwandan "Interahamwe" forces the means and bases to attack Rwandan forces.[24]
— *CIA World Factbook,* 10 January 2006

As of 31 May 2006, 74 U.N. peacekeepers had been killed in the DRC since their mission was set up in 1999. One Nepalese soldier was killed and seven others reported missing as the Congolese troops they were supporting tried to disarm members of the Nationalist and Integrationist Front (FNI) led by Peter Karim. Most of the trouble has been in country's east and southeastern Katanga Province.[25]

Peace Only Possible through a "Grass-Roots" Approach

To slow the flow of Africa's fighters to local wars or Iraq, the West must provide its people with a better way of life. There is no way to "free" them through hastily staged and poorly monitored elections. Most African societies are tribal and only mildly interested in national identity. To make matters worse, they lack a non-biased source of information and the education to use it.

Nor is there a way for the Western World to successfully occupy African soil. The place is too vast, and the desperation of the people too great. *Sepah / Hezbollah, al-Qaeda,* and the communist factions feed off this degree of desperation. Through its manipulation, they have learned how to win both wars and elections.

207

The most the West can hope to do in Africa is to give the majority of its citizens a bare minimum of basic services and a means of support. Once that is done, those citizens will be able to say "no" to local oppressor and *jihadist* recruiter alike. They will chart their own course to a lasting democracy.

Within Africa, food, water, sewage, inoculations, and security are the most important of the basic services. Lt.Gen. Ghormley, the head of the U.S. Marine "Horn of Africa" contingent, has concentrated on providing the first four. In a videotaped interview, he indicated that his Marines were "waging peace instead of war."[26] As has already been mentioned, they spend a fair share of their time digging wells and administering inoculations. In a continent so desperately in need of help, the Marines have set a good example for others to follow.

> Mismanagement, limited resources, and environmental damage had combined to deny 1.1 billion people [about 1/5 the world's population] access to safe water, a U.N. report said Thursday.
> Sub-Saharan Africa is one of the hardest-hit areas where [many things] . . . have led to water shortages exacerbating poverty, disease and drought, the report said. . . .
> Globally, diarrheal diseases and malaria kill around 3.1 million people a year. The U.N. said 1.6 million could be saved if they had safe drinking water, sanitation, and hygiene.[27]
> —Associated Press, 7 March 2006

As for African security, the West will have to replace its usual format of electronic surveillance and bombardment with the more 4GW-friendly combination of mantracking and arrest. That way, there will be less local perception of occupation, and more of law enforcement.

14 ___ **Urban Tracking**

- Can footprints be followed in a built-up area?
- How is it possible to see them?

IN A DRY CLIMATE, URBAN COMBAT CREATES DUST

(Source: FM 90-10-1 [1982], p. E-13)

4GW Is Much Like Police Work

If the U.S. were seriously interested in helping an oppressed people, it would do more from the bottom up than from the top down. Those people are no different from Americans. They value most their families and some semblance of local security. Widespread local security is only possible where a few GIs are allowed to live in each town or neighborhood. It does not automatically result from grandiose attempts to rebuild national government or infrastructure. Those GIs must be able to help local security personnel to apprehend resident terrorists. That takes urban tracking skill.

How Urban Landscape Differs from Rural

The areas between buildings in a city are only partially covered with pavement. Following footprints there is like doing so across occasional patches of rock—something that native Americans could do. While their techniques may have been forgotten, others can be developed through visualization and experimentation. The first part of this chapter has been devoted to the former. The rest is the advice of instructors at a world-famous mantracking school. Urban tracking would make a good "signature" capability for the U.S. Marine Corps' new Special Operations Command. (See Figure 14.1.)

Figure 14.1: New U.S. Marine "Special Operator"
(Source: Courtesy of Orion Books, from *Uniforms of Elite Forces*, © 1982 by Blandford Press Ltd., Plate 6, No. 16)

A Brief Look at the Overall Problem

Hard surfaces are not as easily disturbed as soft ones. If they hold any evidence of human passage, it is on the order of a dislodged pebble, modified residue, shoe dropping, or scuff mark. To the untrained eye, all would be invisible. Thus, the aspiring urban tracker must first work on his ability to spot details at varying distances. Knowing what to look for is only half the battle. He must have vision correctable to 20/20 and do a couple of eye exercises while walking. The first is to identify tiny ground abnormalities 20 yards ahead and then instantly shift one's gaze.[1] The second is to sequentially focus on something distant, 10-15 feet ahead, and then at one's feet. Skilled trackers only look down occasionally; they spend most of their time looking ahead to the farthest point at which they can still see sign.[2] (See Figure 14.2.) In the city, the occasional street, alleyway, parking lot, or sidewalk would pose little problem if they were not heavily used. One would only have to spot where similar footprints picked up on the other side. Unfortunately, they often are heavily traveled, so the tracker must be intimately familiar with the unique characteristics of his quarry's shoe print. He would also have to be good at judging a track's age.

Luckily, most urban surfaces provide an aid to tracking that is not normally available in the woods. That aid is dust. Because of the dust imprint (or transference) possibility, one should not disturb

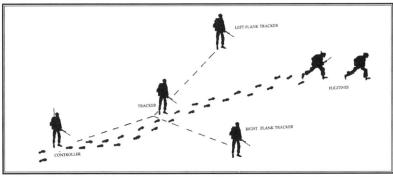

Figure 14.2: "Y"-Shaped Formation
(Source: Courtesy of Paladin Press, from *Tactical Tracking Operations*, © 1998, by David Scott-Donelan. p. 63)

211

Figure 14.3: "Track Traps" and Transference
(Source: FM 90-10 (1979), p. G-4)

a paved or cement area that has been crossed. With proper side-lighting (like from a flashlight at the end of a stick), the trail may become visible.

In urban terrain, the most effective tracking formation is still the "Y" (with flankers slightly ahead of the tracker on either side and a controller behind him). (Refer back to Figure 14.2.) Amidst multistory buildings, the flankers must keep a particularly close watch on the windows above each other. As in the country, it is wise to add a fifth "optics man" behind the controller. Through his binoculars, he can watch for trouble ahead. In the city, there is more risk of long-range machinegun or sniper fire from several blocks away. In urban tracking, a rear/overhead/underneath security man is also advisable. Cities have ready-made ways of ambush from rear, top, and below.

What Do Mantracks Look Like in the City?

In most cities, there is dust everywhere. What isn't caused by the vehicular crushing of dirt, precipitates out of the smog. When that dust is disturbed or transferred onto another surface, it leaves a print. Dust is not the only thing that can be "transferred" in a built-up area. There is also mud, blood, water, oil, tar, and refuse. Thus, the city is filled with trails. (See Figure 14.3.) The principal difference between following a person in the city and in the country is what to do when the trail goes cold. In urban terrain, the tracks often come to an end because the quarry passed over an ostensibly clean and impenetrable surface. The tracker then needs special techniques to rediscover those tracks on the other side of that surface. As that "other" side may be some distance away, those techniques must not be too time consuming.

Much of what appears below has been extracted from an urban-tracking package developed by Mark Sexton, Rick Adrian, and the famous David Scott-Donelan.[3]

Urban "Track Traps"

A track trap is defined as an area of any medium (soil, sand, dust, vegetation, etc.) that leaves distinct evidence of human passage. That means any one the following: (1) lawn, (2) flower garden, (3)

213

crop area, (4) just-watered plot, (5) park, (6) vacant lot, (7) bicycle/foot path, (8) dirt road, (9) muddy street, (10) roadside shoulder/dust, (11) mud puddle, (12) gutter sediment, (13) steep incline, (14) gravel embankment, (15) slippery stream bank, (16) construction site, (17) garbage dump, (18) alleyway refuse, (19) parking-area oil, (20) molten asphalt, (21) sewage pipe seepage, (22) drainage ditch run-off, (23) community water point spillage, (24) industrial-site residue, or (25) children's playpen/sandbox. In addition, any segment of urban setting becomes a track trap when covered by fallen leaves, pollen, dew, frost, snow, or particulate smog. Then, even a brick/concrete wall, paved street, or railroad track/tie might be included.

In grassy areas, there will be depressed blades. In gardens and cultivated patches, there will be the compacting of soft soil. Both mediums attract dew and frost. Further, people slip while negotiating steep inclines or road embankments, leaving a characteristic skid mark. In dump sites, cardboard, paper, styrofoam, and trash bags leave a footwear impression when stepped on. When fallen leaves are crossed, some get crushed. The tops and sides of brick/concrete walls are easily scuffed.

There will be a good chance of transference of material onto the next hard surface every time the quarry exits a track trap. (Refer back to Figure 14.3.) Near a gutter, there will be traces of mud or water. Where a street abuts a vacant lot, there will be dirt particles or grass stains.

More Emphasis on Print Peculiarities

In the city, the tracker must commit to memory a thorough "search image" of what he is looking for. Much of his success will depend on his knowledge of local habits and footwear. Some outsole patterns will be more common than others due to current fads and shared designs. Wherever an IED has been detonated, all print peculiarities must be recorded. Was the probable bomber wearing an unusually soled shoe? Did his left foot pitch out, or right foot drag a toe? As in police work, these are the things that will lead to his apprehension.

Wherever there are twist/pivot marks, the quarry may have abruptly changed direction. That happens often in the city—every time someone turns a corner.

Where someone squatted (feet apart with fingers on the ground) or dug, there may be an observation post or impromptu toilet. Only a student of the local culture could easily sense the difference. Evidence of kneeling (knee impressions between toe- and foot-prints) has more significance. A nearby row of upturned soil might contain a wire, or a patch of dry turf, a mine. Needless to say, any sign of construction should be taken seriously.

Third-World Cities Are Different from Those in the U.S.

Throughout the developing world, the cities are often a conglomerate of new and old construction. Throughout that construction are patches of unimproved land. Outside the inner city are very few sidewalks. Amidst the taller vegetation beside such "streets" are the same examples of sign as in the woods: (1) broken twigs, (2) displaced root bark, (3) stripped leaves, (4) changes in foliage color, (5) crushed/bent/scratched/intertwined branches, (6) broken spider webs, (7) disturbed ant trails, and (8) dislodged insect nests. In addition, a quarry will often inadvertently brush dust or dew from the plants. Once he enters a paved area, the art of trailing him is of the new variety. If that trail goes cold, specialized methods will be required to rediscover it.

Urban "Lost-Spoor" Techniques

As the tracker moves forward along the quarry's trail, he scans the ground ahead and advances from indicator to indicator. All the while, he keeps track of where the last visible spoor was. If he cannot see a subsequent sign, he marks the last known spoor or asks the controller to stand behind it. Then, without moving, he visually inspects the most likely avenue of advance out to the farthest point at which can identify tracks (30-40 feet). If he still sees nothing, he institutes his lost spoor procedures to include other possible routes. The most obvious "line of drift" (path between the buildings) should always be included. In the city, those lost spoor procedures are as follows: (1) "quick scan," (2) "likely lines wedge out," (3) "tracker 360," (4) "flank 360," and (5) "box search." If time is a factor, he also has several shortcuts: (1) "crossover," (2) "track trap," and (3) "alleyway scan."

215

In the "quick scan," he surveys everything from ground level to his own height in an imaginary three-quarter cylinder that is 10-to-15-feet deep. He does so while standing behind the last recognizable print and facing in the probable direction of march. On the most likely side, he first looks 45 degrees behind him out to about 10-15 feet. He then moves his gaze up and down across the entire breadth of the imaginary cylinder, looking for both ground and aerial spoor. (See Figure 14.4.)

In the "likely lines wedge out" search pattern, the tracker physically inspects possible routes—one at a time. First, he moves forward about 30-40 yards alongside the most likely line of advance, closely examining the ground as he goes. If he fails to find anything, he returns over the same ground he traveled to the last known spoor. He then runs the procedure along the closest alternative route. As long as the lines to be searched are always at a greater angle from the original, he can repeat the process as many times as he deems necessary.[4] (See Figure 14.5.)

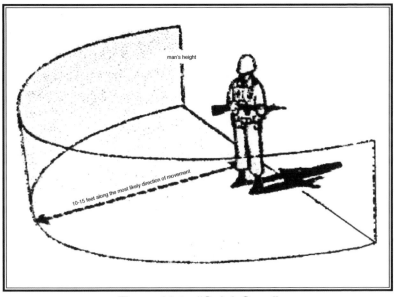

Figure 14.4: "Quick Scan"
(Source: Courtesy of David Scott-Donelan, Mark Sexton, and Rick Adrian, from "Urban Tracking" [a powerpoint presentation rough], December 2005)

To do the "tracker 360," the tracker moves out about 30 yards alongside a possible line of travel and begins a circular search pattern. Often the first loop barely includes that last known spoor. If it fails to produce evidence, the tracker incrementally increases the size of subsequent loops. Attempting to intersect the trail on a perpendicular (so as not to disturb it), he can stretch the spiral's diameter to as many as 500 yards.[5] (See Figure 14.5 again.)

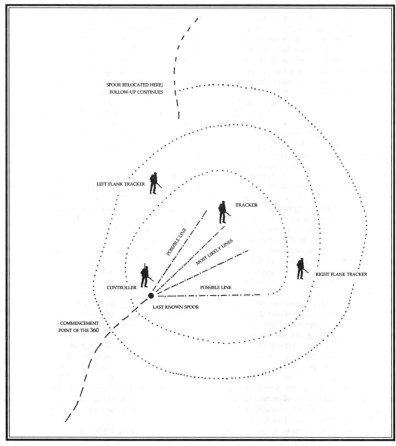

SPOOR RELOCATED HERE;
FOLLOW-UP CONTINUES

LEFT FLANK TRACKER

TRACKER

POSSIBLE LINE

MOST LIKELY LINES

RIGHT FLANK TRACKER

CONTROLLER

POSSIBLE LINE

LAST KNOWN SPOOR

COMMENCEMENT
POINT OF THE 360

Figure 14.5: "Likely Lines Wedge Out" Then "Tracker 360"
(Source: Courtesy of Paladin Press, from *Tactical Tracking Operations*, © 1998, by David Scott-Donelan, p.48)

In the "flank 360," the controller has both flankers conduct their own circular searches beyond where the tracker did his. The circles should overlap to insure that the ground has been fully covered.[6] (See Figure 14.6.)

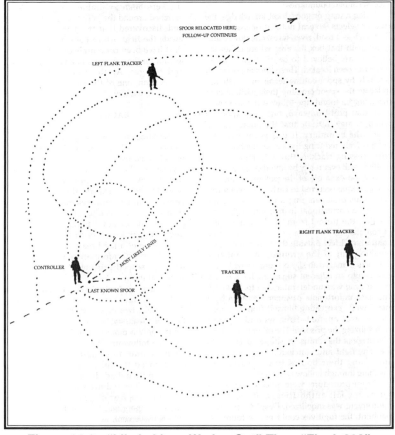

Figure 14.6: "Likely Lines Wedge Out" Then "Flank 360"
(Source: Courtesy of Paladin Press, from *Tactical Tracking Operations,* © 1998, by David Scott-Donelan, p.49)

The "box search" is what its name implies. The area through which the quarry has most probably traveled is in a large box bounded by lines of drift—drainage ditches, footpaths, roads, and alleyways. First, the periphery of that box is searched for where the trail has emerged. As considerable distances may be involved, two sign-cutting teams can be utilized simultaneously. If no sign is found, the teams have two options. The peripheries of progressively smaller boxes can be walked, or the original box can be crisscrossed at various distances from the last known print.[7]

The shortcuts are "crossover," "track trap," and "alleyway scan." In the crossover, the flankers switch sides looking for the lost trail. To employ the second shortcut, the tracker must move ahead of a clearly marked "last identifiable print" to inspect track traps along the most likely direction of travel. In the third, the flankers check for where the trail may have left a street as they scan between-building spaces for signs of an ambush. Meanwhile, the tracker and an assistant follow along behind looking for the lost trail in the street itself.[8]

Another shortcut might be for a single tracker to move forward alongside the most likely line of travel and then repeatedly cross over it in a snakelike pattern. In wartime, any urban mantracking operation will be much safer when closely monitored by overhead-cover teams. (See Figure 14.7.)

Tire Tracks

As tire tracks and vehicular configurations vary, so do the prints they leave. Contributing characteristics are as follows: (1) tread depth, (2) impression depth, (3) tread pattern, (4) wear pattern, (5) tire width, (6) four-tire mixture, (7) direction of travel, (8) oil/fuel leaks, (9) substance transference, (10) emotions/habits of the driver, and (11) vehicle type.

The width of the tire varies according to tire size, tire pressure, vehicle type, vehicle weight, and load weight. In combination, that many variables leave a distinctive signature.

The direction of travel can be determined from the following: (1) tread pattern, (2) pebbles pushed forward slightly and then kicked back, (3) flattening/distorting of tires after hitting a bump, (4) dust/mud/water thrown outward and slightly back, (5) vegetation bent forward, and (6) an uncertain line while in reverse. When a vehicle is traveling at moderate speed, the following are displaced forward: (1) soil and snow droppings (stuff between the treads), and (2) splashes from puddles and stains. When that vehicle is just starting to move forward, those substances are displaced backwards.[9]

There is also a substance transfer when a vehicle moves onto pavement from soft soil. When that vehicle is at rest, it will sometimes leak oil or air-conditioning condensation. In relation to the tire prints, that leak's location will indicate which direction the vehicle was pointing when it started (and probably left).

Depending on the disposition and mental state of the driver, a vehicle may leave characteristic skid marks as it starts/stops too suddenly or corners too fast. Its veering from side to side will cause tire tracks that do not precisely align.

Figure 14.7: Overwatch Protection for Urban Trackers
(Source: FM 5-103 [1985], p. D-9)

Vehicles have different numbers of wheels and means of loco-
motion. They can vary from multi-axled trucks to motorcycles and
horse-drawn carts. Wheels, though sharing the same axle, can also
operate independently of each other. If not, one would leave a nar-
rower, partial impression every time its opposite negotiated a small
curb or ridge in the road. Vehicular tracks are every bit as varied
as footprints and a lot larger. That means they can be followed.

All That Can Be Accomplished in the City

Sometimes, the object is not to catch up with the individual who
made a trail, but just to see where it leads. It may lead to a spider
hole or hidden bunker. Then, the following of that trail would facilitate the seizure of intelligence or ammunition. On the other hand,
the trail may lead to the secret, tiny entrance to a large, underground
hide facility. In that case, the tracking would result in the discovery
of something of tremendous strategic significance—the subterranean
waystation on one of the enemy's major infiltration routes. Within
that underground facility, there is a further need for tracking procedure. By "side-lighting" the floors and walls with a flashlight,
one may find a hidden trapdoor to the still-hidden thoroughfare.
Along that thoroughfare would be other waystations, arms' stores,
escape corridors, and safe-house access ladders. None of this will
be possible without formally trained trackers. How much easier the
battle for Iwo Jima would have been if the Marines of that era had
realized this.

What has happens above ground is also more obvious to an
experienced tracker. There may be 40 ways to detonate an IED,
but there is only one way to position it. By sending a "sign-cutting"
patrol up both sides of a road every morning, one could tell if that
road had been mined overnight. After every IED detonation, there
is a trail to be followed. It leads initially to the perpetrator and
eventually to the manufacturer. Due to the climate, most Middle
Eastern cities are dusty. That makes unusual sole patterns easy
to follow.

To escape bombardment, America's foes prefer to fight at close
quarters. For any form of short-range combat, there are subtle signs
of the enemy's presence. If U.S. leaders were really interested in
saving the lives of their subordinates, they would give them better
observation skills. The requisite attention to detail becomes auto-

matically available to every school-trained tracker. No amount of technology can provide the same capability. But, true proficiency at short range also involves many other things. Now prerequisite to winning 21st-Century wars, they will be the ultimate focus of the final chapter.

15 TO TRULY WIN IN A PLACE LIKE IRAQ

- Do Muslim revolts need a constant influx of alien fighters?
- How does the Maoist method subvert democratization?

IT'S ALL ABOUT THE BASIC SERVICES

(Source: Corel Gallery, Totem Graphics, Man #28V028)

The Glaring Need to Redefine "Victory"

In Iraq and Afghanistan, America has gotten its first good look at 4GW. As in Palestine, the hidden foe has been attacking through four mediums at once: (1) battle, (2) politics, (3) psychology, and (4) infrastructure. To defeat that foe, the U.S. must redefine what it means to win. In a 4GW conflict, it is more important to restore food, water, electricity, and sewage than to kill enemy combatants. Providing alternative basic services is central to the *Sepah/Hezbollah/Hamas* method. Each neighborhood's security is important too, but not at the cost of its

223

residents' lives or livelihoods. As of February 2006, Coalition forces had only been able to police 30% of all populated areas in Iraq.[1] Most of the rest are "protected" by fundamentalist militias. To insure a viable recruiting base and safe area, radical Islamists specifically target the urban "downtrodden and dispossessed." Those Islamists cannot be defeated without a widespread, "grass-roots" program to assist the poor, unemployed, and disenfranchised. While such reasoning makes sense to most readers, the U.S. and Israeli governments have allowed the average Palestinian's desperate plight to worsen since *Hamas* won the election.[2]

To limit the Islamists' subjugation of Africa, America must do what the Marines have been doing in Djibouti—dig wells, give inoculations, and fight hunger. Only then, will the flow of new fighters abate. Within the Marines' method is the answer to 4GW—more "good works" and less "bombardment." In an active war zone, the latter requires something that America lacks—tactically refined (light) infantrymen.

> Every gun that is made, every warship launched, every rocket fired signifies, in the final sense, a theft from those who hunger and are not fed.[3]
> — President Dwight D. Eisenhower, 1952

In any tribal setting from Africa to South Asia, America cannot make the same mistake that Portugal did in Angola and Mozambique. Just to look good in the polls, U.S. leaders cannot opt for "force protection" over neighborhood participation and assailant apprehension. Otherwise, they will create an overly armored, overly centralized, and overly regulated force that will be at the mercy of any quick moving, decentralized, and initiative-wielding adversary. Having commandos is not enough. (See Figure 15.1.) The Russians depended almost entirely on some very proficient SPETSNAZ commandos in Afghanistan. To beat Eastern guerrillas, America will need true light infantry (of the East-Asian variety).

America's Strategy in Relation to That of the Enemy

America's priority in the "War on Terror" has been to disrupt *al-Qaeda's* highest echelon. If it were a Western, "top-down" organization, such an approach might work. But, *al-Qaeda* has evolved

Figure 15.1: Portuguese Commando, 1974
(Source: Courtesy of Orion Books, from *Uniforms of Elite Forces*, © 1982 by Blandford Press Ltd., Plate 13, No. 38)

into a dummy headquarters. It functions only as an umbrella over a number of obscure parties, agencies, and movements. It routinely takes credit for what they do to absolve them of any complicity. To the extent that it needs infrastructure, it uses theirs. While *al-Qaeda* also supports hundreds of tiny terrorist cells, those cells have no direct link with its leaders. Their job is to create a diversion while the larger entities—like *Sepah, Hezbollah,* and Pakistani ISI—create more Islamic states. *Al-Qaeda* depends upon regional militias to protect its lightly manned "support centers." Those centers do little more than dispatch recruiters and trainers. So, every time the United States kills a "leader" of *al-Qaeda*, it does very little to disrupt the everyday operations of a "bottom-up" entity.

225

When Osama bin Laden's people were asked to leave Sudan in 1996, some went to the Chitral region of Pakistan and others to Somalia. Those in Somalia have been destabilizing the eastern coast of Central Africa, while their Shiite replacements in Sudan have been helping the Muslim Brotherhood to subvert North Africa. *Al-Qaeda* sends new *mujahideen* to Chechnya and Afghanistan by ship from Bosaso, while *Hezbollah / Sepah* sends new *baseej* to Iraq by plane from a Sudanese airstrip (or ship from Port Sudan).

That the Sunni and Shiite fundamentalists have been cooperating should be fairly apparent to almost everyone. The same Muslim Brotherhood than spawned *al-Qaeda* in Afghanistan and *Hamas* in Palestine is now the ruling political party in Sudan. Its government is patterned after the one in Tehran. Like China, it believes that "revolution" is an integral part of regional growth. Also like China, one would never guess this from what its leaders say.

One More Bureaucratic Bridge to Cross

Al-Qaeda and the largest entities beneath its umbrella are "bottom-up" organizations. They can only be beaten from the bottom up. To limit *al-Qaeda's* effect, America must focus on the equivalent of cells. Nothing bigger than a squad can sneak up on a cell. To produce squads that can survive that long alone, U.S. commanders would have to change how they train and operate their units. Unfortunately, most lack enough leeway. The U.S. military has so centralized control over the last few years that established procedure has become sacrosanct. "Headquarters" now dictates every training and operational detail. Any "break with faith" might be grounds for dismissal. A yearly, service-wide symposium on all procedures could usefully be coupled with local authority to amend some.

Traditionally, America has depended almost entirely on its technological edge. Some say it does so to capitalize on its wealth and scientific advantage. Others say it does so to stimulate its economy. Whatever the reason, this fascination with technology has become an impediment. All Eastern armies and movements now know that the West cannot fight any other way. They have further discovered that—within deployed units—the new equipment drives the tactics instead of the other way around. Any past or present U.S. infantryman will confirm that the way to defeat IEDs is to get off the vehicles and outpost the neighborhoods. Yet, the Pentagon has instead launched a multi-billion dollar campaign to defeat IEDs technologically. One U.S. battalion commander's request to dismount was flatly denied.[4]

While not as brutal, the U.S. way of war is very much like that of Russia. It discourages short-range resistance through overwhelming bombardment. Within the Muslim world, indirect fire—of whatever degree of accuracy—generates *"jihadic"* duty, multi-generational vendetta, suicide fighter, and car bomb. America should have learned that from its Beirut experience in 1983. It now has a choice—change how it fights at short range or run the risk of losing every future Eastern conflict. In the Global War on Terror, allowing the "ward bosses" of fundamentalist-controlled neighborhoods to steal an election does not constitute victory.

Will the U.S. Way of War Work for the Iraqis?

If Iraq's army and police are to defeat its insurgency, they will need enough organizational integrity and military expertise to do so. They will enjoy little of the first, because both systems are being heavily infiltrated by Islamists. For the insurgents, this creates both intelligence bonanza and tactical advantage.

At issue then is whether the U.S. military can impart enough military expertise to compensate for intelligence leaks, unlocked gates, and "inside jobs." For decades, it has approached its mission through enforced loyalty, technological superiority, and overwhelming firepower. Iraqi security forces won't enjoy any of the three. Even if they could afford the latest technology, they wouldn't know how to use it. Nor could they withstand the public backlash from misdirected "smart" bombs. Instead, they must restore order like policemen do—through minimal force by widely dispersed contingents. That takes more skill at short range than most U.S. military units possess. How, then, will those units teach the Iraqis? Many veterans of Korea and Vietnam still think that local forces did poorly because of cultural weakness and unit corruption. The first sentiment is nothing more than propaganda-inspired racism. The second turns a blind eye to what routinely passes as technological advancement in the Pentagon. Might the indigenous forces have fared poorly against guerrillas because of having to copy the U.S. style of war?

That America has the best style of government and economy does not necessarily mean that it has the most flexible military. Only the most prideful of Vietnam War veterarns still blame the media or Congress for its loss. Most have since come to realize that it takes decentralized control over training and operations to defeat an Eastern insurgent or 4GW warrior.

For the U.S. infantryman or policeman, technology can help to detect an enemy presence. But it can also facilitate a false signature. When the GI must patrol by vehicle and wear a 70-pound wrap-around flak jacket, technology becomes his enemy.[5] The brass, or whoever has been coming up with such loving ideas, should try to stay alive while fully exposed and totally "cocooned" on a 120-degree day. The GI's unloved adversary may appear less professional, but he is also less encumbered.

For U.S. Leaders, One Last Chance to Reassess Options

Within the context of 4GW, martial force has its limitations. By now, those limitations should be fairly obvious to soldiers and politicians alike. For many, leadership has come to mean protecting their subordinates/constituents from news of setbacks. Not sensing the interface between battle and diplomacy, they have yet to realize that aerial bombs, overzealous interrogation, assassination, and subversion, are simply fanning the flames. (See Figure 15.2.) To project less force, they need a replacement for firepower. The most obvious candidate is "state-of-the-art" assault techniques for all U.S. infantry squads. Each could generate enough surprise to remove the need for preparatory bombardment.

Tracing Each Resistance Fighter to His Point of Origin

The way to limit collateral damage is not to overpower each person who resists, but rather to trace him to his point of origin. When one fights this way "at the bottom," he has several advantages. First, he can see what his opponent is really up to. Those who deal in "death by 1,000 cuts" are hard to spot in the standard headquarters' "big-picture." With a little combat tracking experience, the average GI could provide much of his own intelligence. He would know when his perimeter was about to be attacked. He could locate enemy infiltration routes. He could apprehend IED riggers. He could better tell when he was approaching a fully camouflaged enemy strongpoint. In short, he could better survive and win. Combat trackers can prevent incursion into secured areas by walking "sign-cutting" arcs across the most likely avenues of intrusion. This is especially important where the area is unlevel and expansive. Like a wild animal, the enemy scout approaches an American camp through its watershed ditches. Those ditches provide easy proof of passage. Other types of microterrain provide additional "track traps."

To the extent that guerrillas need reinforcement and resupply, they depend upon infiltration routes. Whenever U.S. forces learn of a personnel or materiel delivery to a certain place, they should backtrack the handlers/porters. If they do so far enough, they would find themselves on the Iraqi or Afghan equivalent to the Ho Chi Minh Trail. That's the reason for all of the map enlargements in Chapter 4. They reveal trails, quarries, and depressions that would not otherwise be visible. Backtracking along the Euphrates would locate far more caches and underground waystations than technology ever could. However, to cripple an insurgency, all of Iraq's infiltration routes would have to be sabotaged at once. In the Eastern world, the most obvious of those routes may partially function as a diversion.

The Syrian Conduits May Now Be Distractions

Neither Iran, nor the Baathists, nor *al-Qaeda* need to bring many more foreign *jihadists* into Iraq. The war has now reached the stage where enough everyday fighters can be recruited locally. Guerrillas either learn or die. Their on-the-job training works better than most because of its lack of impediments and automatic assessment procedure.

That Iran is behind much of the Iraqi trouble in is no longer speculation. It may count on Lebanese *Hezbollah* and the Euphrates infiltration route to draw attention away from what is occurring along its own border with Iraq.

Iran's Revolutionary Guards have set up a network of

Figure 15.2: Architecture Worth Saving
(Source: DA Pam 550-175 [1989], p. xxxvii)

secret smuggling routes to ferry men and equipment into Iraq for attacks on coalition troops, according to an exiled opposition group.

The smuggling is said to be orchestrated by the guards' elite Quds Force, which has its HQ in the southern Iranian city of Ahwaz.

The National Council of Resistance of Iran (NCRI) says commanders are sending a steady stream of agents and bomb-making equipment from a base code-named "Fajr" into Iraq, where roadside attacks are carried out against coalition troops.

After The Sunday Telegraph revealed in August [2005] that Iran was supplying infrared [guided] bombs to Iraqi insurgents, the Government held the Iranians responsible for the deaths of at least eight British soldiers.

Last week, Tony Blair condemned Iran as a "threat to world security" after President Mahmoud Ahmadinejad, a former Revolutionary Guards commander, declared that Israel should be "wiped off the map."

Western intelligence agencies have reported a sharp increase in Iran's involvement in insurgent operations since Mr. Ahmadinejad was elected in June.

The agencies believe that the guards use a network of routes along Iran's 620-mile border with Iraq.

Documents seen by The Sunday Telegraph show three principal routes, two near the Iraqi cities of Basra and Amara[h], and a third via the Iranian town of Mehran.

A main route is thought to be through the marshland surrounding the Shatt al-Arab waterway in southern Iraq, which enables guard units to plan attacks against British forces in Basra.

Other routes lead to central Iraq, where United States military intelligence believes that Iranian agents are involved in attacks against U.S. troops, 2,000 of whom have died since the invasion.

Details of the routes have been compiled by the . . . (NCRI), and passed to British and American intelligence officers.

NCRI is regarded as one of the most informed and effective Iranian opposition groups. It was recently responsible for revealing details of Iran's secret nuclear bomb programme, which led to the latest crisis in relations between Iran and the West.

According to the NCRI's latest report Iranian agents travel to Iraq dressed as local Arabs to spy on and film British and American patrols.

The report states that each reconnaissance group is formed of 20 members and, apart from monitoring the activities of coalition forces, they are also tasked with linking up with local Shia groups involved in the insurgency.[6]

—*Daily Telegraph* (London), 29 October 2005

Iran's involvement in Iraq has become increasingly flagrant. There were reports of 80 Iranians fighting with al-Sadr in Najaf in the summer of 2004.[7] There was proof of Iran providing Iraqi resistance fighters with sophisticated IEDs in the summer of 2005.[8] In May 2006, the missile that downed a British helicopter in Basra was determined to have come from Iran.[9]

Recapturing the Momentum in Iraq

To solve a chronic problem, one must try nontraditional solutions. If Americans' expectations are not being met in Iraq, their governmental representatives must implement new policies, strategies, and tactics. By constitutional mandate, U.S. military leaders must accept their country's foreign policies. They have no such obligation to stick with traditional strategies and tactics. Today's enemy is different from the one in WWII. As a member of an independent cell or group, he is unencumbered by orders and regulations. His learning is dynamic. He requires little, if any, logistical support. And, with the most limited of strategic guidance, he can make a real contribution to the war effort. To defeat him, one must enter his everyday environment and operate at his dimensional scale.

U.S. line outfits have been prepared for all-out, conventional war, not the blanketing a foreign city with self-sufficient squads. Unfortunately, most Eastern armies and movements have now discovered how to expel a Western occupier. They have only to operate on a scale with which Western leaders have little experience and deem unimportant (each of the "1,000 cuts"). Their fighters are largely able to operate because of the restrictions placed on their Western counterparts. Those counterparts are generally only allowed to report sightings, follow orders, and operate weapons. To make matters worse, they are encased in buttoned-up vehicles and/or 70-pound, unventilated flak jackets. The insurgents have only to wait for the U.S. to get tired of its unit maneuver/deployment and declare victory. For the U.S. military, winning has come to mean entering a hot zone, fighting for a while without any particular objective, overestimating the number of enemy killed by supporting arms, and leaving.

If America's brigade commanders can't figure out how to fight more effectively at short range, they should defer to the collective wisdom of those who do it for a living—their rifle squad leaders. Any good SNCO could facilitate that wisdom. (See Figure 15.3.) By simply decentralizing control over training and operations (and

Figure 15.3: U.S. Special Forces Sergeant First Class
(Source: Courtesy of Orion Books, from *World Army Uniforms since 1939*, © 1975, 1980, 1981, 1983 by Blandford Press Ltd., Part II, Plate 142)

making subordinates do likewise), those commanders could surprise more enemy. Their casualty ratio might not improve because of the higher incidence of close combat, but they would have preserved the hearts, minds, and infrastructure required for final victory. If time makes a more assertive approach necessary, they could require all companies to follow the squad training method that Posterity Enterprises has spent the last 20 years perfecting.[10]

Many U.S. military members have come to believe that ordinary Americans do not care about the sacrifices that they have made in Iraq and Afghanistan. This could not be further from the truth. Ordinary Americans do realize their sacrifices and care deeply. It is the system within which those GIs live and work that can be a little short on caring. That it contains good people at the higher echelons does not change that. The system has simply placed too much emphasis on making the military into a career. How many of those careerists have asked that the troops be allowed to get off the vehicles to outpost Iraqi neighborhoods in a counter-*Sepah* methodology? How many have demanded that their people be allowed to wear whatever facilitates their mission? A senior commander in Vietnam went to his grave convinced that the *New York Times* had lost the war. Newspapers don't lose wars, nor does Congress. Armies lose wars. Perhaps, one can only "win" relative to the enemy's way of fighting. Through it all, one process irresistibly continues. It is the very real and ongoing evolution of tactical technique. Until the U.S. military catches up with its Eastern counterparts in tactical technique, true victory at short range will not be possible.

The Missing Ingredient Is Not the Fault of Someone Else

Instituting democracy throughout the Middle East—with the intent of turning armed conflict into political strife—is a lofty goal. It ignores the prevailing tribal thought process,[11] but it could work. Its success would depend on the local security forces being able to suppress fundamentalist insurrection. Until U.S. forces acquire more light-infantry ability themselves, they will be unable to impart that type of knowledge. If their government does not require them to evolve tactically, there will emerge an Iranian-orchestrated (and nuclear-armed) *"al-Qaeda"* Crescent that extends from Afghanistan to Somalia. As its revolutionary goal will be the creation of new Islamic states all along its periphery, the Western world will experience 150 more years of brush fire war. While this may make the U.S. arms manufacturers happy, it won't do much for world stability. Another Muslim Empire will emerge, but this time it will take in not only oil-rich Saudi Arabia, but also mineral-rich Central Africa. Perhaps it's time for ordinary Americans to demand that their duly elected government officials replace the so-far counterproductive "smart" bombs with infantry squads that can single-handedly avoid detection, escape encirclement, and exercise mercy.

Only light infantry can teach foreign armies and police how to counter insurgency. The current generation of GIs has been hamstrung tactically in Iraq just as their fathers were in Vietnam. Until America admits that, there will be no reason to develop the world-class small-unit tactics that would be required to win an unconventionally fought WWIII. There is every indication that, like the French in 1917, the U.S. government (through pressure from its military/industrial complex) has made the conscious decision to discourage tactical innovation.

Within the two U.S. infantry branches, company and battalion leaders are buried in uninterpreted intelligence, bureaucratic red tape, and politically expedient rumor. Many are under the following misconceptions:

- That U.S. infantry has continued to evolve tactically.
- That lives are saved by bombarding all frontal resistance.
- That frontal, bottom-floor assault is the safest in buildings.
- That tight stacks are best way to enter buildings or rooms.
- That U.S. units fight offensively.
- That there is only one kind of infantry.
- That giving every infantryman his own optics will help.
- That all U.S. efforts are working in Iraq and Afghanistan.
- That the American press is hurting the war effort.
- That U.S. military intelligence is comprehensive.
- That fundamentalist Shiites and Sunnis won't cooperate.

Once an American (of whatever job description) learns how to identify hasty research and intentional disinformation, the press becomes his or her closest ally. The press at least attempts to get at the truth. Western-style military bureaucracies often have more pressing priorities—like keeping from getting swallowed up by a sister service or underfunded by Congress. If the U.S. military establishment had been searching for truth, it would have noticed that

235

much its small-unit tactical technique had fallen 90 years behind the state of the art. Military bureaucracies generate a "positive outlook" to create the impression that their mission is always being accomplished. Good things are always happening (as in fact they are through a lot of hard work and dedication), yet the organization itself and its corporate memory remain relatively unchanged.

To blame for the apparent disconnect is the military "system" itself. It contains too many procedures that have outlived their usefulness. It is those procedures that do not adequately protect the troops, not their seniors per se. Until the U.S. military adopts a way of training and operating that allows enlisted infantrymen to reach their full battlefield potential, America should not expect to win any more wars. For a Western military establishment to develop advanced squad tactics, it must decentralize control. To decentralize control, it must first admit that headquarters is not getting the job done. Some say that the war in Iraq has been lost for over a year. Others say it could still be won with a CAP (Combined Action Platoon) counter-*Sepah* deployment throughout the major urban areas. For those who consider it their leadership responsibility to say that the war is going well despite evidence to the contrary, there are pitfalls. From what they have said, subordinates will be less likely to try other strategies and tactics. From what they have said, history may draw some very unpleasant conclusions.

There Is No More Room for Error

Now that there's evidence that Iran has been behind much of the trouble in Iraq, U.S. leaders will have to explain why they have facilitated pro-Iranian regimes in Iraq, Afghanistan, and Palestine. An overly centralized administration might have trouble adapting foreign policy and military strategy to a rapidly changing situation.

If the U.S. now decides to take military action against Iran, it must do so in a way that does not provoke a worldwide epidemic of suicide bombings. Instead of a bombardment of peripheral installations, it must attempt an advanced maneuver against the enemy's center of gravity. The most promising is the lotus blossom or "inside-out" urban assault. The standard U.S. format (no matter how well infused with precision ordnance) would, in all likelihood, result in an extended guerrilla war in Iran and diversions throughout the world. As this book shows, the Chinese are clearly cooperating with Iran, the Muslim Brotherhood, and *al-Qaeda* in Sudan, Nigeria, and elsewhere in Africa. It is the Chinese who trained ANC, PAC, and FRELIMO guerrillas in Tanzania. It is the Chinese who just gave a $2 billion line of credit to Angola and signed oil contracts with Nigeria. And it is the Chinese who blocked Darfur-related U.N. sanctions against Sudan and nuclear-related resolutions against Iran.[12] The unfortunate pattern is there; it will not go away by ignoring it.

> China is pursuing a troubling, tricky alliance with radical, right-wing Islam, or Islamism, despite concerns about its own restive Muslim population.[13]

While democratization of the region is a noble goal, it has pre-requisites. One is the prospective voters' level of education. Another is their access to unbiased information. Still another is their inter-est in nationalism. Most importantly, they must be protected from pre-election intimidation and post-election retaliation. These are things that do not normally exist in many parts of Africa. There, vote fraud is a fact of life. So far, the West has been "surprised" by communist-backed factions winning elections in Zimbabwe, South Africa, Namibia, and Angola. It has further been surprised by fun-damentalist Muslims winning elections in Iraq, Iran, and Palestine. Did not Hitler come to power in the early 1930's through an exacer-bation of the democratic process? Political conflict is more produc-tive than its martial alternative, but the West must do a better job of countering electoral subversion. It must also do a better job of providing alternative basic services. While the instigators of terror are being tracked down and arrested, the indigenous populations will need clean water, sewage, vaccines, and food. Only then, will actual democracy take hold in Africa. Should the West attempt a more militaristic solution, most of Africa and the Middle East will end up as the latest addition to the growing fundamentalist Muslim bloc of nations.

The "Information Age" Challenge for U.S. Leaders

The internet has made possible an explosion of timely informa-tion from all over the world. America's leaders can no longer get away with policy that can't keep pace with events. Now that the arenas of diplomacy and warfare have merged, they must pay more attention to the collective wisdom of their lower-echelon, foreign service and military professionals. If they don't, the Islamist and communist "bottom-up" way of operating will more quickly adapt to a fluid situation and continue to succeed.

U.S. military personnel have long known about what goes on in the Pentagon but have generally kept quiet about it while still on active duty. In short, the Pentagon's pricey obsession with technology has overridden any cost-free responsibility for tactical reform. What a properly trained infantry squad can accomplish became impossible to ignore with the German Stormtrooper techniques of 1917. To this day, they are the "state of the art" for both offense and defense. To win a 4th-Generation war, America will need more light infantrymen—those who can attack or repel any number of enemy with just one squad. Those 4GW warriors must look more like Mohicans than electronics-draped extensions of their commander. As again proven in Iraq, no amount of firepower or "vehicularization" can take the place of community involvement. That takes infantry squads with enough training to coexist with local counterparts in each village or neighborhood.

To the U.S. leaders' credit, foreign dictators are less often supported in the face of popular discontent. Unfortunately, that insensitive policy has given way to one that is too naive. It is naive to think that democratization (without its many prerequisites) can quickly solve all of an underdeveloped country's ills. If it were just the Islamists that America were confronting, that oversight would only cost extra billions and years. But China—the acknowledged master of deception—is also involved. It is again using the illusion of democracy to pursue its expansionist goals. Those not personally aware of the extent and method of these goals could usefully research the term, "Greater China Co-Prosperity Sphere." While Westernized thinkers might have trouble imagining a Sino-Islamic "coalition of convenience," they can certainly relate to Muslim pawns in a Chinese chessboard. They can also see how a different perspective on human rights might lead to two, distinct camps.

The Enemy's Pro-Democracy Ruse

After massive "pro-democracy" demonstrations at Kathmandu

in late April 2006, Nepal's king agreed to reactivate the parliament and "return executive powers to the people."[14] He had disbanded that parliament in February 2005, because it wasn't doing enough to quell the Maoist revolt.[15]

Nepal is not overpopulated and poor like its southern neighbor. Thus, its Maoist rebellion springs from something other than popular discontent. Nepal borders on Chinese-occupied Tibet and is just a few hundred miles from an Indian Ocean seaport. Though inside a democratic nation, that seaport lies within a communist state and has a city government that is communist.[16] Another Maoist revolt has been occurring in northeast India for decades.[17] All of this adds up to only one thing: Chinese expansionism. But, the evidence of expansion is not what's disturbing. What is disturbing is how its proponents have taken advantage of the West's unbridled quest for democracy.

In 1994, the Nepal Communist Party won midterm elections and formed a minority government. In 1996, the Maoist United People's Front officially launched a "people's war." In June 2001, all but the crown prince of the ruling family were murdered, and the crown prince declared king. In August 2003, the Maoists broke the truce and resumed fighting.[18] In November 2005, they reentered the political arena of an obviously 4GW environment.

> The Maoists entered into a 12-point understanding last November, committing to multiparty democracy, with the seven-party alliance that called for the current strike.[19]
> — *Christian Science Monitor,* 18 April 2006

On 21 April 2006, that seven-party alliance rejected the king's offer to return to the parliamentary system. Their most influential member wanted nothing short of an end to the monarchy.[20] Through "unconditional constituent-assembly elections,"[21] the Maoists wanted immunity from attack. That they suspended all hostilities nationwide during the protests should be adequate proof that they planned them.[22] After the king's concession, the Maoists agreed to lift the blockades of all major highways into Kathmandu, if the political parties immediately rewrote the constitution to limit or eliminate the monarchy's power.[23] At that point, the king was still the commander in chief of the army. On 4 May, the Nepalese cabinet dropped all terrorism-related charges against the communist insurgents.[24] This concession might have been viewed as productive, if Maoist chairman Pranchanda's principal demand had not been "unconditional constituent assembly elections."[25] Pranchanda is a *nom de guerre* meaning "fierce one." The chairman's real name is Pushpa Kamal Dahal.[26]

On 12 May, under the advice of a seven-party alliance commission and threat of renewed violence, the new government acted.

> [Parliament] arrested five senior ministers of the king, restricted the rest from leaving Kathmandu, and suspended chiefs of three security agencies: the regular police, the armed police, and the central intelligence department. The parties have also indicated their intent to end the king's control over the Army.[27]
> — *Christian Science Monitor,* 15 May 2006

It was as if a slow-motion coup were occurring under the guise of democratic reform. While the West was engrossed in Iran's nuclear grandstanding, China was quietly making its move on the jewel of Southeast Asia. To meet the Maoist rebels' demands for taking part in the upcoming elections, the newly reinstalled parliament took the army away from the king and nullified provisions of the existing constitution on 18 May. But, this was not enough for Pranchanda. According to him, a ceremonial role for the monarchy "goes against the people's desire for a republic."[28] He had learned how—with catch words—to appease the West. The individual freedoms of Nepal's wonderful people were now very much in doubt. On 16 June, the two sides signed a deal "dissolving both the parliament and rebel-run local governments" so that a new constitution could be written and coalition government formed. The Maoists were "pushing the argument that the [10,000 man] PLA [People's Liberation Army] is the legitimate state army while the Nepali army is the residue of a rejected regime."[29] Those who would continue to resist Chinese or Islamic expansionism anywhere in the world should study these refinements to the takeover variant.

Too Many Similarities with the Past

The parallels between these events in Nepal and those in southern Africa fifteen years ago should serve as a warning to America.

Communist nations see themselves as democratic. They too (at least theoretically) support the will of the people. When China finally makes her bid to remove all Western influence from the Asian mainland, one of her instruments will be the Democratic People's Republic of Korea (DPRK). The Chinese have become skilled at deceiving the West. While many of the African resistance movements of the late 20th Century had the word "People's" or "Liberation" in their titles, those of today have "Democratic." China's communist regime is not America's friend, nor is it her arch rival. It is simply a country with a mushrooming need for natural resource, little regard for human rights, a knack for deception, and expansionist tendencies. Those tendencies must be countered wherever possible. For those who have not studied the Asian thought process or recent Chinese history, there is a contemporary warning. As of June 2006, China was still monthly returning hundreds of North Korean refugees to almost certain death in their homeland.[30] For over two years, there has been evidence of a gas chamber at North Korea's largest concentration camp near the Russian border.[31]

As of 21 April 2006, the People's Republic of China possessed a 2.5-million member military establishment and had made double-digit military spending increases almost every year since the early 1990's.[32] Now devoid of any border threat, China must have something else in mind.

China has been sending more than just peacekeepers to Africa. It has also been sending "election observers."[33] One of its allies (South Africa) has been combining peacekeeper security with election "training" in the outlying villages of DRC. According to Human Rights Watch, there are problems with such an approach. "The institutions that are organizing the elections are politicized."[34] How many more "Chinese-style" elections will the West permit, and Africa have to endure?

> China's "comprehensive warfare" strategy wears down [an] enemy using non-military means. . . .
> . . . [Chinese] National Defense University Senior Col. Meng Xiansheng . . . defined the term as "the means of defeating enemies without waging a war through deploying a wide range of political, economic, cultural, diplomatic and military tactics."
> [Col.] Meng said "comprehensive warfare" advocates the

use of non-violent means in handling state-to-state disputes,
. . . but [it] also fits with China's grand strategy of "peaceful
development."[35]
— *Geostrategy-Direct,* 2 August 2006

Unless considered in the 4GW context, China's new, expanded
involvement in Africa might be seen as a positive development. Yet,
the West must never forget the genocides that a disregard for human rights have already produced on that beleaguered continent.
No matter how convenient, America cannot afford to relinquish its
African responsibilities to Red China.

The Chinese advance . . . [is] government-backed, led by
state-run corporations and propelled by the drive to secure
oil supplies. . . .
Tradespeople from Cape Verde to Namibia complain
about a Chinese invasion.[36]
— *The Financial Times,* 28 February 2006

That the Chinese now pose a significant threat to the region is
no longer speculation. "In less than 10 years China has secured oil
production and exploration deals in a swathe of countries reaching
across Africa from the Red Sea to the Gulf of Guinea."[37]

Other Examples of Chinese Excess

China has been sending "election planners" to various nations.
There's proof it helped *Hamas* to win in Palestine. China doesn't
maintain diplomatic relations with Israel, but it does with the Palestinian National Authority. That embassy is in Ramallah.[38]

A Chinese intelligence officer is engaged in covertly aiding the ruling Palestinian Hamas terrorist group. . . . Gong
Xiaosheng . . . [is the] Chinese Ministry of State Security
(MSS) official who has worked out of Ramallah since Nov.
2002, first with Yasser Arafat and latterly helping Hamas.
It was Gong who arranged for Mahmoud al-Zahar to be
invited to Beijing shortly after his appointment as Hamas
foreign minister. . . .

... As far back as 2004, the Chinese MSS pegged the Islamist terrorist group as an up-and-coming force heading for Palestinian rule. . . . Our sources disclose that the Chinese intelligence officer is very close to Hamas prime minister Ismail Haniya, a-Zahar, and Muhammed Jaabari, chief of the Hamas armed wing, Ezz e-Din al-Qassam. They habitually consult him [the Chinese officer] for advice. Hamas's actions and decisions are there[fore] not merely influenced by its relations with . . . other parts of the Muslim world. The Hamas-Gaza, Beijing connection is no less influential.[39]
— Israeli Intelligence Bulletin, 19 June 2006

Proof That Communists Exporting Light-Infantry Skills

The FBI calls *Hezbollah* the best light infantry in the world.[40] It's not of course, but the presence of a DPRK embassy in Mousaitbeh (West Beirut) is still troubling. North Korea has others in Nepal, India, Pakistan, Syria, Egypt, Ethiopia, and South Africa.[41] It also has its own 100,000-man Light Infantry Training Guidance Bureau.[42] A few of its members can double as infantry attachment or commando team. Should that bureau be helping *Hezbollah,* the entire region would be impacted. It is *Hezbollah* that is thought to be still training replacements for Iraq and Palestine in Sudan and the Bekaa Valley.

It is now apparent that North Korea has helped *Hezbollah* to design its Israeli-border "defense zone." The underground-strongpoint matrix is the cornerstone of the modern light-infantry defensive tactics.

Hezbollah is . . . benefiting from . . . North Korean advisers, according to a July 29 report in *al-Sharq al-Awsat.* The report quotes a high-ranking Iranian Revolutionary Guards officer, who stated that North Korean advisers had assisted Hezbollah in building tunnel infrastructure, including a 25 kilometer underground tunnel. . . . The report also provides specifics on Iran's assistance to Hezbollah, such as . . . the construction of underground command and control centers, [and] . . . underground weapons depots.[43]
— Jamestown Foundation journal, 1 August 2006

An Appropriate U.S. Response

The Global War on Terror is far from over. With any luck, U.S. leaders have learned a few things from their Iraqi experiment. To blame any particular segment of a multi-sided society is to sow the seeds of civil war. The UIA is culturally spliced into the revolutionary government of Iran. Allowing its candidates to run unopposed in a loosely monitored election is, at best, naive.

The West's . . . assumption that democratically elected governments will be cooperative and pro-Western need not hold true in non-Western societies where electoral competition can bring anti-Western nationalists and fundamentalists to power.[44]

In underdeveloped and tribal regions, makeshift elections simply facilitate a takeover by Islamist or communist elements.

The Administration's top-down approach of assuming that elections will solve problems has been too simplistic. You also need educational institutions and economic development.[45]

— Foreign policy chief, Brookings Institute, July 2006

America might have more luck promoting environments within which democracy can take root. The key to such an environment is local security. Without it, the elections will not be fair, and the people cannot be expected to help the government.[46] With light-infantry skills, U.S. troops could prepare local forces for that role. Then, the perpetrators of terror could be tracked down and arrested without disturbing the local population or ruining their infrastructure. Light infantrymen depend more on surprise than on firepower. They don't need a lot of ordnance. If the Pentagon were to dedicate—to well drilling and water purification—one tenth of what it wastes on counterproductive ammunition, it could save/create millions of pro-Western voters in sub-Saharan Africa alone.

The solution is the same no matter how many communist nations and Islamist movements are involved in the expansionism. To defeat it, America's leaders must override their cultural impulse to "think big" and start "thinking small." It will all come down to the basics—basic 4GW skills for U.S. troops and basic services for op-pressed populations. That means humanitarian light infantrymen instead of infrastructure destroying and *jihadist*-generating smart bombs. Some squads would anchor neighborhood security through CAP platoons, while others mantracked and arrested perpetrators. Only then will the cycle of violence be broken.

Conclusion

The inescapable conclusion of this study is twofold. One per-tains to the Middle East, and the other to Africa and the rest of the world.

In the Middle East, America and Israel have been unintention-ally fanning the flames of terrorism through their firepower-depen-dent approach to war. That's why the U.S. State Department had to stop publishing *Patterns of Global Terrorism*. To effectively counter Chinese and Islamist expansionism, the United States and its al-lies will have to do two things: (1) admit that Iran and Lebanese *Hezbollah* have had more to do with destabilizing the region than *al-Qaeda,* and (2) demand that their own militaries tactically evolve at the infantry squad level. Upon Zarqawi's death, Richard Clarke former U.S. anti-terrorism czar—admitted that *Al-Qaeda in Iraq* had a few hundred members and was only one of 14 groups fight-ing.[47] On the other hand, it is William S. Lind who has produced the 3GW and 4GW handbooks that the U.S. military has been trying so hard to ignore. He says that 4GW can automatically defeat a 2GW proponent (one with so much firepower as to need self-sufficient squads).[48]

In 4GW, the neighborhoods have tremendous strategic value. They cannot be secured by occasionally driving through them. They must be outposted by tiny, contingents of U.S. and local forces that can survive on their own without resupply or having to resort to supporting arms. That takes more skill than most American infan-trymen and special operators currently possess.

In Africa, the U.S. has shown more restraint. In league with the U.N. and Britain, it has converted much of the continent's martial strife into political debate. Unfortunately, this "democratic approach" to every problem has resulted in a "hands-off" response to the Rwanda massacre and one-party rule in many nations.

245

Through a failure to first work on the prerequisites for democracy, the West has failed to provide more freedom and basic services to the African people. In essence, the communists, Islamists, and dictators have learned how to rig elections. There is only one way to produce the so-far-elusive, security prerequisite. Local forces must be shown how to protect their towns and neighborhoods with minimal force while badly outnumbered. They must also be shown how to track down and *arrest* miscreants. That will not be possible without U.S. trainers who themselves know a wide assortment of Eastern-style light-infantry techniques. It is only through such techniques that Eastern insurgents, terrorists, and 4GW warriors can be suppressed. (See Figure 15.4.)

Figure 15.4: That All May Live in Peace
(Source: Corel Gallery, Landmarks, Corel #26A020)

Notes

SOURCE NOTES

Illustrations

Pictures on pages 5, 24, 32, 42, 82, 96, 135, 140, 161, 166, 176, 178, 184, 198, and 233 reprinted after written assurance from Orion Books, London, that the copyright holders for *WORLD ARMY UNIFORMS SINCE 1939,* text by Andrew Mollo and Digby Smith, color plates by Malcolm McGregor and Michael Chappell, can no longer be contacted. They are from Part II (Plates 110, 81, 117, 113, 38, 118, 96, 63, 99, 98, 106, 132, 90, 124, and 142, respectively) of the Orion publication. Copyright © 1975, 1980, 1981, 1983 by Blandford Books Ltd. All rights reserved.

Pictures on pages 103 and 115 reprinted after written assurance from Pan Macmillan, London, that the copyright holders for *MILITARY UNIFORMS OF THE WORLD,* written and illustrated by Preben Kannick, can no longer be contacted. The illustrations are from Plate 382 (58th Rutlandshire Foot Private, 1880) and Plate 381 (Boer Army Sharpshooter, 1880-1902) of the Pan Macmillan publication, respectively. Copyright ©1968 by Blandford Press Ltd. All rights reserved.

Pictures on pages 120, 211, 217, and 218 reprinted with permission of Paladin Press, Boulder, CO, from *TACTICAL TRACKING OPERATIONS,* by David Scott-Donelan. The illustrations are from pages 6, 63, 48, 49 of the Paladin publication, respectively. Copyright © 1998 by David Scott-Donelan. All rights reserved.

Pictures on pages 131, 151, 202, 210, and 225 reprinted after written assurance from Cassell PLC, London, that the copyright holders for *UNIFORMS OF THE ELITE FORCES,* text by Leroy Thompson, color plates by Michael Chappell, can not longer be contacted. The illustrations are from Plate 23 (Nos. 68 & 69), Plate 32 (No. 95), Plate 6 (No. 16), and Plate 13 (No. 38) of the Cassell publication, respectively. Copyright © 1982 by Blandford Press Ltd. All rights reserved.

Maps on pages xxi, 6, 7, 10, 19, 30, 43, 117, 133, 136, 141, 153, 201, and 206 reprinted after written assurance from GENERAL LIBRARIES OF THE UNIVERSITY OF TEXAS AT AUSTIN that they are in the public domain.

Maps on pages 47-52, 57-60, and 65-73 reprinted after written assurance from the UNIVERSITY OF CALIFORNIA AT BERKELEY LIBRARY that the copyright owner can no longer be determined for map designator "8085/iraq/200k/i38_20.jpg," 1:200,000, Topographic Map, Soviet Union, Sovetskaia Armiia, Generalnyi shtab, 1972-1991. Copyright ©. All rights reserved.

Map on page 191 reprinted with permission of DIGITALGLOBE, INC., from the USAID portion of the General Libraries of the University of Texas at Austin collection for Sudan. Copyright © 2004 by DigitalGlobe, Inc. All rights reserved.

Text

Reprinted after asking permission of *REUTERS* from the following article(s): (1) "U.S.-Led Forces Arrest Top Militia Commander in Iraq," 7 July 2006. Copyright © 2006 by Reuters. All rights reserved.

Reprinted with permission of East-West Services, Springfield, VA, publishers of *GEOSTRATEGY-DIRECT* and *WORLD TRIBUNE,* from the following article(s): (1) " 'White Man' Training Al Qaida Terrorists in Wilderness Camp near Kenya," by Bill Gertz, 14 December 2004; (2) "Insurgents Using New Advanced Russian RPG from Iran," 11 May 2006; (3) "Hamas Army Recruited Thousands for Holy War to Destroy Israel," 7 March 2006; (4) "China's 'Comprehensive Warfare' Strategy Wears Down Enemy Using Non-Military Means," 2 August 2006. Copyrights © 2004 and 2006 by East-West Services. All rights reserved.

Reprinted with permission of EMERGENCY RESPONSE AND RESEARCH INSTITUTE, Chicago, IL, from the following article(s): (1) "Islamists Training in Somalia," by Bill Gertz, 31 December 2005. Copyright © 2005 by Emergency Response and Research Institute. All rights reserved.

Reprinted with permission of Lt.Col. R.F. Reid-Daly, from *PAMWE CHETE.* Copyright © 1999 by R.F. Reid-Daly. All rights reserved.

ENDNOTES

Introduction

1. Faiza Saleh Ambah, AP, "Iraq: Spinning Off Arab Terrorists," *Christian Science Monitor,* 8 February 2005, p. 6.
2. "Islamists Training in Somalia," ERRI Daily Intelligence Report, vol. 11, no. 363, Emergency Net News, 31 December 2005, from Bill Gertz, through *Geostrategy-Direct.*
3. "Pirates off Somali Coast Take Cargo Ship, Kill Member of Crew," World Briefs Wire Reports (AP), *Jacksonville Daily News* (NC), 8 May 2006, p. 4A; ABC's Nightly News, 5 November 2006; Marc Lacey, New York Times, "Somalia's Pirates Scare Toughest of Sailors," *Raleigh News Observer,* 3 July 2006.
4. "Piracy Increase 'Alarming'," from AP, 16 November 2005, through news24.com (South Africa).
5. "Pirates Hijack Ship off Somalia," from AFP, 7 December 2005, through news24.com (South Africa).
6. Jim Krane, AP, "U.S. Navy Seizes Suspected Pirate Ship," *Jacksonville Daily News* (NC), 23 January 2006, p. 4A.
7. Rohan Gunaratna, *Inside al-Qaeda: Global Network of Terror* (Lahore: Vanguard, 2002), pp. 154, 158.
8. Abraham McLaughlin, "Rebuilding African Tourism," *Christian Science Monitor,* 8 November 2005, p. 6.
9. "Marine General Warns Somalia a Terrorist Haven," from AP, *Jacksonville Daily News* (NC), 14 May 2005. p. 4A.
10. Ibid.
11. "Deny Shooting First at Navy in Skirmish with Pirates," from AP, *Jacksonville Daily News* (NC), 20 March 2006, p. 4A.
12. Gunaratna, *Inside al-Qaeda,* pp. 154-156.
13. "Ambush in Mogadishu," written, produced, and directed by William Cran, PBS's *Frontline,* in conjunction with WGBH, Boston, 2002, videotape.
14. Ibid.
15. Gunaratna, *Inside al-Qaeda,* p. 156.
16. *Patterns of Global Terrorism, 2003 Report* (Washington, D.C.: U.S. Dept. of State, April 2004), s.v. "Al-Itihaad al-Islamiya."
17. "Eliminating Terrorist Sanctuaries: The Case of Iraq, Iran, Somalia and Sudan," Center for Defense Information (Washington, D.C.), 10 December 2001.
18. "Passed Death Sentence on Killers of Aid Workers," official news release, 13 November 2005, from Somaliland government website.
19. James Brandon, "To Fight Al Qaeda, US Troops in Africa Build Schools Instead," *Christian Science Monitor,* 9 January 2006, pp. 1, 4.

20. Bill Gertz, " 'White Man' Training Al Qaida Terrorists in Wilderness Camp near Kenya," *Geostrategy-Direct,* week of 14 December 2004.

21. Chris Thomlinson, AP, "U.S. Backing Somali Militants against Islamic Extremists, *Jacksonville Daily News* (NC), 10 April 2006, p. 3A.

22. Harun Hassan, "Somalia Twists in the Wind," from harowo.com, 13 April 2006, through access@g2-forward.org; "Militia Hunt Al-Qaeda in Somalia," from Agence France Presse, 5 May 2006.

23. Edward Girardet, "Clashes Worsen Somalia Food Crisis As Drought Sets In," *Christian Science Monitor,* 19 April 2006, p. 4.

24. Rob Crilly, "Islamist-Warlord Clashes Hinder Somalia's New Government," *Christian Science Monitor,* 5 June 2006, p. 4.

25. ABC's Nightly News, 5 June 2006.

26. "Somali Islamists Seize Rival Base," *Khartoum Monitor,* 2 June 2006, p. 6.

27. Crilly, "Islamist-Warlord Clashes Hinder Somalia's New Government," p. 4.

28. Chris Thomlinson, "Video Shows Arabs Fighting in Somalia," from AP, 5 July 2006.

29. "Chanting, 'We Don't Want Islamic Courts . . . '," World News in Brief, *Christian Science Monitor,* 7 June 2006, p. 7.

30. "Hundreds of Soldiers from Neighboring Ethiopia Crossed into Somalia," World News in Brief, *Christian Science Monitor,* 19 June 2006, p. 7.

31. Rob Crilly, "Foreign Intervention in Somalia," *Christian Science Monitor,* 21 June 2006, pp. 1, 2.

32. "Ethiopian Troops Lend Aid to Somali Allies," World Briefs Wire Reports, *Jacksonville Daily News* (NC), 21 July 2006, p. 4A.

33. Rob Crilly, "Somalia on the Edge of Full-Scale War," *Christian Science Monitor,* 25 July 2006. p. 7.

34. "Islamic Militia Plans to Seize Somali Base," World Briefs Wire Reports, *Jacksonville Daily News* (NC), 21 July 2006, p. 5A.

35. "Al Qaida Now Controls Somalia," *Geostrategy-Direct,* Middle East Report, 30 June 2006.

36. Hassan, "Somalia Twists in the Wind"; "Militia Hunt Al-Qaeda in Somalia," from Agence France-Presse.

37. Al Qaida Now Controls Somalia."

Chapter 1: *Baseej from North Africa*

1. John Hunwick, "Africa and Islamic Revival: Historical and Contemporary Perspectives," extracted verbatim from MSA News by Univ. of Georgia, p. 7; *Britannica.com,* s.v. "Muslim Brotherhood."

2. *Wikipedia Encyclopedia,* s.v. "Wahhabi" and "Salafi."

3. Stephen E. Hughes, *Warring on Terrorism: A Comprehensive Dispatch Briefing,* Part I, (unpublished work, Soda Springs, ID, 2005), p. 6.

4. Ibid.

5. Ibid.

6. Gunaratna, *Inside al-Qaeda,* p. 153.

7. Ibid., p. 153.

8. Ibid., p. 151.

9. Hunwick, "Africa and Islamic Revival," p. 1.

10. Gunaratna, *Inside al-Qaeda,* p. 158.

11. "Eliminating Terrorist Sanctuaries," Center for Defense Information, 10 December 2001.

12. Gunaratna, *Inside al-Qaeda,* pp. 152, 153; Paul Clammer, *Sudan (*Bucks, England: Bradt Travel Guides Ltd., 2005), p. 37.

13. Samuel P. Huntington, *The Clash of Civilizations and the Remaking of World Order* (London: Simon & Schuster UK, 1997), p. 177; Aaron Mannes, *Profiles in Terror: Guide to Middle East Terror Organizations* (Lanham, MD: Rowman & Littlefield, 2004), p. 22; Hughes, *Warring on Terrorism,* pp. 10, 36; Gunaratna, *Inside al-Qaeda,* p. 139.

14. Ibid.

15. Yossef Bodansky (Director of Research of the Internat. Strategic Studies Assoc. and Congressional Task Force on Terrorism and Unconventional Warfare), *Offensive in the Balkans* (Alexandria, VA: Internat. Media Corp., 1995), chapt. 8, pp. 71-78, from "In Bosnia the West . . . Took the Side of . . . Fundamentalist Islam," at the Serbian Network website, www.srpska-mzeza.com; excerpt from (Israeli Project for the Research of Islamist Movements website, www.e-prism.org, in "The State Sponsorship of the Islamic Terrorist Network," by Stephen E. Hughes (unpublished study, Salt Lake City, 2003).

16. Ibid.

17. Hughes, *Warring on Terrorism,* p. 36.

18. Aaron Mannes, *Profiles in Terror: Guide to Middle East Terror Organizations* (Lanham, MD: Rowman & Littlefield, 2004), p. 22.

19. "Al-Qaeda's New Front," PBS's *Frontline,* NC Public TV, 25 January 2005.

20. Bodansky, *Offensive in the Balkans,* pp. 71-78.

21. "National Islamic Front" and "Hassan al-Turabi," *Who's Who: Significant People and Organizations,* Sudan Update (West Yorkshire, England), from its website, www.sudanupdate.org. (These works will henceforth be cited as "National Islamic Front" and "Hassan al-Turabi.")

22. Hunwick, "Africa and Islamic Revival," p. 8; "National Islamic Front."

23. Dr. Mohammed Mahmoud, Tufts Univ., "Islam and Islamization in Sudan: The Islamic National Front," from *Religion, Nationalism, and Peace in Sudan* (paper presented at U.S. Inst. of Peace Conference, 16-17 September 1997), p. 4.

24. Kenneth Katzman, *Warriors of Islam: Iran's Revolutionary Guard* (Boulder, CO: Westview Press, 1993), pp. 82-84.

25. H. John Poole, *Tactics of the Crescent Moon: Militant Muslim Combat Methods* (Emerald Isle, NC: Posterity Press, 2004), p. 187.

26. "Muslims," PBS's *Frontline,* 120 min. (Wellspring, n.d.), DVD #WSP757.

27. Ali Jalali and Lester W. Grau, *Afghan Guerrilla Warfare: In the Words of the Mujahideen Fighters* (St. Paul, MN: MBI Publishing, 2001), first published as *The Other Side of the Mountain* (Quantico, VA: Marine Corps Combat Development Cmd., 1995), p. 409.

28. John L. Esposito, *Unholy War: Terror in the Name of Islam* (London: Oxford Univ. Press, 2002), pp. 15-17.

29. Robin Batty and David Hoffman, "Afghanistan: Crisis of Impunity," *Human Rights Watch,* vol. 13, no. 3(c), July 2001, p. 28.

30. Ramit Plushnick-Masti, AP, "Militant Groups Join Forces, Get Hezbollah Help," *Jacksonville Daily News* (NC), 28 October 2003, p. 1A; Jason Keyser, AP, "Israel Bombs Syria," *Jacksonville Daily News* (NC), 6 October 2003; *Patterns of Global Terrorism, 2002* (Washington, D.C.: U.S. Dept. of State, April 2003), s.v. "Popular Front for the Liberation of Palestine–General Command (PFLP-GC)."

31. Ibid.

32. Ibid.

33. Abdul Hussein al-Obeidi, AP, "Holy City Najaf Fighting Worst Since Saddam Fell," *Jacksonville Daily News* (NC), 7 August 2004, pp. 1A, 4A.

34. C.J. Chivers, "Threats and Responses . . . ," *New York Times,* 13 January 2003, and "Here Is the Kurdish Al-Qaeda," *Financial Times Information,* 7 January 2003, in "Iraqi Wahhabi Factions Affiliated with Abu Musaab al Zarqawi," by Deanna Linder, Rachael Levy, and Yael Shahar, Internat. Policy Inst. for Counter-Terrorism, November 2004; Michael Rubin, "Ansar al-Sunna: Iraq's New Terrorist Threat," *Middle East Intelligence Bulletin,* vol. 6, no. 5, May 2004; "Translation of Ansar al-Sunna Army's 'Banners of Truth' Video," TIDES World Press Reports, in "Ansar al-Sunna," by Rubin; "Hizbullah Suspected of Joining Sunni Insurgents," *Iraqi News,* 17 February 2005.

35. "Shiite Radicals Join with Sunni Insurgents in Ramadi," *DEBKAfile,* 7 April 2004.

36. Huntington, *The Clash of Civilizations and the Remaking of World Order,* p. 176; Musharraf, "Speech at OIC Conference," *World Report,* CNN, 31 May 2005; Makhdoom Babar, "President Envisages Vibrant OIC to Face New Challenges," *Daily Mail* (Islamabad), 30 May 2005, pp. 1, 5.

37. Gunaratna, *Inside al-Qaeda,* pp. 158, 159.

38. Mannes, *Profiles in Terror,* p. 22; Huntington, *The Clash of Civilizations and the Remaking of World Order,* p. 176.

39. Gunaratna, *Inside al-Qaeda,* p. 31.

40. "Al-Qaeda's New Front."

41. Gunaratna, *Inside al-Qaeda,* p. 100.

42. Esposito, *Unholy War,* p. 10.

43. Bodansky, *Offensive in the Balkans,* p. 40.

44. Chris Suellentrop, "Abdullah Azzam—The Godfather of Jihad," slate.msn.com; Esposito, *Unholy War,* pp. 7, 94, 95; *Encyclopedia.com,* s.v. "Muslim Brotherhood."

45. Neamatollah Nojumi, *The Rise of the Taliban in Afghanistan: Mass Mobilization, Civil War, and the Future of the Region* (New York: Palgrave, 2002), p. 85.

46. Edgar O'Ballance, *Afghan Wars: Battles in a Hostile Land, 1839 to Present* (Karachi: Oxford Univ. Press, 2002), pp. 16, 131; Nojumi, *The Rise of the Taliban in Afghanistan,* pp. 101, 189.

47. Ibid.

48. Amir Mir, *The True Face of Jihadis* (Lahore: Maktaba Jadeed Press, 2004), p. 104.

49. Excerpt from the (Israeli) Project for the Research of Islamist Movements' website, www.e-prism.org, in "The State Sponsorship of the Islamic Terrorist Network," by Stephen E. Hughes (unpublished study, Salt Lake City, 2003).

50. Huntington, *The Clash of Civilizations and the Remaking of World Order,* p. 189; *Sudan Country Study,* DA PAM 550-27, Area Handbook Series (Washington, D.C.: Hdqts. Dept. of the Army, 1992), p. 260; "China Puts 700,000 Troops on Alert in Sudan," newsmax.com (West Palm Beach, FL), 27 August 2000; Bill Gertz, "Notes from the Pentagon," *Washington Times,* 5 March 2004.

51. "Iran Shifting Its Attention . . . ," *New York Times,* 13 December 1991, p. A7.

52. Mannes, *Profiles in Terror,* p. 21.

53. Interview, U.S. intelligence community, February 2000, in *Inside al-Qaeda,* by Rohan Gunaratna, p. 158.

54. Gunaratna, *Inside al-Qaeda,* p. 158.

55. Ibid., pp. 154, 158.

56. Ibid., p. 159.

57. *Wikipedia Encyclopedia,* s.v. "Foreign Relations of Sudan."

58. Huntington, *The Clash of Civilizations and the Remaking of World Order,* p. 177; Katzman, *Warriors of Islam,* p. 177.
59. Ibid.; Esposito, *Unholy War,* p. 10.
60. Ibid., p. 7.
61. Azzam, as quoted in *Unholy War,* by Esposito, p. 7.
62. *Wikipedia Encyclopedia,* s.v. "Foreign Relations of Sudan."
63. *Sudan Country Study,* DA PAM 550-27, p. 262.
64. Paul Clammer, *Sudan* (Bucks, England: Bradt Travel Guides Ltd., 2005), pp. 37, 38; *Wikipedia Encyclopedia,* s.v. "Foreign Relations of Sudan"; Michael Koma, "Sorry, Madam Teny," *Khartoum Monitor,* 31 May 2006, p. 3.
65. Clammer, *Sudan,* p. 37.
66. Ibid., p. 38.
67. Azam S. Ahmed, "Analysis: What Next in Darfur," UPI, 9 June 2005.
68. "Sudan, Eritrea Discuss Eastern Conflict," *Sudan Tribune,* 12 June 2006.
69. Ibid.
70. Huntington, *The Clash of Civilizations and the Remaking of World Order,* p. 137.
71. McLaughlin, "Tensions Rise in the Horn of Africa," *Christian Science Monitor,* 20 October 2005, p. 6.
72. Abraham McLaughlin, "Africa Wary of New Border War," *Christian Science Monitor,* 27 December 2005, p. 6; Mohamed Sheikh Nor, AP, "Mysterious Plane Lands in Somalia," *Jacksonville Daily News* (NC), 27 July 2006, p. 5A.
73. "Worries That the Powerful Muslim Militia . . . ," World News in Brief, *Christian Science Monitor,* 24 August 2006, p. 7.
74. Katherine Shrader, AP, "Search for bin Laden Continues along Border," *Jacksonville Daily News* (NC), 24 April 2006, p. 1A.
75. Simon Robinson and Daniel Pepper/Tawila, "The Front Lines of Genocide," *Time,* 8 May 2006, p. 45; ABC's Morning News, 28 April 2006.
76. ABC's Nightly News, 28 April 2006.

Chapter 2: *Bilad as-Sudan*

1. Clammer, *Sudan,* p. 3.
2. Memo for the record from H.J. Poole.
3. Huntington, *The Clash of Civilizations and the Remaking of World Order,* p. 137; Clammer, *Sudan.*
4. Baptist Stanislaus, "There Is a Lot of Money in this Country," *Khartoum Monitor,* 31 May 2006, p. 5.
5. Gunaratna, *Inside al-Qaeda,* p. 159; *Wikipedia Encyclopedia,* s.v. "Carlos (Ilich Ramírez Sánchez)."

6. Watts Roba Gibia Nyirigwa, "Why 2011 Referendum Is the Only Hope for South Sudanese: Part One," *Khartoum Monitor,* 31 May 2006, p. 5; *Wikipedia Encyclopedia,* s.v. "National Congress (Sudan)"; "Sudan Unity Requires Secular State," *Khartoum Monitor,* 1 June 2006, p. 4.

7. U.N. Mission in Sudan website, unmis.org, s.v. "Political Parties."

8. Ibid., s.v. "Hassan al-Turabi."

9. "Sudan's Turabi Calls for Popular Uprising," *Sudan Tribune,* 19 May 2006.

10. *Wikipedia Encyclopedia,* s.v. "Hassan al-Turabi."

11. "Sudan's Turabi Calls for Popular Uprising."

12. H. John Poole, *Militant Tricks: Battlefield Ruses of the Islamic Insurgent* (Emerald Isle, NC: Posterity Press, 2005), pp. 91-93, 120-124.

13. Memo for the record from H.J. Poole.

14. *Wikipedia Encyclopedia,* s.v. "History of Sudan"; "South Sudan Leader Defends Aid to Ugandan Rebel LRA," *Sudan Vision,* 31 May 2006, p. 1.

15. "Sudan Ex-Rebels Show Unity with Khartoum Despite Differences," *Sudan Vision,* 31 May 2006, p. 2.

16. "NCP-SPLM Partners Proposed Four Options to the Abyei Issue," *Sudan Vision,* 31 May 2006, p. 4.

17. Watts Roba Gibia Nyirigwa, "Why 2011 Referendum Is the Only Hope for South Sudanese: Part Two," *Khartoum Monitor,* 1 June 2006, p. 5.

18. "Sudan: Disagreements over Implementation of Peace Accord," from IRIN (Nairobi), *The Citizen* (Khartoum), 1 June 2006, p. 4.

19. "SPLM Demands Construction of Oil Refinery in the South," *Sudan Tribune,* 31 May 2006, p. 2.

20. *Wikipedia Encyclopedia,* s.v. "History of Sudan."

21. Nyirigwa, "Why 2011 Referendum Is the Only Hope for South Sudanese: Part One," p. 5; *Wikipedia Encyclopedia,* s.v. "United Nations Mission in Sudan."

22. "NCP-SPLM Partners Proposed Four Options to the Abyei Issue," p. 4.

23. *Wikipedia Encyclopedia,* s.v. "List of Political Parties in Sudan."

24. Michael Koma, "Sorry, Madam Teny," *Khartoum Monitor,* 31 May 2006, p. 3.

25. "LRA Attacks Village Killing One," *Khartoum Monitor,* 1 June 2006, p. 1.

26. "South Sudan Leader Defends Aid to Ugandan Rebel LRA," *Sudan Vision,* 31 May 2006, p. 1.

27. Nyirigwa, "Why 2011 Referendum Is the Only Hope for South Sudanese: Part One," p. 5.

28. John Lemi Stephen, "The NCP/SPLM Took a Bold Step," *Sudan Tribune*, p. 5; Nyirigwa, "Why 2011 Referendum Is the Only Hope for South Sudanese: Part One," p. 5.

29. Memo for the record from H.J. Poole.

30. Hotel car driver in Khartoum, in conversation with author on 1 June 2006.

31. Memo for the record from H.J. Poole.

32. "The Four Feathers," by A.E.W. Mason, directed by Alexander Korda (Samuel Goldwyn Co., 1939), technicolor film.

33. "Darfur's Peace Plan: the View from the Ground," *Sudan Tribune*, 31 May 2006, p. 12; "Sudan Signs Off on Darfur Peace Plan, Will the Rebels," from Reuters and AP, *Christian Science Monitor*, 1 May 2006, p. 4.

34. "New Concessions Designed to Appeal to Darfur Rebels," World News in Brief, *Christian Science Monitor*, 4 May 2006, p. 7; "Darfur Rebels Face Deal Deadline," *Khartoum Monitor*, 1 June 2006, p. 1.

35. "Government, Main Rebels Sign Pace Accord in Nigeria," World Briefs Wire Reports, *Christian Science Monitor*, 6 May 2006, p. 5.

36. Katherine Houreld and Claire Soares, "Next Steps to Peace in Darfur," *Christian Science Monitor*, 8 May 2006, pp. 1, 11.

37. *Wikipedia Encyclopedia*, s.v. "Justice and Equality Movement."

38. "Darfur's Peace Plan: the View from the Ground," p. 12.

39. Ibid.

40. "Al-Qaida Deputy Al-Zawahiri Calls for Holy War in Darfur," *Sudan Tribune*, 10 June 2006.

41. "Darfur's Peace Plan: the View from the Ground," p. 12.

42. Abraham McLaughlin and Claire Soares, "Oil Wealth and Corruption at Play in Chad's Rebellion," *Christian Science Monitor*, 21 April 2006, p. 6.

43. "Sudan Arrested Chadian Rebel to Support of His Rival," *Khartoum Monitor*, 1 June 2006, p. 1.

44. "China Winning Resources and Loyalties of Africa," *The Financial Times* (UK), 28 February 2006.

45. "Drought Management, an Alternative Solution to Darfur's Armed Conflicts," *Sudan Tribune*, 1 June 2006, p. 5.

46. *Wikipedia Encyclopedia*, s.v. "United Nations Mission in Sudan."

47. Ibid., s.v. "History of Sudan."

48. "China Puts 700,000 Troops on Alert in Sudan," newsmax.com (West Palm Beach, FL), 27 August 2000.

49. Bill Gertz, "Notes from the Pentagon," *Washington Times*, 5 March 2004.

50. "China Winning Resources and Loyalties of Africa."

51. NPR Morning News, 1 May 2006.

52. "China Winning Resources and Loyalties of Africa."

53. Longtime owner of Khartoum hotel, in conversation with author on 31 May 2006.

54. Hotel car driver in Khartoum, in conversation with author on 1 June 2006.

55. Longtime owner of Khartoum hotel.

56. "China Praises Achievements of Sudan's National Congress Party," from Xinhua, *Peoples Daily on Line*, 24 November 2005.

57. "China to Construct 25 Locomotives for Sudan," *Sudan Tribune,* 10 June 2006.

58. "China Winning Resources and Loyalties of Africa"; Andrew Jeffrey, "Lifeline to Angola's Future," BBC News, 16 December 2004.

59. Chinese senior citizen (victim of class relocation period), in conversation with author in 2001.

60. Terry Leonard, AP, "Africa Looks to China for Help Financially, Politically," *Casper Star Tribune,* 10 August 2006.

61. "Zimbabwe: Shadows and Lies," *Frontline/World,* NC Public TV, 27 June 2006; "SA Favors Stability over Democracy in Zimbabwe," *The Egyptian Gazette,* 29 May 2006, p. 4.

62. *Wikipedia Encyclopedia,* s.v. "African National Congress."

63. South African lawyer who had been working in England, in conversation with author on 3 June 2006.

64. "SA, Sudan Hopeful Darfur Peace Deal Will Last," *Sudan Vision,* 31 May 2006, p. 1.

65. "SA to Sign Treaty with Sudan," *Sudan Vision,* 31 May 2006, p. 2.

66. Ibid.

67. Michael Wines, "In South Africa, Democracy May Breed One-Party Rule," *New York Times,* 14 April 2004.

68. Rachel L. Swarns, "Disillusion Rises Among South Africa's Poor," *New York Times,* 31 December 2002.

69. Sarah Hudleston, "South Africa: Racism under the Colour of Law Enforcement," *Business Day* (Johannesburg), n.d., as republished in *Sudan Vision,* 31 May 2006, p. 10.

70. South African lawyer.

71. "Sudan Suspends All U.N. Mission Work in Darfur," *Sudan Tribune,* 25 June 2006.

Chapter 3: *Levant Passage*

1. ExO or CO of 2d Battalion, 7th Marines, in conversation with author during training evolution of 14, 15 January 2005.

2. "Iraqi Medicines on the Black Market," Radio Free Iraq, 8 September 2000, through KurdishMedia.com.

3. "Hezbollah Fighters Said to Be in Iraq," *World Net Daily* (Medford, OR), 21 June 2004, through www.intelmessages.org.

4. "Hamas Army Recruited Thousands for Holy War to Destroy Israel," *World Tribune* (Springfield, VA), 7 March 2006.

5. Sam Ghattas, AP, "Israel Unleashes More Military Power in Lebanon," AOL News, 13 July 2006.

6. Memo for the record from H.J. Poole.

7. Christopher Dickey, Kevin Peraino, and Babak Dehghanpisheh, "The Hand That Feeds the Fire," *Newsweek,* 24 July 2006, p. 29.

8. ABC's Nightly News, 26 January 2006.

9. Peter Baker (*Washington Post* leader), on PBS's *Washington Week in Review,* NC Public TV, 27 January 2005.

10. ABC's Morning News, 23 or 24 January 2006.

11. Lee Glendinning, "The Secret World of Palestinian Tunnels," *Times Online* (UK), 27 June 2006.

12. ABC's Morning News, 12 July 2006.

13. Christopher Dickey and Babak Dehghanpisheh, "Torn to Shreds," *Newsweek,* 31 July 2006, p 24; Barry Schweid, AP, "Plan to Help Train Lebanese Army Approved," *Jacksonville Daily News* (NC), 4 August 2006, p. 8A.

14. Kevin Peraino, Babak Dehghanpisheh, and Christopher Dickey, "Eye for an Eye," *Newsweek,* 14 August 2006, p. 23; Steven R. Hurst, AP, "Israelis Isolating Lebanon," *Jacksonville Daily News* (NC), 5 August 2006, pp. 1A, 5A; ABC's Morning News, 12 August 2006.

15. Aron Heller, AP, "Hezbollah, Israel Step Up Attacks," *Jacksonville Daily News* (NC), 7 August 2006, pp. 1A, 2A; "Iran Provides Hizbullah High-Tech Surveillance . . . ," *Geostrategy-Direct,* 19 April 2006.

16. Abraham Rabinovich, "Militants Seen As Able to Hit Tel Aviv," *Washington Times,* 18 July 2006.

17. Sam Ghattas, AP, "Nine Israeli Soldiers Killed in Fighting in South Lebanon," *Jacksonville Daily News* (NC), 27 July 2006, pp. 1A, 2A.

18. Ibid.; ABC's Nightly News, 18-20 July 2006.

19. ABC's Nightly News, 28 July 2006.

20. Ibid.

21. Embassy World, s.v. "Embassy Listings for North Korea," from its website, www.embassyworld.com; British private website, http://uk.geocities.com/hkgalbert/kpdo.htm.

22. Ghattas, AP, "Nine Israeli Soldiers Killed in Fighting in South Lebanon," pp. 1A, 2A.

23. Hala Jaber, "Hezbollah: We've Planned This for 6 Years," *The Sunday Times* (London), 30 July 2006.

24. Hamza Hendawi, "Israel Hits Beirut; Hezbollah Rockets Israel," from AP, 3 August 2006.

25. "Hizbullah Using Tunnels, Bunkers to Frustrate Israelis' Advance," *World Tribune* (Springfield, VA), 7 August 2006.
26. Ibid.
27. Nicholas Blanford, Daniel McGrory, and Stephen Farrell, "Tactics That Have Kept the Middle East's Most Powerful Army at Bay," *The Times* (UK), 10 August 2006.
28. Peraino, Dehghanpisheh, and Dickey, "Eye for an Eye," p. 22; Ravi Nessman, AP, "Israelis Step Up Offensive," *Jacksonville Daily News* (NC), 10 August 2006, p. 2A.
29. Blanford, McGrory, and Farrell, "Tactics That Have Kept the Middle East's Most Powerful Army at Bay."
30. Edward Cody and Molly Moore, "Analysts Attribute Hezbollah's Resilience to Zeal, Secrecy and Iranian Funding," *Washington Post*, 14 August 2006.
31. Nicholas Blanford, "Hizbullah's Resilience Built on Years of Homework," *Christian Science Monitor*, 11 August 2006, p. 4.
32. Scott Peterson, "Unresolved: Disarming Hizbullah," *Christian Science Monitor*, 15 August 2006, pp. 1, 10.
33. Steven R. Hurst, AP, "Mideast Cease-Fire Holds," *Jacksonville Daily News* (NC), 15 August 2006, p. 2A.
34. ABC's Morning News, 18 August 2006.
35. Peterson, "Unresolved: Disarming Hizbullah," pp. 1, 10.
36. Sam F. Ghattas, AP, "Israelis Step Up Withdrawal," *Jacksonville Daily News* (NC), 18 August 2006, pp. 1A, 5A.
37. Lauren Frayer, AP, "Lebanese Army Moves In," *Jacksonville Daily News* (NC), 18 August 2006, pp. 1A, 2A.
38. "Strong Sentiment," caption for front page photograph, *Jacksonville Daily News* (NC), 18 August 2006.

Chapter 4: *Euphrates Pipeline*

1. Andrew and Leslie Cockburn, *One Point Safe* (New York: Doubleday, 1997), pp. 202, 214, 223.
2. Ibid., pp. 210-212.
3. Ibid., p. 214.
4. Lee Keath, AP, "Chaos Grips Iraq," *Jacksonville Daily News* (NC), 10 April 2004, p. 5A.
5. Jim Krane, AP, "Occupied, Not Subdued," *Jacksonville Daily News* (NC), 14 November 2004, pp. 1A, 9A.
6. Tini Tran, AP, "Insurgents Hit Mosul Police Stations," *Jacksonville Daily News* (NC), 15 November 2004, p. 1A.
7. NPR's Morning News, 15 November 2004.

8. H. John Poole, *The Tiger's Way: A U.S. Private's Best Chance of Survival* (Emerald Isle, NC: Posterity Press, 2003), pp. 116-124.

9. "Iraq Arrests 17 Suspected Antiquity Smugglers," from Xinhua, *People's Daily Online* (China), 2 August 2005.

10. "Iraqi Medicines on the Black Market," Radio Free Iraq, 8 September 2000.

11. Ibid.

12. "Iraqi Resistance Report for . . . 28 February 2005," trans. and compiled by Muhammad Abu Nasr, member, editorial board, the Free Arab Voice, from www.albasrah.net. (This work will henceforth be cited as "Iraqi Resistance Report.")

13. Abdul-Ahad Ghaith, "Outside Iraq but Deep in the Fight: A Smuggler of Insurgents. . . ," *Washington Post,* 8 June 2005, p. AO1.

14. Ibid.

15. "Marines Unearth Weapons Caches; Tipsters Lead Troops to More Caches," from Armed Forces Press Service, *Camp Lejeune Globe* (NC), 5 January, 2006, p. 1A.

16. Mariam Fam, "U.S. Troops Raid Iraqi Smuggling Ring," from AP, 12 April 2005; CBS's News on Line, 12 April 2005.

17. Mohammed Barakat, AP, "U.S. Wraps Up Offensive near Syrian Border," *Jacksonville Daily News* (NC), 15 May 2005, p. 4A.

18. "Hunt for Insurgents near Syria Ends," CNN, 14 May 2005.

19. Ibid.; "100 Militants Killed in Iraq," CBS News on Line, 9 May 2005; Charles Recknagel, "Iraq: U.S. Forces Attacking Insurgents in West Face Well-Trained Foe," Radio Free Europe/Radio Liberty, 11 May 2005; "Seven killed in Baghdad bombings," *Middle East On Line* (London), 10 May 2005.

20. Rick Jervis, "Iraqi Insurgents Take U.S. Troops by Surprise," *USA Today,* 5 October 2005.

21. Charles Recknagel, "Iraq: U.S. Forces Attacking Insurgents in West Face Well-Trained Foe," Radio Free Europe/Radio Liberty, 11 May 2005.

22. Jervis, "Iraqi Insurgents Take U.S. Troops by Surprise."

23. Enlisted member of 3d Battalion, 2d Marines (Anbar Province veteran), in conversation with author on 22 March 2006.

24. Bill Roggio, "Steel Curtain Update: Slugging it out in Ubaydi," *Threats Watch,* 15 November 2005.

25. "Iraqi Resistance Report."

26. Joseph L. Galloway, "U.S. Won't Quickly Change a Thousand Years of Tradition in Iraq," Knight Ridder, 11 January 2006.

27. J.B. Sameer, *As Qurans Burn: Ideas & Identities of India Pakistan,* "#60," 23 April 2003, from website, www.chowk.com.

28. John Grant, "Deja-vu in Baghdad," Iraqi Water Project Press Update, December 2003.

29. Jacob Silberberg, AP, "Iraqi, U.S. Troops Hit Insurgent Stronghold," *Jacksonville Daily News* (NC), 11 September 2005, p. 7A.

30. Jacob Silberberg, AP, "Militants Flee Tal Afar in Wake of U.S.-Iraqi Offensive," *Jacksonville Daily News* (NC), 12 September 2005, p. 3A.

31. CBS's "60 Minutes," 12 March 2006.

32. "The Insurgency," PBS's *Frontline,* NC Public TV, 21 February and 24 April 2006.

33. Dan Murphy, "Iraq's Foreign Fighters: Few But Deadly," *Christian Science Monitor,* 27 September 2005, pp. 1, 10; "The Insurgency," PBS's *Frontline.*

34. Ibid.

35. Galloway, "U.S. Won't Quickly Change a Thousand Years of Tradition in Iraq."

36. Bill Roggio, "River Gates," *The Fourth Rail,* 6 October 2005.

37. Ron Harris, St. Louis Post-Dispatch, "Marines Return to Violent City," *Jacksonville (NC) Daily News* (NC), 19 April 2004, p. 5A.

38. Ron Harris, St. Louis Post-Dispatch, "5 Marines, Scores of Iraqis Die in Battle," *Jacksonville Daily News* (NC), 18 April 2004, p. 4A; company commander in 3d Battalion, 7th Marines, in conversation with author during training session of 15, 16 January 2005.

39. Scott Peterson, "New Iraq Strategy: Stay in Hot Spots," *Christian Science Monitor,* 23 November 2005, pp. 1, 10; Robert H. Reid, AP, "Suicide Bomber Kills 21 after Drawing Police to Scene," *Jacksonville Daily News* (NC), 23 November 2005, p. 10A.

40. Roggio, "Steel Curtain Update."

41. Jacob Silberberg, AP, "Troops Press Fight," *Jacksonville Daily News* (NC), 19 June 2005, pp. 1A, 2A.

42. Peterson, "New Iraq Strategy," pp. 1, 10.

43. Jill Carrol, "Marines Assault Rebel Border Town," *Christian Science Monitor,* 3 October 2005, pp. 6, 7.

44. Ibid.

45. Robert H. Reid, AP, "U.S.-Iraqi Operation Takes Aim at Car Bomb Builders," *Jacksonville Daily News* (NC), 1 December 2005, p. 8A.

46. Charles Crain, "Counterinsurgency Strategy: Staying Put," *Christian Science Monitor,* 7 June 2006, p. 6; Barakat, "U.S. Wraps Up Offensive near Syrian Border," p. 4A.

47. Crain, "Counterinsurgency Strategy," p. 6; Carrol, "Marines Assault Rebel Border Town," p. 6.

48. Robert H. Reid, AP, "5 Marines Die in Iraq Fighting," *Jacksonville Daily News* (NC), 17 November 2005, pp. 1A, 2A.

49. Peterson, "New Iraq Strategy," pp. 1, 10.

50. Robert H. Reid, AP, "5 Marines Die in Iraq Fighting," pp. 1A, 2A.

51. Jill Carroll, "Next Job: Keeping Rebels Out," *Christian Science Monitor,* 21 November 2005, p. 6.

52. Ibid., pp. 5, 6.
53. Crain, "Counterinsurgency Strategy," p. 6.
54. Robert H. Reid and Jim Krane, AP, "Bombs Biggest Killer for U.S. in Iraq," *Jacksonville Daily News* (NC), 7 August 2005, pp. 1A, 4A; ABC's Nightly News, 3 August 2005; Lee Hockstader, "Israeli Army Suffers Pair of Sharp Blows," *International Herald Tribune,* 16 February 2002, reprinted from *Washington Post,* n.d.
55. "Attacks on Rise As Iraqis View Constitution," from AP, *Jacksonville Daily News* (NC), 7 October 2005. p. 4A.
56. Bill Roggio, "The Islamic Republic of Haditha," *The Fourth Rail,* 24 August 2005; NCO of 3d Battalion, 2d Marines, in conversation with author during training session of March 2006.
57. C.J. Chivers, "Threats and Responses . . . ," *New York Times,* 13 January 2003, and "Here Is the Kurdish Al-Qaeda," *Financial Times Information,* 7 January 2003, in "Iraqi Wahhabi Factions Affiliated with Abu Musaab al Zarqawi," by Deanna Linder, Rachael Levy, and Yael Shahar, Internat. Policy Inst. for Counter-Terrorism, November 2004; Michael Rubin, "Ansar al-Sunna: Iraq's New Terrorist Threat," *Middle East Intelligence Bulletin,* vol. 6, no. 5, May 2004; "Translation of Ansar al-Sunna Army's 'Banners of Truth' Video," TIDES World Press Reports, in "Ansar al-Sunna," by Rubin; "Hizbullah Suspected of Joining Sunni Insurgents," *Iraqi News,* 17 February 2005, from www.iraqinews.com.
58. Christian Lowe, "Ramadi Killings Not the Only Sniper Losses," *Times* (UK), 12 June 2006.
59. Roggio, "The Islamic Republic of Haditha?"
60. Cpl. Michael R. McMaugh (photographer), caption with picture #051227-M-8530M-015, 2d Marine Division release, 27 December 2005.
61. Antonio Castaneda. AP, "Iraqi Troops to Secure Deadly City." *Jacksonville Daily News* (NC), 27 October 2005, p. 4A.
62. Peterson, "New Iraq Strategy," pp. 1, 10.
63. Dan Murphy, "In Iraq with 'Reservists That Fight'," *Christian Science Monitor,* 24 March 2005, p. 4.
64. "Iraq, U.S. Operate near Syria (Operation Koa Canyon)," *Middle East Newsline,* 22 January 2006; "Iraq Soldiers, U.S. Marines Take Insurgents by Storm," by L.Cpl. Peter R. Miller, *Camp Lejeune Globe* (NC), 2 February 2006, p. 7A.
65. Ibid.
66. "Operation Koa Canyon Update," by Maj. Eric Dent, 2d Marine Division Press Release #0123-06-1004, 23 January 2006.
67. Michael Ware, "The View from the Front Lines," *Time,* 5 December 2005, pp. 44, 45.
68. Bill Roggio, "Ramadi: North, South, East and West, and Operation Panther," *Threats Watch,* 17 November 2005; "Lejeune Marines Find Weapons near Ramadi," News Briefs Wire Reports (AP), *Jacksonville Daily News* (NC), 17 January 2006, p. 3A.

69. "Lejeune Marines Stay Busy Finding Weapons Caches," by Cpl. Joseph DiGirolamo, *Camp Lejeune Globe* (NC), 27 April 2006, p. 10A; Antonio Castaneda, AP, "Troops Meet Little Resistance," *Jacksonville Daily News* (NC), 19 June 2006, p. 4A; Antonio Castaneda, AP, "American, Iraqi Forces Muscle Way into Eastern Ramadi," *Jacksonville Daily News* (NC), 20 June 2006, p. 4A.

70. Todd Pitman, AP, "Lejeune Marines Repulse Assault," *Jacksonville Daily News* (NC), 18 April 2006, pp. 1A, 2A.

71. Todd Pitman, AP, "Don't Stop, They'll Shoot," *Jacksonville Daily News* (NC), 24 April 2006, p. 2A; "Insurgents Still a Major Force in Ramadi," access@g2-forward.org, 23 May 2006.

72. Ellen Knickmeyer, "U.S. Will Reinforce Troops in West Iraq," *Washington Post,* 29 May 2006; Pamela Hess, "Ramadi Poses Tactical Challenge for U.S.," UPI, 30 May 2006.

73. Alex Rodriguez, "Retaking Ramadi, 1 District at a Time," *Chicago Tribune,* 9 July 2006.

74. Ibid.

75. Silberberg, "Troops Press Fight," pp. 1A, 2A.

76. CBS's News on Line, 12 April 2005.

77. Barakat, "U.S. Wraps Up Offensive near Syrian Border," p. 4A.

78. Carrol, "Marines Assault Rebel Border Town," pp. 6, 7.

79. Bill Roggio, "Operation Steel Curtain Continues," *Threats Watch,* 18 November 2005.

80. Bill Roggio, "The Anbar Campaign Revisited," *The Fourth Rail,* 8 August 2005.

81. Peterson, "New Iraq Strategy," pp. 1, 10.

82. Jeff (member of 3rd Battalion, 1st Marine Regiment), in widely circulated internet newsletter of 17 December 2005.

83. Ibid.

84. "Operation Red Bull Disrupts Terrorism in Triad Area," by Cpl. Adam C. Schnell, 2d Marine Division Story Identification #20061822216, 9 January 2006.

85. "Combat Engineers Unearth More Than 500 Weapons Cache[s], Save Lives in Iraq," by Cpl. Adam C. Schnell, *Camp Lejeune Globe* (NC), 30 March 2006, p. 11A.

86. Robert H. Reid, AP, "19 Iraqi Soldiers Killed by Roadside Bomb, Ambush," *Jacksonville Daily News* (NC), 4 December 2005, pp. 1A, 4A.

87. Robert Burns, AP, "Blast Kills 10 Marines in Iraq," *Jacksonville Daily News* (NC), 3 December 2005, pp. 1A, 4A; ABC's Morning News, 3 December 2005.

88. ABC's Nightly News, 24 November 2004.

89. NPR's Morning News, 15 November 2004.

90. Krane, "Occupied, Not Subdued," pp. 1A, 9A.

91. Tran, "Insurgents Hit Mosul Police Stations," p. 1A.

92. NPR's Morning News, 15 November 2004.

93. Scott Peterson, "Marine, Insurgent Tactics Evolve," *Christian Science Monitor,* 17 November 2004, p. 6.

94. Murphy, "In Iraq with 'Reservists That Fight'," p. 4.

95. Antonio Castaneda, AP, "Marines Capture Weapons in Iraq," *Jacksonville Daily News* (NC), 5 June 2005, p. 1A.

96. Davis, 2dLt. Joseph W. (member of 1st Battalion, 6th Marines and Iraq veteran), in conversation with author on 15 December 2005.

97. Reid, "5 Marines Die in Iraq Fighting," pp. 1A, 2A.

98. NPR's Morning News, 3 April 2005; ABC's Nightly News, 5 April 2005; "Abu Ghraib Attack," CENTCOM news release, 6 April 2005.

99. Steven R. Hurst, AP, "Iraq Violence Limited to 3 Provinces, U.S. Says," *Jacksonville Daily News* (NC), 24 March 2006, p. 5A.

100. "Insurgents Using New Advanced Russian RPG from Iran," *World Tribune* (Springfield, VA), 11 May 2006.

101. *Wikipedia Encyclopedia,* s.v. "RPG-29."

102. "Insurgents Using New Advanced Russian RPG from Iran."

Chapter 5: *The Ongoing War in Iraq*

1. Jalal Muhammad, "Hizb al-Khatf," *Al-Majalla,* 20 April 1988, from "Islamism in Lebanon: A Guide," by A. Nizar Hamzeh, in *Middle East Quarterly,* vol. 1, no. 3, September 1997.

2. Robert H. Reid, AP, "Iran Demands British Withdraw," *Jacksonville Daily News* (NC), 18 February 2006, p. 6A.

3. ABC's Morning News, 14 December 2006.

4. Sami Moubayed, "In Iraq, Chaos by Another Name," *Asia Times Online,* 3 May 2006; Michael Hastings, "The Death Squad War," *Newsweek,* 27 February 2006, p. 44; Robert H. Reid, AP, "5 Marines Die in Iraqi Fighting," *Jacksonville Daily News* (NC), 17 November 2006, pp. 1A, 2A.

5. Robert H. Reid, AP, "Ex-Prime Minister: Iraqi Abuses As Bad As Saddam," *Jacksonville Daily News* (NC), 28 November 2005, p. 6A.

6. Sam Knight, "Al-Askariya Shrine: 'Not just a Major Cathedral'," *Times on Line* (UK), 22 February 2006.

7. Robert H. Reid, AP, "Curfews Ordered in Iraq," *Jacksonville Daily News* (NC), 24 February 2006, pp. 1A, 2A; Dan Murphy, "Iraqi Leaders Sidestep All-Out Civil War," *Christian Science Monitor,* 27 February 2006, pp. 1, 11; Aparisim Ghosh, "An Eye for an Eye," *Time,* 6 March 2006, pp. 16-21; Steven R. Hurst, AP, "Death Toll Rises after Curfew Ends in Iraqi Capital," *Jacksonville Daily News* (NC), 1 March 2006, p. 5A; ABC's Morning News, 1 March 2006.

8. Aparisim Ghosh and Christopher Allbritton, "The Wild Card," *Time,* 6 March 2006, pp. 22, 23.

9. Ibid.

10. Alexandra Zavis, AP, "Security Measures Don't Halt Violence," *Jacksonville Daily News* (NC), 27 February 2006, pp. 1A, 2A.

11. Babak Dehghanpisheh, Michael Hastings, and Michael Hirsh, "War of the Mosques," *Newsweek,* 6 March 2006, pp. 24-27.

12. Ramachandra Guha, "Could Partition Have Been Made Less Bloody," *The Hindu* (Madras), 28 August 2005.

13. Hamza Hendawi, AP, "Al-Zarqawi's Death May Not Matter," *Jacksonville Daily News* (NC), 12 June 2006, pp. 1A, 2A.

14. Nicholas Blanford, "Mideast 'Axis' Forms against West," *Christian Science Monitor,* 20 April 2006, pp. 1, 12.

15. Muqtada al-Sadr, in interview with Scott Johnson, from " 'I Demand a Timetable'," *Newsweek,* 8 May 2006, p. 41.

16. ABC's Nightly News, 26 March 2006; Rod Nordland, "Al-Sadr Strikes," *Newsweek,* 10 April 2006, pp. 45-47.

17. Charles Levinson, "Ballot-Box Win Boosts Iraqi Radical," *Christian Science Monitor,* 30 January 2006, pp. 1, 11; Dan Murphy, "A Militia Tightens Grip on Heathcare," *Christian Science Monitor,* 25 May 2006, pp. 1, 12.

18. Ibid.

19. Mahan Abedin, "The Supreme Council for the Islamic Revolution in Iraq (SCIRI)," *Middle East Intelligence Bulletin,* autumn 2003.

20. Mariam Fam, AP, "Iraq in 'Undeclared Civil War'," *Jacksonville Daily News* (NC), 9 April 2006, p. 1A.

21. Scott Johnson, Babak Dehghanpisheh, and Michael Hastings, "No More Illusions," *Newsweek,* 10 October 2005, pp. 40-42.

22. Dan Murphy, "Zarqawi Message: 'I'm Still Here'," *Christian Science Monitor,* 27 April 2006, p. 6.

23. Lee Keath, AP, "Shiites Nominate New Premier," *Jacksonville Daily News* (NC), 22 April 2006., p. 5A.

24. Abedin, "The Supreme Council for the Islamic Revolution in Iraq (SCIRI)."

25. Robert H. Reid, AP, "Baghdad Is Rocked by a String of Car Bombings," *Jacksonville Daily News* (NC), 25 April 2006, p. 8A.

26. Moubayed, "In Iraq, Chaos by Another Name," 3 May 2006.

27. Howard Lafranchi, "More Iraqis Look to Vote Secular," *Christian Science Monitor,* 5 December 2005, pp. 1, 11.

28. Richard A. Oppel, Jr., and Khalid W. Hassan, "Iraqi Recruits Reportedly Balk at Postings Away from Home," *New York Times,* 2 May 2006.

29. Scott Johnson, "Phantom Force," *Newsweek,* 24 April 2006, pp. 36, 37.

30. Ibid.

31. Dan Murphy, "A Militia Tightens Grip on Heathcare," *Christian Science Monitor,* 25 MAY 2006, pp. 1, 12.

32. Dexter Filkins, "In Iraq, Armed Police Carry Out Militias' Work," *International Herald Tribune,* 25 May 2006, p. 4.

33. Dan Murphy, "Iraq's Neighborhood Councils Are Vanishing," *Christian Science Monitor,* 25 February 2005, pp. 1, 5.

34. M.Sgt. Mark Mosher (Ramadi veteran), in telephone conversation with author on February 2006.

35. Daniel McGrory, "Exodus of the Iraqi Middle Class," *The Times* (UK), 11 May 2006.

36. Levinson, "Ballot-Box Win Boosts Iraqi Radical," pp. 1, 11.

37. McGrory, "Exodus of the Iraqi Middle Class."

38. Robert H. Reid, AP, "U.S., Iraqi Units Rescue 7 Abducted Sunnis," *Jacksonville Daily News* (NC), 12 May 2006, p. 4A.

39. Filkins, "In Iraq, Armed Police Carry Out Militias' Work," p. 4.

40. PBS's News Hour with Jim Lehrer, 22 May 2006.

41. Patrick Quinn, AP, "Iraqis Focus on War," *Jacksonville Daily News* (NC), 22 May 2006, pp. 1A, 2A.

42. Meer N. Yacoub, "4GW: Al-Qaida Blueprint for Conflict," from AP, 15 June 2006, through access@g2-forward.org.

43. Scott Peterson, "A Picture of a Weakening Insurgency," *Christian Science Monitor,* 16 June 2006, pp. 1, 10.

44. "U.S.-Led Forces Arrest Top Militia Commander in Iraq," from Reuters, 7 July 2006.

45. Michael R. Gordon, "Iran Aiding Shiite Attacks Inside Iraq, General Says," *New York Times,* 23 June 2006.

46. Jim Garamone, "Pace Says Iran Fighting Proxy Wars against Iraq, Israel," *Camp Lejeune Globe* (NC), 17 August 2006, p. 1A.

47. "Shiite Radicals Join with Sunni Insurgents in Ramadi," *DEBKAfile* (Israel), 7 April 2004.

48. "Iranian Soldiers Captured in Iraq," from Reuters, 1 July 2006.

49. Kim Gamel, AP, "Two Missing U.S. Soldiers Found Dead in Iraq," AOL News, 21 June 2006.

50. Glendinning, "The Secret World of Palestinian Tunnels," 27 June 2006.

51. ABC's Morning News, 12 July 2006.

52. ABC's Evening News, 26 July 2006.

53. Joshua Mitnick, "Hostilities Rise in Gaza," *Christian Science Monitor,* 26 June 2006, pp. 1, 11.

54. "5,000 More U.S. Troops May Be Sent to Baghdad," from AP, *Jacksonville Daily News* (NC), 28 July 2006, p. 4A.

55. Qassim Abdul-Zahra, AP, "Iraqi Leader Angry over U.S. Raid on Militia Stronghold," *Jacksonville Daily News* (NC), 8 August 2006, p. 5A.
56. Ibid.

Chapter 6: *Iran's Growing Militancy*

1. NPR's Morning News, 14 December 2005.
2. "18 of Iran's 21 New Ministers Hail from Revolutionary Guards, Secret Police," Iran Report, vol. 8, no. 34, *Radio Free Europe/Radio Liberty,* 29 August 2005.
3. "Iran's New Elite Army Chief Had Lebanese Terror Ties," Iran Focus, 24 August 2005.
4. "Iran's Intelligence Service Occupies Key Iraq City," Iran Focus, 4 September 2005.
5. "Iraqi Paper Claims Iranians Fighting There," from UPI, 10 May 2006.
6. "Iraqi Forces Find Iranian Arms Cache," UPI, 12 April 2006.
7. Laurie Copans, AP, "Hamas Defends Tel Aviv Suicide Bombing That Kills 9," *Jacksonville Daily News* (NC), 18 April 2006, p. 4A.
8. "Hamas Army Recruited Thousands for Holy War to Destroy Israel."
9. Ibid.
10. ABC's Morning News, 17 April 2006.

Chapter 7: *Zulu Double-Envelopment*

1. "Zulu and Zulu Wars," in *Reader's Companion to Military History* (Boston, MA: Houghton Mifflin, College Division, n.d.). (This work will henceforth be cited as "Zulu and Zulu Wars.")
2. "Scouting in South Africa, 1884-1890," as extracted from *Scouting with Baden-Powell,* by Russell Freedman (New York: Holiday House, 1967), at www.pinetreeweb.com. (This work will henceforth be cited as "Scouting in South Africa.")
3. "KwaZulu-Natal's Battlefield Experience," Drakensberg (South Africa) Tourism. (This work will henceforth be cited as "KwaZulu.")
4. Ibid.
5. "Zulu," 139 min., Platinum Disc Corp., 2000, videocassette #02863.
6. "Zulu and Zulu Wars."
7. Ibid.
8. "Zulu," videocassette #02863, dust cover text.
9. "Zulu and Zulu Wars."

10. "Zulu," videocassette #02863.
11. "Scouting in South Africa."
12. "Battle of Ulundi, 1879," artwork caption by William Maxwell, 1902, at www.war-art.com.
13. Ibid.
14. "Scouting in South Africa."

Chapter 8: *Boer Stalking Attack*

1. Gregory Fremont-Barnes, *The Boer War: 1899-1902* (Oxford, England: Osprey, 2003), p. 13.
2. Ibid.
3. "KwaZulu."
4. Fremont-Barnes, *The Boer War,* pp. 15-22.
5. "Scouting in South Africa."
6. David Scott-Donelan, *Tactical Tracking Operations* (Boulder, CO: Paladin Press, 1998), p. 6.
7. "KwaZulu."
8. Ibid.
9. Fremont-Barnes, *The Boer War,* p. 37.
10. Ibid., p. 39.
11. Ibid.
12. Ibid., p. 27.
13. Ibid., p. 43.
14. Thomas Pakenham, *The Boer War* (New York: Avon Books, 1979), p. 213.
15. Ibid., p. 215.
16. Ibid., p. 242.
17. Ibid., p. 228.
18. Ibid., p. 231.
19. Fremont-Barnes, *The Boer War,* p. 44.
20. Pakenham, *The Boer War,* p. 247.
21. Fremont-Barnes, *The Boer War,* p. 57.
22. Pakenham, *The Boer War,* p. 229.
23. Fremont-Barnes, *The Boer War,* p. 59.
24. Ibid., p. 64.
25. Ibid., p. 7.
26. Ibid., p. 24.
27. Winston Churchill, as quoted in *The Boer War,* by Gregory Fremont-Barnes, p. 26.
28. Fremont-Barnes, *The Boer War,* p. 7.
29. *The Defense of Duffer's Drift,* by Ernest D. Swinton, FMFRP 12-33 (Quantico, VA: Marine Corps Combat Development Cmd., 1989), p. 17.

30. "Zulu and Zulu Wars."
31. "Scouting in South Africa."
32. Lucille Davie, "Thomas Pakenham, the Boer War and the Old Fort," City of Johannesburg.
33. "KwaZulu."
34. Lt.Col. R.F. Reid-Daly, *Pamwe Chete: The Legend of the Selous Scouts* (Weltevreden Park, South Africa: Covos-Day Books, 1999), p. 414.

Chapter 9: *South African Reconnaissance*

1. *CIA—The World Factbook,* as updated 10 January 2006, s.v. "Zimbabwe." (The overall work will henceforth be cited as *CIA World Factbook.)*
2. *CIA World Factbook,* s.v. "Zambia."
3. Peter Stiff, *The Silent War: South African Recce Operations, 1969-1994* (Alberton, South Africa: Galago Publishing, 1999), p. 30.
4. Gertz, "Notes from the Pentagon."
5. MEF operator (recent traveler to Nigeria), in conversation with author on 31 March 2006.
6. M.Gy.Sgt. Jim Gardiner (former Horn of Africa contingent logistics chief), in conversation with author on 16 April 2006.
7. Bikash Sangraula, "Nepal Grapples with Next Steps," *Christian Science Monitor,* 2 May 2006, p. 6; Stiff, *The Silent War,* p. 315.
8. Stiff, *The Silent War,* p. 17.
9. Ibid., p. 18.
10. Ibid.
11. *Azania Combat,* issue 16, p. 9, in *The Silent War,* by Peter Stiff, p. 19.
12. *Country Profiles: A Guide to Africa,* BBC News, s.v. "Namibia" (Time Line). (The overall work will henceforth be cited as *BBC Country Profiles.)*
13. Stiff, *The Silent War,* p. 36.
14. Ibid., p. 53.
15. Ibid., p. 96.
16. John Stockwell, *In Search of Enemies* (n.p.: Andre Deutsch, 1978), p. 67, in *The Silent War,* by Peter Stiff, p. 101.
17. Stiff, *The Silent War,* p. 101.
18. Ibid., pp. 100, 351.
19. Ibid., p. 100.
20. Ibid., p. 121.
21. Ibid., p. 120.
22. Ibid., p. 125.

23. Ibid., pp. 124-129, 135.
24. Ibid., p. 137.
25. Ibid., pp. 144, 145.
26. Ian Greig, *The Communist Challenge to Africa* (Johannesburg: South African Freedom Foundation, 1977), p. 36, in *The Silent War,* by Peter Stiff, p. 149.
27. Stiff, *The Silent War,* p. 149.
28. Ibid., p. 182.
29. Ibid., p. 191.
30. Ibid., p. 192.
31. Ibid., p. 196.
32. Ibid., pp. 203, 204.
33. Ibid., pp. 208-215.
34. Ibid., pp. 222-226.
35. Greig, *The Communist Challenge to Africa,* p. 103, in *The Silent War,* by Peter Stiff, p. 47.
36. Stiff, *The Silent War,* p. 46.
37. Ibid., pp. 47, 48.
38. Ibid., p. 85.
39. Ibid., p. 86.
40. Ibid., p. 93.
41. Ibid., p. 98.
42. Ibid., pp. 155, 156.
43. David Hoile, *Mozambique—A Nation in Crisis* (London: Claridge Press, 1989), p. 36, in *The Silent War,* by Peter Stiff, p. 156.
44. *CIA World Factbook,* s.v. "Mozambique."
45. Stiff, *The Silent War,* p. 180.
46. Ibid., p. 281.
47. Ibid., p. 243.
48. Ibid., pp. 270, 271.
49. Ibid,, p. 283.
50. Ibid., p. 281.
51. Ibid., p. 283.
52. Ibid., p. 30.
53. Ibid., p. 285.
54. Ibid., p. 282.
55. Ibid., p. 244.
56. Ibid.
57. Ibid., p. 245.
58. Ibid., pp. 239-241.
59. Ibid., p. 244.
60. Ibid., p. 246.
61. Ibid., p. 248.
62. Ibid., p. 251.
63. Ibid., p. 253.

64. Barbara Cole, *The Elite — The Story of the Rhodesian Special Air Service* (Transkei, South Africa: Three Knights, 1984), pp. 393-409, in *The Silent War,* by Peter Stiff, p. 285.

65. Stiff, *The Silent War,* p. 289.

66. Wikipedia Encyclopedia, s.v. "Zimbabwe."

67. Stiff, *The Silent War,* p. 315.

68. Peter Stanton (former Selous Scout) interview of 1981, in *The Silent War,* by Peter Stiff, p. 88.

69. Stiff, *The Silent War,* p. 315.

70. Ibid., pp. 289, 290.

71. Ibid.

72. Ibid., pp. 17, 315.

73. Ibid., pp. 314, 316.

74. Ibid.

75. Ibid., pp. 335, 341.

76. Ibid., p. 351.

77. Ibid., p. 357.

78. Ibid., pp. 358-364.

79. Ibid., p. 530.

80. Ibid.

81. Ibid., p. 532.

82. Fred Bridgland, *War for Africa* (Gibraltar: Ashanti, 1991), p. 17, and Helmoed-Romer Heitman, *War in Angola — The Final South African Phase* (Gibraltar: Ashanti, 1990), pp. 15-16, in *The Silent War,* by Peter Stiff, p. 533.

83. Stiff, *The Silent War,* p. 548.

84. Ibid., p. 552.

85. Ibid., p. 560.

86. Ibid., p. 584.

87. *BBC Country Profiles,* s.v. "Angola."

88. Stiff, *The Silent War,* p. 532.

89. *BBC Country Profiles,* s.v. "Angola."

90. Ibid.

91. Ibid., (Time Line).

Chapter 10: *Selous Scout Infiltration*

1. Reid-Daly, *Pamwe Chete,* p. ii.

2. His Holiness John Paul II, *Crossing the Threshold of Hope* (New York: Alfred A. Knopf, 1995), pp. 205, 206.

3. *Catechism of the Catholic Church* (New York: Doubleday, 1994), par. 2309, p. 615.

4. Chris Vermaak, "Rhodesia's Selous Scouts," *Armed Forces (Journal),* May 1977.

5. Reid-Daly, *Pamwe Chete,* pp. 204, 205.
6. *Selous Scouts,* "External Operations," from website maintained by T.A.L. Dozer, at http://members.tripod.com/selousscouts/home_page.htm. (The overall work will henceforth be cited as *Selous Scouts.)*
7. Vermaak, "Rhodesia's Selous Scouts."
8. Reid-Daly, *Pamwe Chete,* p. 58.
9. Vermaak, "Rhodesia's Selous Scouts."
10. Reid-Daly, *Pamwe Chete,* p. ii.
11. Leroy Thompson, *Dirty Wars: Elite Forces vs. the Guerrillas* (Devon, England: David & Charles, 1991).
12. Reid-Daly, *Pamwe Chete,* p. 3.
13. Ibid., p. 67.
14. Ibid., p. 3.
15. Ibid., pp. 71-73.
16. Ibid., pp. 59, 60.
17. Ibid., p. 47.
18. Ibid., p. 157.
19. Ibid.
20. Ibid., pp. 198, 199.
21. Peter Stiff, as quoted in "The Selous Scout Regiment," from *Selous Scouts.*
22. David Scott-Donelan (former member of Selous Scouts and SA Recce), in telephone conversation with the author on June 2004; Vermaak, "Rhodesia's Selous Scouts."
23. "Bushcraft," *Selous Scouts.*
24. Ibid.
25. Reid-Daly, as quoted in Vermaak, "Rhodesia's Selous Scouts."
26. Thompson, *Dirty Wars.*
27. Reid-Daly, *Pamwe Chete,* pp. 182, 183.
28. Ibid., p. 342.
29. Thompson, *Dirty Wars.*
30. Jim Simpson, "Scouts to the Rescue," *Defense Watch,* 17 September 2003.
31. Thompson, *Dirty Wars.*
32. Ibid.
33. Ibid.
34. Ibid.
35. Ibid.
36. Ibid.
37. Reid-Daly, *Pamwe Chete,* p. 151.
38. "External Operations, *Selous Scouts.*
39. Reid-Daly, *Pamwe Chete,* pp. 212-224.
40. Ibid., pp. 224-231.
41. Ibid., p. 205; Stiff, *The Silent War,* p. 241.

42. Reid-Daly, *Pamwe Chete,* p. 204.

43. Ibid., pp. 234, 235.

44. Ibid., p. 236.

45. Ibid., p. 1240.

46. ZANU HQ, Chimoio, "Report on the Massacre at Nyadzonya by the Rhodesian Forces on 9 August 1976," dated 19 August 1976 (captured by the SAS during Chimoio Raid on 23/11/1977), in *Pamwe Chete,* by Lt.Col. R.F. Reid-Daly, pp. 241-247.

47. Ibid., p. 241.

48. Stiff, *The Silent War,* pp. 268, 281.

49. Ibid., p. 241.

50. Photo by Jill Shephard, *The Struggle for Zimbabwe,* in *The Silent War,* by Peter Stiff, p. 241.

51. Reid-Daly, *Pamwe Chete,* pp. 436-445.

Chapter 11: *African-Style Guerrilla Warfare*

1. *Encyclopedia Britannica, 2004,* s.v. "Mau Mau."

2. Ibid., s.v. "Jomo Kenyatta."

3. Ibid.

4. Ibid, s.v. "Mau Mau."

5. Col. McGill Alexander (South African Army), "An African Rapid-Deployment Force for Peace Operations on the African Continent," n.p., July 1995, in "Operation Red Dragon," from Global Security.

6. Ibid.

7. *CIA World Factbook,* s.v. "Mozambique," "Namibia," and "Republic of the Congo."

8. *BBC Country Profiles,* s.v. "Angola."

9. Stiff, *The Silent War,* p. 136.

10. *CIA World Factbook,* s.v. "Angola."

11. Stiff, *The Silent War,* p. 46.

12. *BBC Country Profiles,* s.v. "Tanzania."

13. Maj.Gen. Loots interview of 1987, in *The Silent War,* by Peter Stiff, p. 47.

14. *BBC Country Profiles,* s.v. "Zambia."

15. Ian Greig, *The Communist Challenge to Africa* (Johannesburg: SA Freedom Foundation, 1977), p. 103, in *The Silent War,* by Peter Stiff, p. 47.

16. Stiff, *The Silent War,* p. 151.

17. Ibid.

18. Ibid., p. 47.

19. Ibid., p. 290.

20. Ibid., pp. 17, 315.

21. Ibid., p. 314.

22. Ibid., p. 101.
23. Ibid., pp. 46, 314.
24. Greig, *The Communist Challenge to Africa,* p. 103, in *The Silent War,* by Peter Stiff, p. 47.
25. Stiff, *The Silent War,* p. 315.
26. Ibid., p. 281.
27. Ibid., pp. 243, 244, 281.
28. Ibid., p. 36.
29. Ibid., p. 46.
30. Ibid., p. 155.
31. Ibid., pp. 96-100.
32. Reid-Daly, *Pamwe Chete,* pp. 436-445.
33. Stiff, *The Silent War,* p. 268.
34. Ibid., p. 289; Reid-Daly, *Pamwe Chete,* pp. 67, 436-445.
35. *CIA World Factbook,* s.v. "Republic of the Congo."
36. Ibid., s.v. "Democratic Republic of the Congo."
37. Stiff, *The Silent War,* pp. 101, 126.
38. *CIA World Factbook,* s.v. "Democratic Republic of the Congo."
39. Ibid., s.v. "Zimbabwe."
40. Ibid., s.v. "Angola"; Gertz, "Notes from the Pentagon."
41. ABC's Morning News, 20 April 2006.
42. ABC's Nightly News, 18 April 2006.
43. *CIA World Factbook,* s.v. "Nigeria," "Algeria," "Sudan," "Angola," "Chad," and "Republic of the Congo."
44. Cathy Majtenyi, "China Signs Deal for Kenya Oil Exploration," *VOA* (Nairobi), April 28, 2006.
45. CBS's "60 Minutes," 2 April 2006.
46. Hassan, "Somalia Twists in the Wind."
47. McLaughlin and Soares, "Oil Wealth and Corruption at Play in Chad's Rebellion," p. 6.
48. Daniel Pepper, "From Texas to Chad: Why One Rebel Fights," *Christian Science Monitor,* 20 April 2006, pp. 1, 11.
49. "Iran, Nigeria Strengthening Ties," *World Tribune* (Springfield, VA), 24 March 2006.
50. NPR's Morning News, 1 May 2006.
51. "CCEA Clears OVL's Pipeline Project in Sudan," *Daily Excelsior* (Jammu, India), 25 June 2004.
52. ABC's Nightly News, 18 April 2006.
53. "Islam in Africa Newsletter," vol. 1, no. 1, May 2006, by Moshe Terdman and Reuven Paz, the Project for the Research of Islamist Movements (Israel), from its website, www.e-prism.org; "Tribal Militants Claimed Responsibility for Another Attack on an Energy Installation," World News in Brief, *Christian Science Monitor,* 8 June 2006, p. 7.
54. Ibid.

55. Ibid.

56. William Pasco, "Moscow's Strategy in Southern Africa: A Country by Country Review," Heritage Foundation, 21 July 1986.

57. *CIA World Factbook,* s.v. "Mozambique."

58. *BBC Country Profiles,* s.v. "Angola."

59. Ibid., s.v. "Tanzania."

60. Ibid., s.v. "Zambia."

61. Ibid., s.v. "Angola."

62. *CIA World Factbook,* s.v. "Tanzania."

63. Ibid., s.v. "Zambia."

64. Ibid., s.v. "Zimbabwe."

65. Ibid., s.v. "Angola."

66. Ibid., s.v. "Namibia."

67. "Zimbabwe: No Money to Print Currency," from IRIN (Harare), as reprinted in *Khartoum Monitor,* 31 May 2006, p. 10.

68. Daniel Pepper, "Zimbabwe's Army Takes over Black Farms," *Christian Science Monitor,* 5 June 2006, pp. 1, 10.

69. "China Winning Resources and Loyalties of Africa."

70. Ibid.

71. Stiff, *The Silent War,* p. 289; Reid-Daly, *Pamwe Chete,* pp. 71-73, 242.

72. "Zimbabwe: Shadows and Lies," PBS's *Frontline/World.*

73. Ryan Truscott, "Short Lives Lead to Short-Term Goals in Zimbabwe," *Christian Science Monitor,* 9 June 2006, p. 4.

74. "China Winning Resources and Loyalties of Africa."

75. "Nigeria: Modern Manna from Heaven," *The Voice of the Martyrs* (Bartlesville, OK), August 2005, pp. 6, 7.

76. Njadvara Musa, AP, "At Least 15 Killed in Prophet Protests," *Jacksonville Daily News* (NC), 19 February 2006, p. 6A.

77. "Nigeria," pp. 6, 7.

78. "Nigerians Hail Democratic Victory," *The Citizen* (Khartoum), 1 June 2006, p. 6.

79. "Blood for Oil," *Investor's Business Daily* (Los Angeles), 2 May 2005, as reprinted in *Sudan Tribune,* 3 May 2005 and 15 June 2006; Tristan McConnell, *"Christian Science Monitor,* 13 June 2006, p. 7; McLaughlin and Soares, "Oil Wealth and Corruption at Play in Chad's Rebellion," *Christian Science Monitor,* 21 April 2006, p. 6.

80. "SPLM Demands Construction of Oil Refinery in the South," p. 2.

81. "China, Libya, and Others Investing in Sudan's Booming Economy," *The Citizen* (Khartoum), 1 June 2006, p. 6.

82. "CCEA Clears OVL's Pipeline Project in Sudan," 25 June 2004.

83. "Blood for Oil."

Chapter 12: *Muslim Raids*

1. *Sudan Country Study,* DA PAM 550-27, p. 255.
2. Ibid., pp. 257, 258.
3. *Wikipedia Encyclopedia,* s.v. "United Nations Mission in Sudan."
4. "Sudan Signs Off on Darfur Peace Plan, Will the Rebels," from Reuters and AP, *Christian Science Monitor,* 1 May 2006, p. 4.
5. Robinson and Pepper/Tawila, "The Front Lines of Genocide," pp. 44-46.
6. Ibid.
7. "New Resolution Puts Darfur in U.N. Hands," Word Briefs Wire Reports (AP), *Jacksonville Daily News* (NC), 18 August 2006, p. 6A.
8. "The Constant Gardener," Universal Studios, 2006, DVD, #26292.
9. "The Four Feathers," technicolor film.
10. Ibid.

Chapter 13: *Slowing the Flow of African Fighters*

1. Patrick Poole, "The Muslim Brotherhood 'Project'," *Front Page Magazine,* 11 May 2006, from its website, frontpagemagazine.com.
2. Ibid.
3. Zeyno Baran, "Muslim Brotherhood Takes Up Arms—in Support of Hizbullah," from access@g2-forward.org, 2 August 2006; Syed Saleem Shahzad, "We are just Hit-and-Run Guerrillas," *Asia Times Online,* 10 August 2006.
4. Jon Swain, David Leppard, and Brian Johnson-Thomas, "Iran's Plot to Mine Uranium in Africa." *The Sunday Times* (UK), 6 August 2006.
5. Blake Lambert, "UN Steps Up Peace Efforts in Congo ahead of April Vote," *Christian Science Monitor,* 30 January 2006, p. 4.
6. *CIA World Factbook,* s.v. "Rwanda."
7. "The Scars of Death," *Human Rights Watch,* September 1997.
8. "Lord's Resistance Army," Uganda Civil War, *Global Security,* 2005; Martin Plaut, "Uganda's LRA Rebels," BBC News, 6 February 2004.
9. "Lord's Resistance Army," *Global Security.*
10. Martin Plaut, "Uganda's LRA Rebels," BBC News, 6 February 2004.
11. *Patterns of Global Terrorism, 2003 Report,* s.v. "Lord's Resistance Army."
12. Michael Koma, "Sorry, Madam Teny," *Khartoum Monitor,* 31 May 2006, p. 3.

13. Plaut, "Uganda's LRA Rebels."
14. "The Scars of Death."
15. Ibid.
16. "Lord's Resistance Army," *Global Security.*
17. Ibid.
18. *Patterns of Global Terrorism, 2003 Report,* s.v. "Army for the Liberation of Rwanda (ALIR)."
19. *CIA World Factbook,* s.v. "Rwanda."
20. *Patterns of Global Terrorism, 2003 Report,* s.v. "Army for the Liberation of Rwanda (ALIR)."
21. Simon Robinson and Vivienne Walt, "The Deadliest War in the World," *Time,* 5 June 2006, pp. 38-41.
22. Ibid.
23. NPR's Morning News, 20 August 2006.
24. *CIA World Factbook,* s.v. "Democratic Republic of the Congo."
25. "DR Congo Peacekeepers Missing," *Sudan Vision,* 31 May 2006, p. 10.
26. ABC's Morning News, early 2006.
27. "U.N.: Fifth of the World Lacks Clean Water," World Brief Wire Reports (AP), *Jacksonville Daily News* (NC), 7 March 2006, p. 7A.

Chapter 14: *Urban Tracking*

1. David Scott-Donelan, *Tactical Tracking Operations* (Boulder, CO: Paladin Press, 1998) p. 140.
2. Ibid., p. 35.
3. Mark Sexton, Rick Adrian, and David Scott-Donelan, "Urban Tracking," powerpoint presentation shared with author in December 2005. (This work will henceforth be cited as "Urban Tracking.")
4. Scott-Donelan, *Tactical Tracking Operations,* p. 47.
5. Ibid.,
6. Ibid., p. 49.
7. Ibid., p. 50.
8. Rick Adrian (accomplished tracker and instructor), in e-mail to author on 10 February 2006; "Urban Tracking."
9. "Urban Tracking."

Chapter 15: *To Truly Win in a Place Like Iraq*

1. "The Insurgency," PBS's *Frontline.*
2. "Economic Plight of Palestinians Worsening," *The Egyptian Gazette,* 28 May 2006, p. 4.

3. President Dwight D. Eisenhower, as quoted in "No Excuse for Hunger," by Vincent J. Romano, *Maryknoll,* vol. 96, no. 8., September 2002, p. 15.

4. Battalion commander in 3d Battalion, 7th Marines, in conversation with author during training session of 15, 16 January 2005.

5. Lance Gay, Scripps Howard, "Despite Troops' Grumbling, Pentagon Insists on Side Armor," Capital Notebook, Washington, *Jacksonville Daily News* (NC), 29 January 2006, p. 9A.

6. Con Coughlin, "Smuggling Route Opened to Supply Iraqi Insurgents," *The Daily Telegraph* (London), 29 October 2005.

7. Abdul Hussein al-Obeidi, AP, "Holy City Najaf Fighting Worst Since Saddam Fell," *Jacksonville Daily News* (NC), 7 August 2004, pp. 1A, 4A.

8. Jeffrey Imm, "Some Bombs in Iraq Are Made in Iran, U.S. Says," *New York Times,* 6 August 2005.

9. Thomas Harding, "Iraq: Missile May Have Come from Iran," *Daily Telegraph* (London), 5 May 2006.

10. "Preparing a Company for 4th-Generation Warfare during Short Delays in the Normal Training Schedule," from Posterity Enterprises, overhead transparency presentation, last revised 21 October 2005; H. John Poole, *One More Bridge to Cross: Lowering the Cost of War* (Emerald Isle, NC: Posterity Press, 1999), chapt. 13.

11. Fr. Patrick Gaffney (recognized expert on the Middle East and North Africa), in telephone conversation with author of 20 February 2006.

12. "Russia, China Block Darfur-Related Sanctions," from Associated Press, *Christian Science Monitor,* 19 April 2006, p. 4.

13. "China Forging Strategic Ties to Radical Islam," *China Confidential,* 22 July 2006, through access@g2-forward.org.

14. Bikash Sangraula, "Pressure Rises on Nepal's King," *Christian Science Monitor,* 24 April 2006, pp. 1, 10, 11; ABC's Nightly News, 20-22 April 2006.

15. ABC's Nightly News, 25 April 2006.

16. Memo for the record, from H.J. Poole.

17. Bikash Sangraula, "Nepal Grapples with Next Steps," *Christian Science Monitor,* 2 May 2006, p. 6.

18. Bikash Sangraula, "Key Role of Nepal Security Forces," *Christian Science Monitor,* 18 April 2006, p. 6.

19. Ibid.

20. Sangraula, "Pressure Rises on Nepal's King," pp. 1, 10.

21. Bikash Sangraula, "In Nepal's Democratic Revival, Maoist Rebels Dubious," *Christian Science Monitor,* 26 April 2006, pp. 1, 11.

22. Sangraula, "Pressure Rises on Nepal's King," pp. 1, 10.

23. "The Blockade of Major Highways in Nepal . . . ," World News in Brief, *Christian Science Monitor,* 27 April 2006, p. 7.

24. "Nepalese Cabinet Declares Cease Fire," World Briefs Wire Reports (AP), *Jacksonville Daily News* (NC), 4 May 2006, p. 5A.

25. Sangraula, "In Nepal's Democratic Revival, Maoist Rebels Dubious," pp. 1, 11.

26. Bikash Sangraula, "Nepal's Parliament Sets Fast-Paced Agenda," *Christian Science Monitor,* 15 May 2006, pp. 1, 12.

27. Ibid.

28. Bikash Sangraula, "Nepal's Parliament Asserts Power," *Christian Science Monitor,* 19 May 2006, p. 4.

29. Bikash Sangraula, "Rebel Visit Moves Nepal Closer to Peace," *Christian Science Monitor,* 19 June 2006, pp. 1, 10.

30. "Seoul Train," PBS's *Independent Lens,* NC Public TV, 13 June 2006.

31. Antony Barnett, "Revealed: The Gas Chamber Horror of North Korea's Gulag," *The Observer* (UK), 1 February 2004.

32. Hiroko Tabuchi, AP, "Chinese Spy Planes Have Raised Alerts in Japan, *Jacksonville Daily News* (NC), 21 April 2006, p. 5A.

33. "China Winning Resources and Loyalties of Africa."

34. Daniel Pepper, "Congolese Hopeful Ahead of July 30 Vote," *Christian Science Monitor,* 29 June 2006, p. 7.

35. "China's 'Comprehensive Warfare' Strategy Wears Down Enemy Using Non-Military Means," *Geostrategy Direct,* 2 August 2006.

36. "China Winning Resources and Loyalties of Africa."

37. Ibid.

38. PRC Ministry of Foreign Affairs, s.v. "Chinese Embassies," from its website, www.fmprc.gov.cn.

39. "Strong Chinese-Hamas Intelligence Connection," *DEBKAfile* (Israel), 19 June 2006.

40. Bob Clifford, former FBI Hezbollah unit director, as quoted in "Hezbollah, Illegal Immigration, and the Next 9/11," by Lt.Col. Joseph Myers and Patrick Poole, *Front Page Magazine,* 28 April 2006, from its website, frontpagemagazine.com.

41. Embassy World, s.v. "Embassy Listings for North Korea"; British private website, http://uk.geocities.com/hkgalbert/kpdo.htm.

42. Joseph S. Bermudez, Jr., *North Korean Special Forces* (Annapolis: Naval Inst. Press, 1998), p. 147.

43. "North Koreans Assisted Hezbollah with Tunnel Construction," *Terrorism Focus: The Jamestown Foundation,* vol. III, issue 30, 1 August 2006.

44. Huntington, *The Clash of Civilizations and the Remaking of World Order,* p. 198.

45. Michael O'Hanlon (senior foreign policy fellow at Brookings Institute), as quoted in "The End of Cowboy Diplomacy," by Mike Allen and Romesh Ratnesar, *Time,* 9 July 2006.

46. Brian Calvert, "Afghans Tell Troops: 'No Security, No Help'," *Christian Science Monitor,* 28 June 2006, p. 7.

47. Richard Clarke (former U.S. antiterrorism czar), on ABC's Nightly News, 10 June 2006.

48. William S. Lind (designer of 3GW and 4GW handbooks for the U.S. military), in telephone conversation with the author on 7 June 2006.

Glossary

ABC	American Broadcasting Company	U.S. TV network
AFP	Agence France-Presse	French news agency
AIAI	*Al-Itihaad al-Islamiya*	Somali militia closely linked to *al-Qaeda*
AIM	Armed Islamic Movement	Sudanese alliance of militant groups
ALIR	Army for the Liberation of Rwanda	Once Rwandan army, PALIR's armed wing, became DFLR
ANC	African National Congress	South African political party
APLA	Azanian People's Liberation Army	PAC's military wing, formerly POQO
AU	African Union	African alliance
BBC	British Broadcasting Corporation	British news service
CAP	Combined Action Platoon	U.S. squad with two of local forces
CENTCOM	Central Command	U.S. headquarters for Southwest Asia
CIA	Central Intelligence Agency	U.S. spy organization
CNPC	China National Petroleum Corporation	State-owned Chinese overseas oil company

COSATU	Congress of South African Trade Unions	South African political party
CPA	Comprehensive Peace Agreement	Accord signed by SPLM and Khartoum government in 2005
CPC	Communist Party of China	China's ruling faction
DFLR	Democratic Front for the Liberation of Rwanda	Resistance faction, formerly ALIR
DPA	Darfur Peace Agreement	Accord signed by SLM and Khartoum government in 2006
DPRK	Democratic People's Republic of Korea	North Korea
DRC or DROC	Democratic Republic of the Congo	Equatorial African nation, once Zaire
FAE	Fuel Air Explosive	Flame weapon that also depletes oxygen
FAPLA	People's Armed Forces for Liberation of Angola	MPLA's military wing
FAR	Armed Forces of Rwanda	Rwanda's military, became ALIR
FNI	Nationalist and Integrationist Front	DRC rebel faction
FNLA	National Front for the Liberation of Angola	Angolan resistance movement
4GW	Fourth-Generation Warfare	War that is waged in religious, economic, martial, and political orbs simultaneously
FPS	Facilities Protection Service	Large unofficial security agency in Iraq

FRELIMO	Front for the Liberation of Mozambique	Political party in Mozambique
FUDC	United Front for Democratic Change	Chadian resistance movement
GI	Government Issue	Term of endearment for American soldier
GoSS	Government of South Sudan	SPLM regime in Sudan's autonomous south
GPS	Global Positioning System	Land navigational aid
HIG	*Hezb-i Islami Gulbuddin*	Hekmatyar's militia in Afghanistan today
HIND	Aircraft designator	Eastern bloc helicopter gunship
ICU	Union of Islamic Courts	Al-Qaeda-affiliated fundamentalist faction in Somalia
IDP	Internally Displaced Person	Refugee (phrase most recently applied to Darfur inhabitants)
IED	Improvised Explosive Device	Remote-control bomb
IMB	International Maritime Bureau	World shipping controls agency
INF	Islamic National Front	Sudanese alliance of militant groups, alias of AIM
ISI	Inter-Service Intelligence	Pakistani spy agency
JEM	Justice and Equality Movement	Sudanese rebels at Eritrea border and in Darfur region, al-Turabi linked

JI	*Jamaat i-Islami*	Pakistani religious political party, supports Hekmatyar
JUI/F	*Jamiat-i-Ulema-i-Islam Fazlur Rehman Faction*	Pakistani religious political party, supports the Taliban
LET	*Lashkar e-Toiba*	Military wing of MDI
LRA	Lord's Resistance Army	Separatist faction in northern Uganda
MDI	*Markaz-ud-Dawa-wal-Irshad*	Pakistani group of fundamentalists
MEND	Movement for the Emancipation of the Niger Delta	Nigerian militant faction
MIG-19	Aircraft designator	Old Eastern-bloc fighter-bomber
MIG-23	Aircraft designator	Newer Eastern-bloc fighter-bomber
MK	*Umkhonto we Sizwe*	ANC's military wing
MOIS	Ministry of Intelligence and Security	Iranian spy agency
MONUC	U.N. Organization Mission in the Democratic Republic of the Congo	U.N. agency
MPLA	People's Movement for the Liberation of Angola	Angolan political party
MSS	Ministry of State Security	Chinese spy agency
NCO	Noncommissioned officer	Enlisted leader of 4th or 5th pay grade
NCP	National Congress Party	Ruling political party of Sudan in 2006, created by elements of NIF in 1998

NCRI	National Council of Resistance of Iran	Iranian opposition group
NGO	Non-Governmental Organization	Privately funded agency, term used widely in Africa
NIF	Nationalist Islamic Front	Sudanese political party, linked to the Muslim Brotherhood
NPR	National Public Radio	U.S. nonprofit radio network
OIC	Organization of Islamic Conference	Meeting of Islamic nations, alternative to Arab League
PAC	Pan African Conference	South African political party
PAIC	Popular Arab and Islamic Conference	AIM conferences in Sudan in the 1990's
PALIR	Party for the Liberation of Rwanda	Rwandan political party, parent of ALIR
PBS	Public Broadcasting System	U.S. public-service TV network
PCP	Popular National (Congress) Party	Sudanese political party, split from NCP in 2000, al-Turabi supporters
PDF	Popular Defense Forces	Sudanese equivalent to Iranian *Sepah*
PFLP-CG	Popular Front for the Liberation of Palestine General Command	Palestinian resistance group
PG-29V	Ammunition designator	Tandem warhead, anti-armor/bunker round for RPG-29

PIJ	*Palestinian Islamic Jihad*	Palestinian resistance group, predominantly Sunni
PLA	People's Liberation Army	Maoist guerrilla force in Nepal, communist
PNP	Popular National Party	Turabi-led offshoot of NCP, alias is PCP
POQO	African acronym	PAC's military wing, became APLA
PRC	People's Republic of China	Mainland China
RENAMO	Mozambique National Resistance	Mozambique freedom faction
RPD	Russian acronym	Eastern-bloc light machinegun
RPG	Rocket Propelled Grenade (Launcher)	Eastern-bloc, hand-held rocket launcher
RPG-7	Weapon designator	Prevalent RPG
RPG-29	Weapon designator	Advanced RPG
SA	South Africa or South African	Of the nation at the southern tip of Africa
SA Recce	South African Reconnaissance	SA scouting unit
SACP	South African Communist Party	SA political faction
SADF	South African Defense Forces	South Africa military establishment
SAS	Special Air Service	Term applied in this work to Rhodesian special operators
SCIRI	Supreme Council of the Islamic Revolution in Iraq	Iraqi political party

2GW	Second-Generation Warfare	Overwhelming all foe strongpoints with massive firepower
SLA	Sudanese Liberation Army	Armed wing of SLM
SLM	Sudanese Liberation Movement	Separatist movement in western Sudan
SNCO	Staff noncommissioned officer	Enlisted pay grades E-6 through E-9
SPAF	Sudanese People's Armed Forces	Sudan's military
SPETSNAZ	Russian acronym	Soviet commandos
SPLA	Sudanese People's Liberation Army	Armed wing of SPLM
SPLM	Sudanese People's Liberation Movement	Separatist movement in southern Sudan
SWA	Southwest Africa	Formerly Namibia
SWAPO	Southwest Africa's People's Organization	Southwest African resistance movement
T-62	Weapon designator	Eastern-bloc tank
TBG-29V	Ammunition designator	Thermobaric, anti-personnel round for RPG-29
3GW	Third-Generation Warfare	Bypassing enemy strongpoints to get at supply/control hubs
TV	Television	Visual broadcast
UIA	United Iraqi Alliance	Iraqi political party
UK	United Kingdom	Great Britain
U.N. or UN	United Nations	Global alliance of countries

UNITA	National Union for the Total Liberation of Angola	Angolan political party
UNMIS	United Nations Mission in Sudan	U.N. contingent to monitor 2005 CPA
UPI	United Press International	Global news service
U.S. or US	United States	America
VBIED	Vehicle-Borne Improvised Explosive Device	Conveyance-hauled remote-control bomb
VC	Viet Cong	Vietnam guerrillas
WIFJ	World Islamic Front for the Jihad against Jews and Crusaders	Bin Laden's alliance of militant groups
WMD	Weapons of Mass Destruction	Chemical, nuclear, or biological armaments
WWI	World War One	First global conflict
WWII	World War Two	Second global conflict
WWIII	World War Three	Third global conflict
ZANLA	Zimbabwe African National Liberation Army	Rhodesian resistance movement
ZANU P/F	Zimbabwe African National Union Patriotic Front	Political parent of ZANLA
ZIPRA	Zimbabwe's People's Revolutionary Army	Rhodesian resistance movement

Bibliography

U.S. Government Publications and News Releases

"Abu Ghraib Attack." CENTCOM news release, 6 April 2005.

CIA — The World Factbook. As updated 10 January 2006. From its website, www.odci.gov.

"Combat Engineers Unearth More Than 500 Weapons Cache[s], Save Lives in Iraq." By Cpl. Adam C. Schnell. *Camp Lejeune Globe* (NC), 30 March 2006.

"Crude Oil and Petroleum Imports Top 15 Countries." Energy Information Agency, Dept. of Energy, 29 April 2006. From its website, www.eia.doe.gov.

The Defense of Duffer's Drift. By Ernest D. Swinton. FMFRP 12-33. Quantico, VA: Marine Corps Combat Development Cmd., 1989.

"18 of Iran's 21 New Ministers Hail from Revolutionary Guards, Secret Police." Iran Report, vol. 8, no. 34. *Radio Free Europe / Radio Liberty,* 29 August 2005. From its website, www.rferl.org.

Garamone, Jim. "Pace Says Iran Fighting Proxy Wars against Iraq, Israel." *Camp Lejeune Globe* (NC), 17 August 2006.

"Iraq Soldiers, U.S. Marines Take Insurgents by Storm." By L.Cpl. Peter R. Miller. *Camp Lejeune Globe* (NC), 2 February 2006.

"Lejeune Marines Stay Busy Finding Weapons Caches." By Cpl. Joseph DiGirolamo. *Camp Lejeune Globe* (NC), 27 April 2006.

"Marines Unearth Weapons Caches; Tipsters Lead Troops to More Caches." From Armed Forces Press Service. *Camp Lejeune Globe* (NC), 5 January, 2006.

"Operation Koa Canyon Update." By Maj. Eric Dent. 2nd Marine Division Press Release #0123-06-1004, 23 January 2006.

"Operation Red Bull Disrupts Terrorism in Triad Area." By Cpl. Adam C. Schnell. 2nd Marine Division Story Identification #20061822216, 9 January 2006.

Patterns of Global Terrorism, 2003 Report. Washington, D.C.: U.S. Dept. of State, April 2004. From its website.

Sudan Country Study. DA PAM 550-27. Area Handbook Series. Washington, D.C.: Hdqts. Dept. of the Army, 1992.

Civilian Publications

Analytical Studies

Bermudez, Joseph S., Jr., *North Korean Special Forces.* Annapolis: Naval Inst. Press, 1998.

Catechism of the Catholic Church. New York: Doubleday, 1994.

Clammer, Paul. *Sudan.* Bucks, England: Bradt Travel Guides Ltd., 2005.

Cockburn, Andrew and Leslie. *One Point Safe.* New York: Doubleday, 1997.

Cordesman, Anthony H. and Arleigh A. Burke Chair. "Iran's Developing Military Capabilities." Working draft. Washington, D.C.: Center Strategic Internat. Studies, 14 December 2004.

Country Profiles: A Guide to Africa. BBC News. From its website, news.bbc.co.uk.

Esposito, John L. *Unholy War: Terror in the Name of Islam.* London: Oxford Univ. Press, 2002.

Fremont-Barnes, Gregory. *The Boer War: 1899-1902.* Oxford, England: Osprey, 2003.

Gunaratna, Rohan. *Inside al-Qaeda: Global Network of Terror.* Lahore: Vanguard, 2002.

Hughes, Stephen E. "The State Sponsorship of the Islamic Terrorist Network." Unpublished study. Salt Lake City, 2003. From reload762308@hotmail.com.

Hughes, Stephen E. "Warring on Terrorism: A Comprehensive Dispatch Briefing." Yet-to-be-published study. Soda Springs, ID, 2005. From reload762308@hotmail.com.

Huntington, Samuel P. *The Clash of Civilizations and the Remaking of World Order.* London: Simon & Schuster UK, 1997.

John Paul II, His Holiness. *Crossing the Threshold of Hope.* New York: Alfred A. Knopf, 1995.

Katzman, Kenneth. *Warriors of Islam: Iran's Revolutionary Guard.* Boulder, CO: Westview Press, 1993.

Linder, Deanna and Rachael Levy and Yael Shahar. "Iraqi Wahhabi Factions Affiliated with Abu Musaab al Zarqawi." Internat. Policy Inst. for Counter-Terrorism, November 2004. From its website.

Mannes, Aaron. *Profiles in Terror: The Guide to Middle East Terror Organizations.* Lanham, MD: Rowman & Littlefield Publishers, Inc., 2004.

Mir, Amir. *The True Face of Jihadis.* Lahore: Mashal Books, 2004.

Nojumi, Neamatollah. *The Rise of the Taliban in Afghanistan: Mass Mobilization, Civil War, and the Future of the Region.* New York: Palgrave, 2002.

O'Ballance, Edgar. *Afghan Wars: Battles in a Hostile Land, 1839 to Present*. Karachi: Oxford Univ. Press, 2002.

Pakenham, Thomas. *The Boer War*. New York: Avon Books, 1979.

Pintak, Lawrence. *Seeds of Hate: How America's Flawed Middle East Policy Ignited the Jihad*. London: Pluto Press, 2003.

Poole, H. John. *Militant Tricks: Battlefield Ruses of the Islamic Insurgent*. Emerald Isle, NC: Posterity Press, 2005.

Poole, H. John. *One More Bridge to Cross: Lowering the Cost of War*. Emerald Isle, NC: Posterity Press, 1999.

Poole, H. John. *Tactics of the Crescent Moon: Militant Muslim Combat Methods*. Emerald Isle, NC: Posterity Press, 2004.

Poole, H John. *The Tiger's Way: A U.S. Private's Best Chance of Survival*. Emerald Isle, NC: Posterity Press, 2003.

Reid-Daly, Lt.Col. R.F. *Pamwe Chete: The Legend of the Selous Scouts*. Weltevreden Park, South Africa: Covos-Day Books, 1999.

Scott-Donelan, David. *Tactical Tracking Operations*. Boulder, CO: Paladin Press, 1998.

Selous Scouts. From website maintained by T.A.L. Dozer. At http://members.tripod.com/selousscouts/home_page.htm.

Stiff, Peter. *The Silent War: South African Recce Operations, 1969-1994*. Alberton, South Africa: Galago Publishing (www.galago.co.za), 1999.

Thompson, Leroy. *Dirty Wars: Elite Forces vs. the Guerrillas*. Devon, England: David & Charles, 1991.

Photographs, Videotapes, Movies, TV Programs, and Slide Shows

"Ambush in Mogadishu." Written, produced, and directed by William Cran. PBS's *Frontline*. In conjunction with WGBH, Boston, 2002. Videotape.

Baker, Peter (*Washington Post* leader). On PBS's *Washington Week in Review*. North Carolina public television, 27 January 2005.

Clarke, Richard (former U.S. antiterrorism czar). On ABC's Nightly News, 10 June 2006.

"The Constant Gardener." Universal Studios, 2006. DVD, #26292.

"The Four Feathers." By A.E.W. Mason. Directed by Alexander Korda. Samuel Goldwyn Co., 1939. Technicolor film.

"The Insurgency." PBS's *Frontline*. North Carolina public television, 21 February and 24 April 2006.

McMaugh, Cpl. Michael R. (photographer). Caption with picture #051227-M-8530M-015. 2nd Marine Division release, 27 December 2005.

"Muslims." PBS's *Frontline*. 120 min. Wellspring, n.d. DVD #WSP757.
"Preparing a Company for 4th-Generation Warfare during Short Delays
    in the Normal Training Schedule." From Posterity Enterprises.
    Overhead transparency presentation. Last revised 21 October 2005.
"Al-Qaeda's New Front." PBS's *Frontline*. NC public television,
    25 January 2005.
"Seoul Train." PBS's *Independent Lens*. North Carolina public
    television, 13 June 2006.
Sexton, Mark, Rick Adrian, and David Scott-Donelan. "Urban Tracking."
    Powerpoint presentation shared with author in December 2005.
"Strong Sentiment." Caption for front page photograph. *Jacksonville
    Daily News* (NC), 18 August 2006.
"Zimbabwe: Shadows and Lies." PBS's *Frontline/World*. NC Public TV,
    27 June 2006.
"Zulu." 139 min. Platinum Disc Corp., 2000. Videocassette #02863.

Letters, E-Mail, and Verbal Conversations

Adrian, Rick (accomplished tracker and instructor). In e-mail to author
    on 10 February 2006.
Battalion commander in 3rd Battalion, 7th Marines. In conversation
    with author during training session of 15, 16 January 2005.
Chinese senior citizen (victim of class relocation period). In conversation
    with author in 2001.
Company commander in 3rd Battalion, 7th Marines. In conversation
    with author during training session of 15, 16 January 2005.
Davis, 2dLt. Joseph W. (member of 1st Battalion, 6th Marines and Iraq
    veteran). In conversation with author on 15 December 2005.
Enlisted member of 3rd Battalion, 2nd Marines (Anbar Province
    veteran). In conversation with author on 22 March 2006.
Gaffney, Fr. Patrick (recognized expert on the Middle East and
    North Africa). In telephone conversation with author on
    20 February 2006.
Gardiner, M.Gy.Sgt. Jim (former Horn of Africa contingent logistics
    chief. In conversation with author on 16 April 2006.
Hotel car driver in Khartoum. In conversation with author on 1 June
    2006.
Jeff (member of 3rd Battalion, 1st Marine Regiment). In widely
    circulated internet newsletter (3-1_Dec_05_Newsletter.pdf) of
    17 December 2005.
Lind, William S. (designer of 3GW and 4GW handbooks for the U.S. military).
    In telephone conversation with the author on 7 June 2006.
Longtime owner of Khartoum hotel. In conversation with author on
    31 May 2006.

MEF operator (recent traveler to Nigeria). In conversation with author
    on 31 March 2006.
Mosher, M.Sgt. Mark (Ramadi veteran). In telephone conversation with
    author on February 2006.
NCO of 3rd Battalion, 2nd Marines (Anbar Province veteran).
    In conversation with author during training session of
    March 2006.
Scott-Donelan, David (former member of Selous Scouts and SA Recce).
    In telephone conversation with the author on June 2004.
South African lawyer who had been working in England. In
    conversation with author on 3 June 2006.

Newspaper, Magazine, and Website Articles

Abdul-Zahra, Qassim. Associated Press. "Iraqi Leader Angry over U.S.
    Raid on Militia Stronghold." _Jacksonville Daily News_ (NC),
    8 August 2006.
Abedin, Mahan. "The Supreme Council for the Islamic Revolution in
    Iraq (SCIRI)." _Middle East Intelligence Bulletin,_ autumn 2003.
Ahmed, Azam S. "Analysis: What Next in Darfur?" United Press
    International, 9 June 2005.
Alexander, Col. McGill (South African Army). "An African
    Rapid-Deployment Force for Peace Operations on the African
    Continent." N.p., July 1995. In "Operation Red Dragon." From
    Global Security. At its website, www.globalsecurity.org.
Allen, Mike and Romesh Ratnesar. "The End of Cowboy Diplomacy."
    Time, 9 July 2006.
Ambah, Faiza Saleh. Associated Press. "Iraq: Spinning Off Arab
    Terrorists," _Christian Science Monitor,_ 8 February 2005.
"Attacks on Rise As Iraqis View Constitution." From Associated Press.
    Jacksonville Daily News (NC), 7 October 2005.
Barakat, Mohammed. Associated Press. "U.S. Wraps Up Offensive
    near Syrian Border." _Jacksonville Daily News_ (NC), 15 May
    2005.
Baran, Zeyno. "Muslim Brotherhood Takes Up Arms—in Support of
    Hizbullah." From access@g2-forward.org, 2 August 2006.
Barnett, Antony. "Revealed: The Gas Chamber Horror of North Korea's
    Gulag." _The Observer_ (UK), 1 February 2004.
"Battle of Ulundi, 1879." Artwork caption. By William
    Maxwell, 1902. At www.war-art.com.
Blanford, Nicholas. "Hizbullah's Resilience Built on Years of
    Homework." _Christian Science Monitor,_ 11 August 2006.
Blanford, Nicholas. "Mideast 'Axis' Forms against West." _Christian
    Science Monitor,_ 20 April 2006.

Blanford, Nicholas and Daniel McGrory and Stephen Farrell. "Tactics
That Have Kept the Middle East's Most Powerful Army at Bay."
The Times (UK), 10 August 2006.

"The Blockade of Major Highways in Nepal. . . ." World News in Brief.
Christian Science Monitor, 27 April 2006.

"Blood for Oil." *Investor's Business Daily* (Los Angeles), 2 May 2005.
As reprinted in *Sudan Tribune,* 3 May 2005 and 15 June
2006.

Brandon, James. "To Fight Al Qaeda, US Troops in Africa Build Schools
Instead." *Christian Science Monitor,* 9 January 2006.

Burns, Robert. Associated Press. "Blast Kills 10 Marines in Iraq."
Jacksonville Daily News (NC), 3 December 2005.

Calvert, Brian. "Afghans Tell Troops: 'No Security, No Help'." *Christian
Science Monitor,* 28 June 2006.

Carroll, Jill. "Marines Assault Rebel Border Town." *Christian
Science Monitor,* 3 October 2005.

Carroll, Jill. "Next Job: Keeping Rebels Out." *Christian Science
Monitor,* 21 November 2005.

Castaneda, Antonio. Associated Press. "American, Iraqi Forces Muscle
Way into Eastern Ramadi." *Jacksonville Daily News* (NC),
20 June 2006.

Castaneda, Antonio. Associated Press. "Iraqi Troops to Secure
Deadly City." *Jacksonville Daily News* (NC), 27 October 2005.

Castaneda, Antonio. Associated Press. "Marines Capture Weapons in
Iraq." *Jacksonville Daily News* (NC), 5 June 2005.

Castaneda, Antonio. Associated Press. "Troops Meet Little Resistance."
Jacksonville Daily News (NC), 19 June 2006.

"CCEA Clears OVL's Pipeline Project in Sudan." *Daily Excelsior*
(Jammu, India), 25 June 2004. From its website,
www.dailyexcelsior.com.

"Chanting, 'We Don't Want Islamic Courts . . . '." World News in Brief
(AP). *Christian Science Monitor,* 7 June 2006.

"China Forging Strategic Ties to Radical Islam." *China Confidential,*
22 July 2006. Through access@g2-forward.org.

"China, Libya, and Others Investing in Sudan's Booming Economy."
The Citizen (Khartoum), 1 June 2006.

"China Praises Achievements of Sudan's National Congress Party."
From Xinhua. *Peoples Daily on Line,* 24 November
2005.

"China to Construct 25 Locomotives for Sudan." *Sudan Tribune,* 10 June
2006.

"China Winning Resources and Loyalties of Africa." *The Financial Times* (UK),
28 February 2006.

"China's 'Comprehensive Warfare' Strategy Wears Down Enemy Using
Non-Military Means." *Geostrategy-Direct,* 2 August 2006.

Cody, Edward and Molly Moore, "Analysts Attribute Hezbollah's Resilience to Zeal, Secrecy and Iranian Funding," *Washington Post,* 14 August 2006.

Copans, Laurie. Associated Press. "Hamas Defends Tel Aviv Suicide Bombing That Kills 9." *Jacksonville Daily News* (NC), 18 April 2006.

Coughlin, Con. "Smuggling Route Opened to Supply Iraqi Insurgents." *The Daily Telegraph* (London), 29 October 2005. From its website, telegraph.co.uk.

Crain, Charles. "Counterinsurgency Strategy: Staying Put." *Christian Science Monitor,* 7 June 2006.

Crilly, Rob. "Foreign Intervention in Somalia." *Christian Science Monitor,* 21 June 2006.

Crilly, Rob. "Islamist-Warlord Clashes Hinder Somalia's New Government." *Christian Science Monitor,* 5 June 2006.

Crilly, Rob. "Somalia on the Edge of Full-Scale War." *Christian Science Monitor,* 25 July 2006.

"Darfur Rebels Face Deal Deadline." *Khartoum Monitor,* 1 June 2006.

"Darfur's Peace Plan: the View from the Ground." *Sudan Tribune,* 31 May 2006.

Davie, Lucille. "Thomas Pakenham, the Boer War and the Old Fort." City of Johannesburg. From its website, www.joburg.org.

Dehghanpisheh, Babak, Michael Hastings, and Michael Hirsh. "War of the Mosques." *Newsweek,* 6 March 2006.

"Deny Shooting First at Navy in Skirmish with Pirates." From Associated Press. *Jacksonville Daily News* (NC), 20 March 2006.

Dickey, Christopher and Babak Dehghanpisheh. "Torn to Shreds." *Newsweek,* 31 July 2006.

Dickey, Christopher and Kevin Peraino, and Babak Dehghanpisheh. "The Hand That Feeds the Fire." *Newsweek,* 24 July 2006.

"DR Congo Peacekeepers Missing." *Sudan Vision,* 31 May 2006.

"Drought Management, an Alternative Solution to Darfur's Armed Conflicts." *Sudan Tribune,* 1 June 2006.

"Economic Plight of Palestinians Worsening." *The Egyptian Gazette,* 28 May 2006.

Eisenhower, President Dwight D. As quoted in "No Excuse for Hunger." By Vincent J. Romano. *Maryknoll,* vol. 96, no. 8., September 2002.

"Eliminating Terrorist Sanctuaries: The Case of Iraq, Iran, Somalia and Sudan." Center for Defense Information, Washington, D.C., 10 December 2001. From its website, info@cdi.org.

"Ethiopian Troops Lend Aid to Somali Allies." World Briefs Wire Reports (AP). *Jacksonville Daily News* (NC), 21 July 2006.

Fam, Mariam. Associated Press. "Iraq in 'Undeclared Civil War'." *Jacksonville Daily News* (NC), 9 April 2006.

Fam, Mariam. "U.S. Troops Raid Iraqi Smuggling Ring." From Associated Press, 12 April 2005.

Filkins, Dexter. "In Iraq, Armed Police Carry Out Militias' Work." *International Herald Tribune,* 25 May 2006.

"5,000 More U.S. Troops May Be Sent to Baghdad." From Associated Press. *Jacksonville Daily News* (NC), 28 July 2006.

Frayer, Lauren. Associated Press. "Lebanese Army Moves In." *Jacksonville Daily News* (NC), 18 August 2006.

Galloway, Joseph L. "U.S. Won't Quickly Change a Thousand Years of Tradition in Iraq." Knight Ridder, 11 January 2006. From its website.

Gay, Lance. Scripps Howard. "Despite Troops' Grumbling, Pentagon Insists on Side Armor." Capital Notebook, Washington. *Jacksonville Daily News* (NC), 29 January 2006.

Gertz, Bill. " 'White Man' Training Al Qaida Terrorists in Wilderness Camp near Kenya." *Geostrategy-Direct,* week of 14 December 2004. Through access@g2-forward.org.

Ghaith, Abdul-Ahad. "Outside Iraq but Deep in the Fight: A Smuggler of Insurgents. . . ." *The Washington Post,* 8 June 2005. From its website, washingtonpost.com.

Ghattas, Sam. Associated Press. "Nine Israeli Soldiers Killed in Fighting in South Lebanon." *Jacksonville Daily News* (NC), 27 July 2006.

Ghattas, Sam F. Associated Press. "Israelis Step Up Withdrawal." *Jacksonville Daily News* (NC), 18 August 2006.

Ghosh, Aparisim. "An Eye for an Eye." *Time,* 6 March 2006.

Ghosh, Aparisim and Christopher Allbritton. "The Wild Card." *Time,* 6 March 2006.

Girardet, Edward. "Clashes Worsen Somalia Food Crisis As Drought Sets In." *Christian Science Monitor,* 19 April 2006.

Glendinning, Lee. "The Secret World of Palestinian Tunnels." *Times Online* (UK), 27 June 2006.

Gordon, Michael R. "Iran Aiding Shiite Attacks Inside Iraq, General Says." *New York Times,* 23 June 2006.

"Government, Main Rebels Sign Pace Accord in Nigeria." World Briefs Wire Reports. *Christian Science Monitor,* 6 May 2006.

Grant, John. "Deja-vu in Baghdad." Iraqi Water Project Press Update, December 2003. From its website, www.iraqiwaterproject.com.

Guha, Ramachandra. "Could Partition Have Been Made Less Bloody." *The Hindu* (Madras), 28 August 2005. From its website.

"Hamas Army Recruited Thousands for Holy War to Destroy Israel." *World Tribune* (Springfield, VA), 7 March 2006. From its website, www.worldtribune.com.

Harding, Thomas. "Iraq: Missile May Have Come from Iran." *Daily Telegraph* (London), 5 May 2006. Through access@g2-forward.org.

Harris, Ron. St. Louis Post-Dispatch. "5 Marines, Scores of Iraqis Die in Battle." *Jacksonville Daily News* (NC), 18 April 2004.

Harris, Ron. St. Louis Post-Dispatch. "Marines Return to Violent City." *Jacksonville Daily News* (NC), 19 April 2004.

Hassan, Harun. "Somalia Twists in the Wind." From harowo.com, 13 April 2006. Through access@g2-forward.org.

Hastings, Michael. "The Death Squad War." *Newsweek,* 27 February 2006.

Heller, Aron. Associated Press. "Hezbollah, Israel Step Up Attacks." *Jacksonville Daily News* (NC), 7 August 2006.

Hendawi, Hamza. Associated Press. "Al-Zarqawi's Death May Not Matter." *Jacksonville Daily News* (NC), 12 June 2006.

Hendawi, Hamza. "Israel Hits Beirut; Hezbollah Rockets Israel." From Associated Press, 3 August 2006.

Hess, Pamela. "Ramadi Poses Tactical Challenge for U.S." UPI, 30 May 2006. Through access@g2-forward.org.

"Hezbollah Fighters Said to Be in Iraq." *World Net Daily* (Medford, OR), 21 June 2004. From www.intelmessages.org.

"Hizbullah Suspected of Joining Sunni Insurgents." *Iraqi News,* 17 February 2005. From www.iraqinews.com.

"Hizbullah Using Tunnels, Bunkers to Frustrate Israelis' Advance." *World Tribune* (Springfield, VA), 7 August 2006.

Hockstader, Lee. "Israeli Army Suffers Pair of Sharp Blows." *International Herald Tribune,* 16 February 2002. Reprinted from *Washington Post,* n.d.

Houreld, Katherine and Claire Soares. "Next Steps to Peace in Darfur." *Christian Science Monitor,* 8 May 2006.

Hudleston, Sarah. "South Africa: Racism under the Colour of Law Enforcement." *Business Day* (Johannesburg), n.d. As republished in *Sudan Vision,* 31 May 2006.

"Hundreds of Soldiers from Neighboring Ethiopia Crossed into Somalia." World News in Brief. *Christian Science Monitor,* 19 June 2006.

"Hunt for Insurgents near Syria Ends." Cable News Network, 14 May 2005. From its website, cnn.com.

Hunwick, John. "Africa and Islamic Revival: Historical and Contemporary Perspectives." Extracted verbatim from MSA News, by Univ. of Georgia.

Hurst, Steven R. Associated Press. "Death Toll Rises after Curfew Ends in Iraqi Capital." *Jacksonville Daily News* (NC), 1 March 2006.

Hurst, Steven R. Associated Press. "Iraq Violence Limited to 3 Provinces, U.S. Says." *Jacksonville Daily News* (NC), 24 March 2006.

Hurst, Steven R. Associated Press. "Israelis Isolating Lebanon."
　　Jacksonville Daily News (NC), 5 August 2006.
Hurst, Steven R. Associated Press. "Mideast Cease-Fire Holds."
　　Jacksonville Daily News (NC), 15 August 2006.
Imm, Jeffrey. "Some Bombs in Iraq Are Made in Iran, U.S. Says."
　　New York Times, 6 August 2005.
"Insurgents Still a Major Force in Ramadi." Through
　　access@g2-forward.org, 23 May 2006.
"Insurgents Using New Advanced Russian RPG from Iran." *World
　　Tribune* (Springfield, VA), 11 May 2006. Through
　　access@g-2forward.org.
"Iran, Nigeria Strengthening Ties." *World Tribune* (Springfield, VA),
　　24 March 2006. From its website, www.worldtribune.com.
"Iran Provides Hizbullah High-Tech Surveillance." *Geostrategy-Direct,*
　　19 April 2006. From its website.
"Iran Shifting Its Attention . . . ." *New York Times,* 13 December 1991.
"Iranian Soldiers Captured in Iraq." From Reuters, 1 July 2006.
　　Through access@g2-forward.org.
"Iran's Intelligence Service Occupies Key Iraq City." Iran Focus,
　　4 September 2005. From its website, www.iranfocus.com.
"Iran's New Elite Army Chief Had Lebanese Terror Ties." Iran Focus,
　　24 August 2005. From its website, www.iranfocus.com.
"Iraq Arrests 17 Suspected Antiquity Smugglers." From Xinhua.
　　People's Daily Online (China), 2 August 2005. From its website.
"Iraq, U.S. Operate near Syria (Operation Koa Canyon)." *Middle East
　　Newsline,* 22 January 2006. From its website,
　　www.menewsline.com.
"Iraqi Forces Find Iranian Arms Cache." UPI, 12 April 2006.
"Iraqi Medicines on the Black Market." Radio Free Iraq, 8 September
　　2000. From KurdishMedia.com.
"Iraqi Paper Claims Iranians Fighting There." From UPI, 10 May 2006.
　　Through access@g2-forward.org.
"Iraqi Resistance Report for . . . 28 February 2005." Translated and
　　compiled by Muhammad Abu Nasr, member, editorial board, the
　　Free Arab Voice. From www.albasrah.net.
"Islam in Africa Newsletter," vol. 1, no. 1, May 2006. By Moshe Terdman
　　and Reuven Paz. The Project for the Research of Islamist
　　Movements (Israel). From its website, www.e-prism.org.
"Islamic Militia Plans to Seize Somali Base." World Briefs Wire Reports
　　(AP). *Jacksonville Daily News* (NC), 21 July 2006.
"Islamists Training in Somalia." ERRI Daily Intelligence Report,
　　vol. 11, no. 363. Emergency Net News, 31 December 2005. From
　　Bill Gertz, through *Geostrategy-Direct.*
Jaber, Hala. "Hezbollah: We've Planned This for 6 Years." *The Sunday
　　Times* (London), 30 July 2006.

Jeffrey, Andrew. "Lifeline to Angola's Future." BBC News, 16 December 2004.

Jervis, Rick. "Iraqi Insurgents Take U.S. Troops by Surprise." *USA Today,* 5 October 2005. From its website.

Johnson, Scott. " 'I Demand a Timetable'." *Newsweek,* 8 May 2006.

Johnson, Scott. "Phantom Force." *Newsweek,* 24 April 2006.

Johnson, Scott and Babak Dehghanpisheh and Michael Hastings. "No More Illusions." *Newsweek,* 10 October 2005.

Keath, Lee. Associated Press. "Chaos Grips Iraq." *Jacksonville Daily News* (NC), 10 April 2004.

Keath, Lee. Associated Press. "Shiites Nominate New Premier." *Jacksonville Daily News* (NC), 22 April 2006.

Knickmeyer, Ellen. "U.S. Will Reinforce Troops in West Iraq." *Washington Post,* 29 May 2006. Through access@g2-forward.org.

Knight, Sam. "Al-Askariya Shrine: 'Not Just a Major Cathedral'." *Times on Line* (UK), 22 February 2006.

Koma, Michael. "Sorry, Madam Teny." *Khartoum Monitor,* 31 May 2006.

Krane, Jim. Associated Press. "Occupied, Not Subdued." *Jacksonville Daily News* (NC), 14 November 2004.

Krane, Jim. Associated Press. "U.S. Navy Seizes Suspected Pirate Ship." *Jacksonville Daily News* (NC), 23 January 2006.

"KwaZulu-Natal's Battlefield Experience." Drakensberg (South Africa) Tourism. From its website, www.drakensberg-tourism.com.

Lafranchi, Howard. "More Iraqis Look to Vote Secular." *Christian Science Monitor,* 5 December 2005.

Lambert, Blake. "UN Steps Up Peace Efforts in Congo ahead of April Vote." *Christian Science Monitor,* 30 January 2006.

"Lejeune Marines Find Weapons near Ramadi." News Briefs Wire Reports (AP). *Jacksonville Daily News* (NC), 17 January 2006.

Leonard, Terry. Associated Press. "Africa Looks to China for Help Financially, Politically." *Casper Star Tribune,* 10 August 2006. Through access@g2-forward.org.

Levinson, Charles. "Ballot-Box Win Boosts Iraqi Radical." *Christian Science Monitor,* 30 January 2006.

"Lord's Resistance Army." Uganda Civil War. *Global Security,* 2005. From its website, globalsecurity.org.

Lowe, Christian. "Ramadi Killings Not the Only Sniper Losses." *Times* (UK), 12 June 2006. Through access@g2-forward.org.

"LRA Attacks Village Killing One." *Khartoum Monitor,* 1 June 2006.

Majtenyi, Cathy. "China Signs Deal for Kenya Oil Exploration." *VOA* (Nairobi), April 28, 2006. Through access@g2-forward.org.

"Marine General Warns Somalia a Terrorist Haven." From Associated Press. *Jacksonville Daily News* (NC), 14 May 2005.

McConnell, Tristan. "Rebuilding South Sudan—from Scratch." *Christian Science Monitor,* 13 June 2006.

McGrory, Daniel. "Exodus of the Iraqi Middle Class." *The Times* (UK), 11 May 2006. Through access@g2-forward.org

McLaughlin, Abraham. "Africa Wary of New Border War." *Christian Science Monitor,* 27 December 2005.

McLaughlin, Abraham. "Rebuilding African Tourism." *Christian Science Monitor,* 8 October 2005.

McLaughlin, Abraham. "Tensions Rise in the Horn of Africa." *Christian Science Monitor,* 20 November 2005.

McLaughlin, Abraham and Claire Soares. "Oil Wealth and Corruption at Play in Chad's Rebellion." *Christian Science Monitor,* 21 April 2006.

Meyers, Lt.Col. Joseph and Patrick Poole. "Hezbollah, Illegal Immigration, and the Next 9/11." *Front Page Magazine,* 28 April 2006. From its website, frontpagemagazine.com.

"Militia Hunt Al-Qaeda in Somalia." From Agence France-Presse, 5 May 2006. Through access@g-2forward.org.

Mitnick, Joshua. "Hostilities Rise in Gaza." *Christian Science Monitor,* 26 June 2006.

Moubayed, Sami. "In Iraq, Chaos by Another Name." *Asia Times Online,* 3 May 2006.

"Mozambiquan War of Independence 1962-1975." At www.onwar.com.

Muhammad, Jalal. "Hizb al-Khatf." *Al-Majalla,* 20 April 1988. From "Islamism in Lebanon: A Guide," by A. Nizar Hamzeh. In *Middle East Quarterly,* vol. 1, no. 3, September 1997.

Murphy, Dan. "A Militia Tightens Grip on Heathcare." *Christian Science Monitor,* 25 May 2006.

Murphy, Dan. "Blasts at Major Shrine." *Christian Science Monitor,* 23 February 2006.

Murphy, Dan. "In Iraq with 'Reservists That Fight'." *Christian Science Monitor,* 24 March 2005.

Murphy, Dan. "Iraqi Leaders Sidestep All-Out Civil War." *Christian Science Monitor,* 27 February 2006.

Murphy, Dan. "Iraq's Foreign Fighters: Few But Deadly." *Christian Science Monitor,* 27 September 2005.

Murphy, Dan. "Iraq's Neighborhood Councils Are Vanishing." *Christian Science Monitor,* 25 February 2005.

Murphy, Dan. "Zarqawi Message: 'I'm Still Here'." *Christian Science Monitor,* 27 April 2006.

Musa, Njadvara. Associated Press. "At Least 15 Killed in Prophet Protests." *Jacksonville Daily News* (NC), 19 February 2006.

"NCP-SPLM Partners Proposed Four Options to the Abyei Issue." *Sudan Vision,* 31 May 2006.

"Nepalese Cabinet Declares Cease Fire." World Briefs Wire Reports (AP). *Jacksonville Daily News* (NC), 4 May 2006.

Nessman, Ravi. Associated Press. "Israelis Step Up Offensive." *Jacksonville Daily News* (NC), 10 August 2006.

"New Concessions Designed to Appeal to Darfur Rebels." World News in Brief. *Christian Science Monitor,* 4 May 2006.

"New Resolution Puts Darfur in U.N. Hands." Word Briefs Wire Reports (AP). *Jacksonville Daily News* (NC), 18 August 2006.

"Nigeria: Modern Manna from Heaven." *The Voice of the Martyrs* (Bartlesville, OK), August 2005.

"Nigerians Hail Democratic Victory." *The Citizen* (Khartoum), 1 June 2006.

Nor, Mohamed Sheikh. Associated Press. "Mysterious Plane Lands in Somalia." *Jacksonville Daily News* (NC), 27 July 2006.

Nordland, Rod. "Al-Sadr Strikes." *Newsweek,* 10 April 2006.

"North Koreans Assisted Hezbollah with Tunnel Construction." *Terrorism Focus: The Jamestown Foundation,* vol. III, issue 30, 1 August 2006. From its website, www.jamestown.org.

Nyirigwa, Watts Roba Gibia. "Why 2011 Referendum Is the Only Hope for South Sudanese." Parts One and Two. *Khartoum Monitor,* 31 May and 1 June 2006, respectively.

Al-Obeidi, Abdul Hussein. Associated Press. "Holy City Najaf Fighting Worst Since Saddam Fell." *Jacksonville Daily News* (NC), 7 August 2004.

"100 Militants Killed in Iraq." CBS's News on Line, 9 May 2005. From its website, CBSnews.com.

Oppel, Richard A., Jr., and Khalid W. Hassan. "Iraqi Recruits Reportedly Balk at Postings Away From Home." *New York Times,* 2 May 2006. From its website.

Pasco, William. "Moscow's Strategy in Southern Africa: A Country by Country Review." Heritage Foundation, 21 July 1986. From its website, www.heritage.org.

"Passed Death Sentence on Killers of Aid Workers." Official news release, 13 November 2005. From Somaliland government website, www.somalilandgov.com.

Pepper, Daniel. "Congolese Hopeful Ahead of July 30 Vote." *Christian Science Monitor,* 29 June 2006.

Pepper, Daniel. "From Texas to Chad: Why One Rebel Fights." *Christian Science Monitor,* 20 April 2006.

Pepper, Daniel. "Zimbabwe's Army Takes over Black Farms." *Christian Science Monitor,* 5 June 2006.

Peraino, Kevin and Babak Dehghanpisheh and Christopher Dickey. "Eye for an Eye." *Newsweek,* 14 August 2006.

Peterson, Scott. "A Picture of a Weakening Insurgency." *Christian Science Monitor,* 16 June 2006, pp. 1, 10.

Peterson, Scott. "Marine, Insurgent Tactics Evolve." *Christian Science Monitor,* 17 November 2004.

Peterson, Scott. "New Iraq Strategy: Stay in Hot Spots." *Christian Science Monitor,* 23 November 2005.

Peterson, Scott. "Unresolved: Disarming Hizbullah." *Christian Science Monitor,* 15 August 2006.

"Piracy Increase 'Alarming'." From Associated Press, 16 November 2005. Through news24.com (South Africa).

"Pirates Hijack Ship off Somalia." From Agence France-Presse, 7 December 2005. Through news24.com (South Africa).

"Pirates off Somali Coast Take Cargo Ship, Kill Member of Crew." World Briefs Wire Reports (AP). *Jacksonville Daily News* (NC), 8 May 2006.

Pitman, Todd. Associated Press. "Don't Stop, They'll Shoot." *Jacksonville Daily News* (NC), 24 April 2006.

Pitman, Todd. Associated Press. "Lejeune Marines Repulse Assault." *Jacksonville Daily News* (NC), 18 April 2006.

Plaut, Martin. "Uganda's LRA Rebels." BBC News, 6 February 2004. From its website, news.bbc.co.uk.

Poole, Patrick. "The Muslim Brotherhood 'Project'." *Front Page Magazine,* 11 May 2006. From its website, frontpagemagazine.com.

"Al-Qaida Deputy al-Zawahiri Calls for Holy War in Darfur." *Sudan Tribune,* 10 June 2006.

"Al Qaida Now Controls Somalia." *Geostrategy-Direct.* Middle East Report, 30 June 2006.

Quinn, Patrick. Associated Press. "Iraqis Focus on War." *Jacksonville Daily News* (NC), 22 May 2006.

Rabinovich, Abraham. "Militants Seen As Able to Hit Tel Aviv." *Washington Times,* 18 July 2006.

Recknagel, Charles. "Iraq: U.S. Forces Attacking Insurgents in West Face Well-Trained Foe." Radio Free Europe/Radio Liberty, 11 May 2005. From its website, www.rferl.org.

Reid, Robert H. Associated Press. "Baghdad Is Rocked by a String of Car Bombings." *Jacksonville Daily News* (NC), 25 April 2006.

Reid, Robert H. Associated Press. "Curfews Ordered in Iraq." *Jacksonville Daily News* (NC), 24 February 2006.

Reid, Robert H. Associated Press. "Ex-Prime Minister: Iraqi Abuses As Bad As Saddam." *Jacksonville Daily News* (NC), 28 November 2005.

Reid, Robert H. Associated Press. "5 Marines Die in Iraqi Fighting." *Jacksonville Daily News* (NC), 17 November 2006.

Reid, Robert H. Associated Press. "Iran Demands British Withdraw." *Jacksonville Daily News* (NC), 18 February 2006.

Reid, Robert H. Associated Press. "19 Iraqi Soldiers Killed by Roadside Bomb, Ambush." *Jacksonville Daily News* (NC), 4 December 2005.

Reid, Robert H. Associated Press. "Suicide Bomber Kills 21 after Drawing Police to Scene." *Jacksonville Daily News* (NC), 23 November 2005.

Reid, Robert H. Associated Press. "U.S.-Iraqi Operation Takes Aim at Car Bomb Builders." *Jacksonville Daily News* (NC), 1 December 2005.

Reid, Robert H. Associated Press. "U.S., Iraqi Units Rescue 7 Abducted Sunnis." *Jacksonville Daily News* (NC), 12 May 2006.

Reid, Robert H. and Jim Krane. Associated Press. "Bombs Biggest Killer for U.S. in Iraq." *Jacksonville Daily News* (NC), 7 August 2005.

Robinson, Simon and Daniel Pepper/Tawila. "The Front Lines of Genocide." *Time,* 8 May 2006.

Robinson, Simon and Vivienne Walt. "The Deadliest War in the World." *Time,* 5 June 2006.

Rodriguez, Alex. "Retaking Ramadi, 1 District at a Time." *Chicago Tribune,* 9 July 2006.

Roggio, Bill. "Operation Steel Curtain Continues." *Threats Watch,* 18 November 2005. From its website, www.threatswatch.org.

Roggio, Bill. "Ramadi: North, South, East and West, and Operation Panther." *Threats Watch,* 17 November 2005. From its website, www.threatswatch.org.

Roggio, Bill. "River Gates." *The Fourth Rail,* 6 October 2005. From its website.

Roggio, Bill. "Steel Curtain Update: Slugging it out in Ubaydi. . . ." *Threats Watch,* 15 November 2005. From its website, www.threatswatch.org.

Roggio, Bill. "The Anbar Campaign Revisited." *The Fourth Rail,* 8 August 2005. From its website.

Roggio, Bill. "The Islamic Republic of Haditha?" *The Fourth Rail,* 24 August 2005. From its website.

Rubin, Michael. "Ansar al-Sunna: Iraq's New Terrorist Threat." *Middle East Intelligence Bulletin,* vol. 6, no. 5, May 2004.

"Russia, China Block Darfur-Related Sanctions." From Associated Press. *Christian Science Monitor,* 19 April 2006.

"SA Favors Stability over Democracy in Zimbabwe." *The Egyptian Gazette,* 29 May 2006.

"SA, Sudan Hopeful Darfur Peace Deal Will Last." *Sudan Vision,* 31 May 2006.

"SA to Sign Treaty with Sudan." *Sudan Vision,* 31 May 2006.

Sameer, J.B. *As Qurans Burn: Ideas & Identities of India Pakistan.* "#60," 23 April 2003. From website, www.chowk.com. Copyrighted by Lewis P. Orans in 1997. At www.pinetreeweb.com.

Sangraula, Bikash. "In Nepal's Democratic Revival, Maoist Rebels Dubious." *Christian Science Monitor,* 26 April 2006.

Sangraula, Bikash. "Key Role of Nepal Security Forces." *Christian Science Monitor,* 18 April 2006.

Sangraula, Bikash. "Nepal Grapples with Next Steps." *Christian Science Monitor,* 2 May 2006.

Sangraula, Bikash. "Nepal's Parliament Asserts Power." *Christian Science Monitor,* 19 May 2006.

Sangraula, Bikash. "Nepal's Parliament Sets Fast-Paced Agenda." *Christian Science Monitor,* 15 May 2006.

Sangraula, Bikash. "Pressure Rises on Nepal's King." *Christian Science Monitor,* 24 April 2006.

Sangraula, Bikash. "Rebel Visit Moves Nepal Closer to Peace." *Christian Science Monitor,* 19 June 2006.

"The Scars of Death." *Human Rights Watch,* September 1997. From its website, www.hrw.org.

Schweid, Bary. Associated Press. "Plan to Help Train Lebanese Army Approved." *Jacksonville Daily News* (NC), 4 August 2006.

"Scouting in South Africa, 1884-1890." As extracted from *Scouting with Baden-Powell,* by Russell Freedman. New York: Holiday House, 1967. At www.pinetreeweb.com.

"Seven killed in Baghdad bombings." *Middle East On Line* (London), 10 May 2005. From its website, www.middle-east-online.com.

Shahzad, Syed Saleem. "We are just Hit-and-Run Guerrillas." *Asia Times Online,* 10 August 2006.

"Shiite Radicals Join with Sunni Insurgents in Ramadi." *DEBKAfile* (Israel), 7 April 2004.

Shrader, Katherine. Associated Press. "Search for bin Laden Continues along Border." *Jacksonville Daily News* (NC), 24 April 2006.

Silberberg, Jacob. Associated Press. "Iraqi, U.S. Troops Hit Insurgent Stronghold." *Jacksonville Daily News* (NC), 11 September 2005.

Silberberg, Jacob. Associated Press. "Militants Flee Tal Afar in Wake of U.S.-Iraqi Offensive." *Jacksonville Daily News* (NC), 12 September 2005.

Simpson, Jim. "Scouts to the Rescue." *Defense Watch,* 17 September 2003. As posted at military.com.

"Somali Islamists Seize Rival Base." *Khartoum Monitor,* 2 June 2006.

"Somali Pirates Unload Food from Hijacked UN Ship." From Xinhua. *People's Daily Online* (China), 19 August 2005. From its website.

"South Sudan Leader Defends Aid to Ugandan Rebel LRA." *Sudan Vision,* 31 May 2006.

"SPLM Demands Construction of Oil Refinery in the South." *Sudan Tribune,* 31 May 2006.

Stanislaus, Baptist. "There Is a Lot of Money in this Country." *Khartoum Monitor,* 31 May 2006.

"Strong Chinese-Hamas Intelligence Connection." *DEBKAfile* (Israel), 19 June 2006.

"Sudan Arrested Chadian Rebel to Support of His Rival." *Khartoum Monitor,* 1 June 2006.

"Sudan: Disagreements over Implementation of Peace Accord." From IRIN (Nairobi). *The Citizen* (Khartoum), 1 June 2006.

"Sudan, Eritrea Discuss Eastern Conflict." *Sudan Tribune,* 12 June 2006.

"Sudan Ex-Rebels Show Unity with Khartoum Despite Differences." *Sudan Vision,* 31 May 2006.

"Sudan Signs Off on Darfur Peace Plan, Will the Rebels?" From Reuters and Associated Press. *Christian Science Monitor,* 1 May 2006.

"Sudan Suspends All U.N. Mission Work in Darfur." *Sudan Tribune,* 25 June 2006.

"Sudan Unity Requires Secular State." *Khartoum Monitor,* 1 June 2006.

"Sudan's Turabi Calls for Popular Uprising." *Sudan Tribune,* 19 May 2006.

Swain, Jon and David Leppard and Brian Johnson-Thomas. "Iran's Plot to Mine Uranium in Africa." *The Sunday Times* (UK), 6 August 2006. Through access@g2-forward.org.

Swarns, Rachel L. "Disillusion Rises Among South Africa's Poor." *New York Times,* 31 December 2002.

Tabuchi, Hiroko. Associated Press. "Chinese Spy Planes Have Raised Alerts in Japan. *Jacksonville Daily News* (NC), 21 April 2006.

Thomlinson, Chris. Associated Press. "U.S. Backing Somali Militants against Islamic Extremists. *Jacksonville Daily News* (NC), 10 April 2006.

Thomlinson, Chris. "Video Shows Arabs Fighting in Somalia." From Associated Press, 5 July 2006. Through access@g2-forward.org.

Tran, Tini. Associated Press. "Insurgents Hit Mosul Police Stations." *Jacksonville Daily News* (NC), 15 November 2004.

"Tribal Militants Claimed Responsibility for Another Attack on an Energy Installation." World News in Brief. *Christian Science Monitor,* 8 June 2006.

Truscott, Ryan. "Short Lives Lead to Short-Term Goals in Zimbabwe." *Christian Science Monitor,* 9 June 2006.

"U.N.: Fifth of the World Lacks Clean Water. World Brief Wire Reports (AP). *Jacksonville Daily News* (NC), 7 March 2006.

"U.S.-Led Forces Arrest Top Militia Commander in Iraq." From Reuters, 7 July 2006.

Vermaak, Chris. "Rhodesia's Selous Scouts." *Armed Forces,* May 1977. As posted at rhodesian.server101.com.

Ware, Michael. "The View from the Front Lines." *Time,* 5 December 2005.

Wines, Michael. "In South Africa, Democracy May Breed One-Party Rule." *New York Times,* 14 April 2004.

"Worries That the Powerful Muslim Militia." World News in Brief. *Christian Science Monitor,* 24 August 2006.

Yacoub, Meer N. "4GW: Al-Qaida Blueprint for Conflict." From Associated Press, 15 June 2006. Through access@g2-forward.org.

Zavis, Alexandra. Associated Press. "Security Measures Don't Halt Violence." *Jacksonville Daily News* (NC), 27 February 2006.

"Zimbabwe: No Money to Print Currency." From IRIN (Harare). As reprinted in *Khartoum Monitor,* 31 May 2006.

"Zulu and Zulu Wars." In *Reader's Companion to Military History.* Boston, MA: Houghton Mifflin, College Division, n.d. From its website, college.hmco.com.

About the Author

After 28 years of commissioned and noncommissioned infantry service, John Poole retired from the United States Marine Corps in April 1993. While on active duty, he studied small-unit tactics for nine years: (1) six months at the Basic School in Quantico (1966); (2) seven months as a rifle platoon commander in Vietnam (1966-67); (3) three months as a rifle company commander at Camp Pendleton (1967); (4) five months as a regimental headquarters company (and camp) commander in Vietnam (1968); (5) eight months as a rifle company commander in Vietnam (1968-69); (6) five and a half years as an instructor with the Advanced Infantry Training Company (AITC) at Camp Lejeune (1986-92); and (7) one year as the SNCOIC of the 3rd Marine Division Combat Squad Leaders Course (CSLC) on Okinawa (1992-93).

While at AITC, he developed, taught, and refined courses on maneuver warfare, land navigation, fire support coordination, call for fire, adjust fire, close air support, M203 grenade launcher, movement to contact, daylight attack, night attack, infiltration, defense, offensive Military Operations in Urban Terrain (MOUT), defensive MOUT, Nuclear/Biological/Chemical (NBC) defense, and leadership. While at CSLC, he further refined the same periods of instruction and developed others on patrolling.

He has completed all of the correspondence school requirements for the Marine Corps Command and Staff College, Naval War College (1,000-hour curriculum), and Marine Corps Warfighting Skills Program. He is a graduate of the Camp Lejeune Instructional Management Course, the 2nd Marine Division Skill Leaders in Advanced Marksmanship (SLAM) Course, and the East-Coast School of Infantry Platoon Sergeants' Course.

In the 13 years since retirement, John Poole has researched the small-unit tactics of other nations and written five other books: (1) *The Last Hundred Yards: The NCO's Contribution to Warfare,* a squad combat study based on the consensus opinions of 1,200 NCOs and casualty statistics of AITC and CSLC field trials; (2) *One More Bridge to Cross: Lowering the Cost of War,* a treatise on enemy proficiency at short range and how to match it; (3) *Phantom Soldier: The Enemy's Answer to U.S. Firepower,* an in-depth look at the highly deceptive Asian style of war; (4) *The Tiger's Way: A U.S. Private's Best Chance of Survival,* a study of how Eastern fire teams and individual soldiers fight; (5) *Tactics of the Crescent Moon: Militant Muslim*

Combat Methods, a comprehensive analysis of the insurgents' battlefield procedures in Palestine, Chechnya, Afghanistan, and Iraq; and *Militant Tricks: Battlefield Ruses of the Islamic Insurgent,* an honest appraisal of the so-far-undefeated *jihadist* method.

As of September 2006, John Poole had conducted multiday training sessions (on how to conduct 4th-Generation Warfare at the small-unit level) for 38 Marine battalions, nine Marine schools, and seven special-operations units from all four U.S. service branches. He has been stationed twice each in South Vietnam and Okinawa. He has visited Japan, Taiwan, the Philippines, Indonesia, South Korea, Mainland China, Hong Kong, Macao, North Vietnam, Myanmar (Burma), Thailand, Cambodia, Malaysia, Singapore, Tibet, Nepal, Bangladesh, India, Pakistan, Russia, East Germany, West Germany, Morocco, Israel (to include the West Bank), Turkey, Iran, Lebanon, Egypt, and Sudan.

Name Index

A

Adrian, Rick 213
Ahmadinejad, President Mahmoud 95, 96, 99
Ahmed, Shekh Sharif xxviii
Aideed, Mohamed Farah xxiii, xxiv, xxv
Alamieyeseigha, Depriye 185
al-Ali, Mustapha 90
Allawi, Prime Minister Iyad 83
Arafat, Yasser 242
Asari, Alhaji Mujahid Dokubo 185
Atef, Mohammed xxiii, xxiv
Aweys, Hassan Dahir xxvii, xxviii
Azhar, Maulana Masood xxiii
Azzam, Addallah Yusuf 11, 13

B

Baden-Powell, Col. Robert S.S. 112, 118
Balaam, Sgt. Andy 169
Bambatha, Chief 129
Barram, Amatzia 86
Barre, President Mohamed Siad xx
al-Bashir, President Omar 190, 192
Bate, Col. Tufty 172
Bilal, Sheikh 200
Bin Laden, Osama xxiii, xxiv, xxiv, xxv, 3, 11, 12, 15, 185

Botha, President Louis 130, 148
Buller, Gen. Redvers 120, 121
Burnham, Maj. Frederick 118, 120

C

Casey, Gen. George W., Jr. 93
Castro, President Fidel 137
Cetshwayo, King 106, 107, 108
Chase, Col. Bob 44
Chelmsford, Lord Frederick A.T. 106, 107, 108, 111
Churchill, Prime Minister Winston 120, 126
Clarke, Richard 245
Colley, Gen. G.P. 118
Conway, Lt.Gen. James 44

D

Dahal, Pushpa Kamal ("Pranchanda") 240
David xxvi
Deby, President Idriss 23
De Wet, Christiaan 126
Dingane, King 105, 129
Dingiswayo, Chief 104
Dinizulu, Chief 112, 113, 129
Dlamini-Zuma 27
Dos Santos, President Eduardo 26, 149, 186
Drury-Lowe 111